Bird
Without Feathers

Bird
Without Feathers

Mike and Karen Derzack
and Cynthia Sterling

Northwest Publishing, Inc.
Salt Lake City, Utah

Bird Without Feathers

The events in this book are based upon true incidents. Some of the names
have been changed to protect the identities of individuals. For dramatic
purposes, the chronology of some events has been compressed or altered.

For information address: Northwest Publishing, Inc.
6906 South 300 West, Salt Lake City, Utah 84047
SCM 09 22 94
Edited by C.C. Robbins

PRINTING HISTORY
First Printing 1994

ISBN: 1-56901-590-2

NPI books are published by Northwest Publishing, Incorporated,
6906 South 300 West, Salt Lake City, Utah 84047.
The name "NPI" and the "NPI" logo are trademarks belonging to
Northwest Publishing, Incorporated.

PRINTED IN THE UNITED STATES OF AMERICA.
10 9 8 7 6 5 4 3 2 1

To our children. As Lord George Byron said and we have learned, adversity is the first path to truth.
                                        —Mike and Karen Derzack

To Savannah, Max, Megan, Maggie, Davey, Bobby, Cara, Jeremy and all of the children who have touched my life— grow strong, stay young, fly free.
                                        —Cynthia Sterling

Acknowledgments

Karen and I did not stand alone in our fight to do what we knew to be right. Along the way we met some fantastic people. We wish we had enough space to thank everyone, but that would be a book in itself.

Although Karen and I strongly believe that our struggle will benefit others, we had no idea how to go about writing our story. Luckily, Cynthia Sterling, our co-author and now our friend, came to our rescue. She listened, she cared and she captured us—both our good side and our less flattering side. Thanks a million.

While Cynthia was busy writing, the Lee Shore Literary Agency was busy marketing and arranging numerous meetings with the media and government officials. Luckily, they landed Northwest Publishing, to whom we are very grateful.

A special thanks to the Lee Shore staff, Megan Davidson and Patrick Freeman.

Tom Sterling was a great help, too. While his wife was writing, he was helping us through with words of encouragement and was searching out people we could talk to about the problems we were facing.

When talking no longer was getting results, the experts, Joan, Arthur, Todd, Bernadette, Karen and those at Rosenberg and Kirshner stepped in to assist us. Although we still have a long way to go, God willing, we hope we can go the distance together.

We also came to discover that motions, court hearings, and lawsuits are meaningless if the laws protecting children are not changed. Karen and I were fortunate enough to have the support of State Senator Melissa Hart and U.S. Congressman Ron Klink—they never forgot the children.

But laws do not get changed without public support. The media was particularly helpful in exposing and questioning the way in which our children are cared for by organizations that were established to protect them. Sometimes, we disagreed with their reporting but all of them were professional and their expert reporting put pressure where it was necessary.

While the press was doing their fact finding, a few brave individuals, namely, Donna, B.B. and Kenny, had their own way of playing sleuth. Their probing into the dark corners of Allegheny County were immensely helpful to us.

During all of the hullabaloo our friends and neighbors stayed by our side. We can never repay their kindness. We thank each and every one of them. A special thanks to the DelMastro, Cook, Steidl, and Roche families; Vi and Rodney, Marilyn and George; the doctors and staff at Sewickley Valley Pediatric Association; Sister Michelle and everyone at the Sisters of Divine Providence, and the teachers and children at Vincentian Preschool and Providence Heights Alpha School.

When we were at our lowest, other foster parents and families wrapped themselves around us, keeping us warm and safe. They are to be admired.

There was, for a short time, a little boy named Baby Charles, who came into our lives, then was ripped away from us. We wish for you a good life.

If it were not for Recco, there would be no fight—you served better than anyone we ever knew.

Karen and I wish we could personally thank each and every person who wrote us a letter, gave us a phone call, or showed us their support. Rest assured, we feel a deep gratitude.

All through our struggle, we never lost trust that a greater power was guiding us. Our faith paid off.

In the child's best interest,

Mike and Karen Derzack

One

SAT AT MY dinner table, trying to make what I knew had to be one of the most important and difficult decisions of my life. I took a bite of chicken. Everyone was looking at me as I chewed—my wife Karen, and our three children, Chris, Connie and Cameron. Dinnertime was always a wild free-for-all at our house, but today it was remarkably quiet.

Not a day ago, Children and Youth Services, or CYS—the child welfare agency of Allegheny County, Pittsburgh—had asked us to take in a very ill baby and provide him with a safe, comfortable home "for just a few days." It seemed simple enough. Karen and the children had already agreed to it, but I still hesitated. I'd have to make my decision soon, and I did not like being hurried.

Karen and I were in the throes of adopting a little boy named Adam, and I didn't want anything to rock the boat. On the other hand, I thought, if we helped CYS, they might help us speed up Adam's adoption.

"Da-ad," Connie whined as she twisted a strand of her long brown hair around her finger. "Have you decided yet?"

I looked at her for a moment and tried to remember a time when she could not talk. I couldn't think of one. I swear, when we adopted her nine years ago, she was talking then. And nine years ago she was only one day old.

"Leave Dad alone," Chris said, shoving a forkful of potato salad into his mouth. "Can't you see he's trying to think?"

"Listen to your older brother," I said, biting down on an ear of corn. "And Chris, don't you talk with your mouth full." I pulled a piece of chicken from the bone and as I popped it in my mouth, I looked around the table at my family. We were a little unconventional. None of us looked alike, except Cameron, who resembled my wife, Karen. But then he was our only natural child.

How different they all were, I thought, not only in looks but in temperament too. Connie was smart-mouthed and sarcastic, Chris was quiet and thoughtful and Cameron... well, he was pretty much a typical four-year-old with plenty of heart. But, as a family, we worked quite well— most of the time.

At Chris' request, Karen scooped out the last of the potato salad, placed it on his plate, then sat back in her chair. Her dark eyes narrowed as she stared at me. "So, Mike, what's your decision?"

I finished my last piece of chicken, put my fork across my empty plate and rested my hands on my stomach. I knew that Chris could not save me this time, nor would he try. I must give Karen my answer.

The kids stopped eating for a moment and stared at me in silence. I could see the concern in Chris' face. He seemed to sense the seriousness of the decision I had been asked to make.

"Yes," I finally answered. I gave a deep sigh of relief. There, it was done. The decision was made. "We'll take the baby in."

"All right!" Connie yelled, throwing her napkin in the air. "Good decision, Dad!"

"Thank you, Connie," I said, giving her hair a tug as I walked over to the kitchen counter and placed my dirty dish in the sink.

"So, Chris, Cameron…what do you think?"

"I don't know, Dad," Chris said with a shrug of his shoulders. "Whatever you think. I just hope you don't forget about Adam."

"I think it's great, Dad," Cameron offered. But then Cameron thought that red ants and green spiders were great too.

"We won't forget about Adam, will we, Mike?" Karen asked.

"Nope," I answered, squirting too much dish detergent into the sinkful of water.

As I scrubbed the supper dishes, I thought about the little boy we were trying to adopt. Adam was a foster child under the care of the Sisters of Divine Providence. My kids, who attended the school at Divine Providence, had fallen in love with Adam and begged us to adopt him. After weeks of hearing about how smart Adam was and how strong Adam was, Karen and I were finally convinced to meet the little boy for ourselves.

How surprised we were to find out that Adam was an African-American. Our kids had failed to mention this to us, perhaps because they had not seen a black child, only a child who needed a family.

After visiting with Adam every day for several weeks, we had decided to adopt him. We didn't make our decision lightly. I personally struggled a long time with the idea of raising a black child. This was a possibility that I had never considered, and I had misgivings regarding my own ability to be a good father to Adam. What if some unknown prejudice or bias lurked inside me? What if I were unable to love a child who looked different from me and my children?

I was uncomfortable and disappointed that I even had to ask myself these questions. For God's sake, a child was in need! But I couldn't shake my deepest, darkest doubts. Karen, on the other hand, had no such struggle. She, like the kids, did not see color, only a child who needed her.

I began to try and imagine the baby that CYS was asking us to look after. The child was what CYS termed an "emergency placement"—a six-day-old premature black infant who was born addicted to crack cocaine and heroin. His mother had deserted him within hours after giving birth. I didn't even know his name.

I wanted to help the youngster, but I still had as many doubts as ever. I closed my eyes and imagined a chubby little dark baby with tight black curls. Weren't all babies incredibly sweet and cute? Even if he was very sick, how bad could it be? We'd only be pinch-hitting for a day or so.

As I washed the last dish and placed it in the rack to dry with the others, I glanced out the window to the field beyond our yard. Two white-tailed deer were grazing on the hillside, a buck and a doe. Any other time, this beautiful sight would give me some feeling of serenity, but today I couldn't help but feel that a hunter, dressed in camouflage, was hiding in the nearby bushes with a loaded gun, poised to shoot.

"I'd better call CYS," Karen said, placing two coffee mugs and three purple plastic tumblers in the soapy warm water. She gave me a quick hug as she made her way to the phone. "Don't look so worried. It'll be fine. Besides, he'll only be here for a couple of days. What's the big deal?"

As I eavesdropped on Karen's half of her phone conversation with the caseworker, I began to get a hollow feeling in the pit of my stomach. "Yes, yes, we understand that it's only for a few days...What, a week? That's no problem. A week will be fine. After you find a home for the baby, we'll still be able to adopt Adam, correct? Good."

What's happening now? I asked myself. First a few days, now a week. Things were moving too fast, and I hoped they would not go out of control.

Karen was unfazed. "Mike, on the counter is the list of things we'll need," she said, placing the receiver in its cradle. "Diapers, formula, receiving blankets…you know the routine. Be sure to get the iron-enriched formula. This baby's six weeks premature and not as strong as he could be. And, Chris, you go with your dad and help him carry things."

I picked up Karen's list, although I didn't really need it: I was very familiar with the needs of a newborn and the commotion a new baby causes. "Come on, Chris, let's go," I said, motioning to him to hurry up.

He grabbed an apple from the refrigerator, then followed me out the door to the car. On the way out he also snagged a piece of chicken, which he neatly wrapped in a paper napkin.

We drove to the shopping mall in silence, punctuated only by the sounds of Chris munching. I had plenty of time to continue thinking about what I had just agreed to do. Hey, it was only going to be for a little while, I kept reminding myself. Then they would allow us to adopt Adam. Maybe they were giving us this child as some sort of test to see if we were actually serious about adopting.

As we reached the mall and I pulled the car into a parking space, Chris turned to me, his eyes as round as golf balls. "They're not going to give us Adam," he said.

"Sure they are."

"No, they're not," he flatly stated.

"What makes you say that?" I asked, sliding my keys and wallet into my pocket.

"I don't know." That was an eleven-year-old's answer for everything.

By now, I knew better than to press any deeper and decided to just accept 'I don't know' as an answer. "Okay," I said, "I'll think about that. Maybe you're right."

Actually, I had some misgivings on that point myself. I had no reason to distrust the caseworker or Children and Youth Services, but everything was moving too quickly for my liking. Here we were, not yet approved to become foster parents (which we had to become before we were allowed to take Adam into our home), and already they were sending us a different child.

Chris and I hurried through our shopping, although he did insist we buy a little stuffed bear which played a nursery rhyme when you pressed its paw. "The baby will need something cute," Chris explained. After that, we didn't waste any time in getting back to the house. The caseworker was to deliver the baby within two hours, and we knew that Karen would need our help in setting up the crib and getting the baby clothes out of storage.

As I turned onto our street, I was surprised to see a white Chevy parked in our driveway, blocking the entrance to the garage. "Anyone you know?" I asked Chris, squeezing my car alongside the Chevy.

"Nope," he answered, getting out of the Land Cruiser. Chris opened the tailgate and piled several bags into my arms, then picked up the remaining packages.

Carefully, we negotiated our way around the white car. I stopped briefly to look at the license plate: It was a county car. They sure didn't waste any time getting here, I thought.

I glimpsed something green and red at my feet—one of Cameron's treasured squirt guns. I moved several of his toys out of my path with my foot and walked through the open garage door. While I struggled to open the door from the garage into the house, dropping a box of diapers in the process, I made a mental note to have a man-to-man talk with Cameron about putting his toys away and remembering to close the garage door. All he had to do was push a button!

"I'll get them, Dad," Chris offered, bending to retrieve the diapers. I half-expected a snicker out of him as he witnessed his father's awkwardness, but he was perfectly serious. Had Connie been helping me instead of Chris, she would have fallen on the floor from laughing so hard.

I entered the kitchen and saw Karen in the foyer, holding the baby close to her breast, gently rocking him back and forth. She was talking with a woman I assumed was the caseworker we had been communicating with off and on over the phone since early morning. The caseworker appeared disheveled. Her navy blue suit was wrinkled and her short brown hair looked as if it had been combed by a tornado. Her face had as many wrinkles as her suit and, although she was smiling and her voice sounded friendly, her left hand betrayed her nervousness: It grasped the doorknob so tightly her knuckles were white.

"Hello," I said, walking into the room. "I'm Mike Derzack." I reached out my hand to shake hers.

She removed her hand from the doorknob and, without looking at me, shook hands and returned my greeting. "Hi. I've gone over everything with your wife," she said, returning her hand to the doorknob.

"Well, why don't we go into the family room and you can go over everything with me?"

"Oh, no, I don't think that will be necessary," the caseworker answered, shaking her head. "I explained everything to Karen. She can bring you up to speed. Besides, I don't want to get too comfortable. I still have one more appointment before I get to go home myself."

I was a little taken back by her comment. She was sticking us with a drug-addicted baby and didn't have the time to cover the particulars with me? Something was wrong with this whole situation. Or was it a normal procedure for CYS to drop off a kid and run?

I was about to voice my concerns when Karen started cooing and talking baby talk to the little stranger.

"Oh, the poor little thing!" There was a deep concern in Karen's voice. "You're not feeling so well, are you? Your Aunt Karen will make you feel better."

I realized then that any questions I had were not going to change the fact that this child was going to be a part of our family, at least for a couple of days, whether I was comfortable with it or not. I told myself to make the best out of the situation. Just a week, I quietly reminded myself, hardly any time at all. Then Karen and I could get on with making preparations for adopting Adam.

I took a quick look at the baby and turned away in shock.

"This kid looks awful!" I blurted. The closest I had come to seeing anyone addicted to drugs was watching a program about addicts on television. The real thing was far more horrifying. The baby's entire body was contracted and his eyes were clenched shut, as if he were in great pain.

"Yeah, he's pretty bad," the caseworker agreed. "That's a pretty bad combination, being addicted and premature. I can't say I've seen much worse. But he'll come around for you."

"How can a mother do this to her child?" Karen asked. Her voice took on a high-pitched quality that happened only when Karen began to get angry or upset.

"Oh, the mother's a hopeless case," the caseworker said, waving her right hand in the air, while the left one still clutched the doorknob. "This is her fifth kid by at least three different fathers, and the woman's only twenty-three years old. There's no telling how long she's been doing drugs."

"Where is she now?" I asked.

"Probably out on some street corner, looking to turn a trick in order to pay for more crack. Who knows for sure? She'll never show up for her kids. She's pretty much a good-for-nothing."

"Where are the other children?" Karen asked, holding the baby a little tighter.

"The great-aunt's got three, the grandmother has the other one."

"Where are the fathers?" Surely, out of all those fathers, one must have cared about his child, I thought.

"That one's father is dead," the caseworker answered, pointing to the baby. "He supposedly got run over chasing a van down the street. He was whacked out on drugs when it happened. Probably didn't feel a thing. The other ones…who knows? Who cares? Could be just johns, for all we know. This so-called family isn't like anything you've seen. Sometimes I wonder if they're still human."

I began to understand why the caseworker looked and acted the way she did. I'd be a little stressed out too, I guess, if I saw on a daily basis the damage that mothers and fathers do to their children.

"Well, I know you're busy, so I'll let you get on with your day," I said, letting the caseworker off the hook. She sighed, apparently quite relieved that I was no longer drilling her for answers.

Before she left, she stuffed a few booklets into my hands. "This information will help you care for the child," she said. "By the way, his name is Byron. I think he was named after his father."

"And a great poet, too," I murmured.

"Huh?" The caseworker stared at me, clearly puzzled.

"Lord Byron, a Romantic poet. You know, 'She walks in beauty like the night…'"

"Oh, well, whatever," sighed the caseworker, unimpressed. The baby could have been called "dirt" for all she cared, I thought.

I escorted her to the front porch steps and watched as she hurried toward her car, almost tripping once on Cameron's assortment of toys. She got in the car, flashed me a big smile through the closed window and waved good-bye as she shifted into drive. In a few seconds she had disappeared down the street. I was glad I didn't have her job.

I understood a little better the kind of pressure the caseworker was under and the desperate need to find families willing to provide an emergency placement for babies like Byron. But, try as I might, I could not shake myself of the dark thoughts that were plaguing me since I first laid eyes on Adam. Accepting a black child as one of my own was, up until now, merely talk. But here I was with a black baby in my home, and suddenly I didn't like the situation at all.

It was difficult for me to look at this child. I didn't want to go back into the house. Why did I feel like going for a run or hiding out at the shop? Why? What was wrong with me? Was it because he was black or because he was sick? Or both? I was afraid, yet obsessed with finding the answer to those questions.

In our many conversations about adopting Adam, Karen had assured me my fatherly instincts were so strong that they would win out over my fears. Her arguments on my behalf were, on a rational level, convincing, but I was dealing with this issue of color on an emotional level. Throughout my life I had never been very comfortable facing my emotions, and as a result they weren't too familiar to me. To make matters worse, I hadn't known any African-Americans when I was growing up, and I had never been very close with any black person.

Finally, I mustered my courage and entered the house. Karen and the children had moved to the kitchen. I could hear the excitement in their voices as they oohed and ahhed at the baby, and decided that my time to join them had come.

Karen was fixing a bottle for little Byron while Christopher held the child in his arms. "He doesn't look at all like Adam," Connie commented as she stroked the baby's head. Once again she had failed to see color. I was proud of her.

"Do you need any help?" I offered.

Karen shook her head and pointed to the family room. That was my cue to get out of the kitchen and to keep out of her way. She sensed that I just wasn't ready to participate, but at some point I knew she would expect me to overcome my reluctance.

I was jealous as I watched everyone scurry about the kitchen, seeing to the needs of this baby, jealous because I was unable to do the same. To redeem myself, I went upstairs to the nursery to see what I could do to make the baby's stay a little more comfortable.

The crib and the dressing table were already assembled, so I busied myself putting piles of baby clothes in the dresser drawers. I found a little bedsheet sprinkled with blue, pink and yellow dinosaurs, neatly folded at the bottom of the laundry basket. It had been Cameron's sheet when he was little, and I held it up to my nose, fully expecting to be able to smell his sweet baby scent. The sheet smelled like laundry soap. I made the bed for Byron, smoothing out every wrinkle until I was certain a coin would bounce off it.

I sat on the big wooden rocking horse, which had been mine as a child, and waited. After a short while I remembered I had put the pamphlets the caseworker had given me in my back jeans pocket, so I pulled them out and studied them: "The Drug Addicted Newborn"; "Cocaine: The Terrible Addiction"; "Heroin: What It Does to Your Body"; and "Caring For the Drug Addicted Newborn." Catchy titles.

I read each pamphlet several times over. One point was particularly startling. The newborn who was addicted to cocaine and heroin had no sense of self. The baby felt as if it were floating helplessly in a dangerous ocean with no anchor or lifeline. Lost.

When I heard the kids saying good night to the baby and Karen, I placed the booklets on the dressing table where Karen would be sure to see them. I listened as my three took their turns washing their faces and brushing their teeth. Such good kids, I thought. Then Connie, in hopes of starting a ruckus, directed a few of her taunting remarks at both Chris and Cameron, but neither gave into her, so she quieted down.

When I was certain that they were all in bed, I began my regular ritual of saying good night. I gave Connie and Cameron a kiss on the forehead. Chris got a pat on the head—he was too old for a kiss.

When I could not hide out any longer I went downstairs.

Karen sat in the rocking chair in the family room: How beautiful she was! Her short black hair shone in the soft glow of the lighted table lamp. One curl had freed itself from her hairband and lay carelessly on her forehead. She

looked like a young, new mother. The whole scene reminded me of a Norman Rockwell-type painting, which in
my mind I titled, *Karen Holding Child.*

"Are you ready to take another look?" Karen asked.
Although I knew she must have been tired from running at
top speed for most of the day, her face did not show her
fatigue. In fact, she looked very content.

I knelt down beside Karen and for the first time took a good
look at Baby Byron. Much to my surprise he wasn't very dark,
and his black hair was thick and straight. He had no eyebrows
or eyelashes. His eyes were closed, and through his delicate
skin I could see his heart beating. He could not move his arms
or legs, and his little neck did not have enough strength to stop
his head from rolling from side to side with just the slightest
movement. His mouth was opened wide, as if he were hungry
or thirsty. He still looked shockingly weak and sick.

"What's wrong with his color?"

"You mean, why isn't he darker?"

I nodded.

Karen laughed softly. "I asked the caseworker the same
thing. She said that it takes a little time for the skin to darken.
The hair will start to curl up later on, too."

"He really is pretty sick, isn't he?" I said, touching his hand.

"Yes, he is." She gave him a little kiss. "He looks like a
baby bird without feathers," Karen whispered under her
breath. Actually, I thought, he looked more like a bird that
had been pushed out of its nest to die.

"The poor little birdie," Karen said softly, placing the
nipple of the bottle in his mouth. "I know he's hungry,
Mike, but he just doesn't have the strength to eat very much
at one time. Sometimes he just forgets how to suck. And you
know something else? He's too weak to cry, so he can't tell
you when something is wrong."

Life sure dealt this kid a tough hand, I thought. "Here,
hon, let me try feeding the little birdie," I said, reaching out
for him. "Maybe we just need a guy's touch, right, Birdie?"

Byron easily fit into my hands and I was shocked at how

truly little he was. I actually couldn't feel the weight of him; he seemed to float in my hands. Easing myself down on my blue leather recliner, I tried to find a comfortable position for both him and me. I knew we were going to be in for a long night.

"I'll make us a fresh pot of coffee," Karen said, walking into the kitchen.

"Just make enough for me," I said, still staring at Byron. "You did enough for one day. Get some rest and leave the night shift to me."

I could smell the coffee brewing and looked forward to having a cup. However, I was not looking forward to pulling an all-nighter, especially because I had to be at the print shop early the next morning.

Karen placed a full mug of coffee on the end table, gave me a kiss and wished both of us good luck. Then, as she turned to walk away, she suddenly stopped and sat down on a footstool in front of me.

"You've got something to tell me, don't you?" I asked. I knew Karen well enough to know that something was really bothering her.

She nodded. "All day I've been thinking about something that happened to me when I was around six or seven years old," she said, scrunching up her face as if in pain. "I guess having Byron here made me remember it. Are you in the mood to listen?"

"Of course," I answered. Karen, throughout our relationship, had told me many stories about her childhood, and I always welcomed any invitation into her life.

"It's not very pretty," Karen said, moving the footstool closer to me.

"That's all right, hon. I'm listening."

Karen hugged her knees close to her chest and reluctantly began her story. "I was playing in the backyard with a few of the neighbor kids. My parents must have been having a picnic or something because one of my cousins, Jimmy Pino, was there, the older man in my life. I guess he was about ten or eleven, and I had this huge crush on him. Anyway, we were playing hide and seek and I hid behind a big oak tree. As I was waiting to be found, I could hear this bird fussing about, making noise and flapping its wings. I looked up and could see a bird's nest in one of the tree limbs.

"Then something fell out of the tree and landed at my feet. At first I wasn't quite sure what it was, but after studying it for a few minutes I realized that it was a baby bird. It looked really strange because it didn't have any feathers at all, just a little fuzz on its wings. But it was alive.

"I yelled to Jimmy for help. He looked at the bird, then walked over behind the garage and came back with a big stone. Without a word, before I could stop him, he dropped the stone on the tiny bird.

"I screamed hysterically and all the adults came running. I lifted the rock and showed them what Jimmy had done. My father explained that mother birds sometimes push their babies from the nest because there wasn't enough food to go around or the baby bird was sick and was going to die anyway. 'If you try to put the baby bird back into its nest,' he said, 'the mother bird will only push it out again.' Is that true, Mike?"

I shrugged. I didn't know much about birds, but her dad's advice seemed to make sense.

"Poor Jimmy," Karen continued. "He tried to explain that he didn't want the bird to suffer and that's why he killed it, while I kept trying to explain that I wanted to be its Mommy and take care of it until it grew feathers on its wings. I kept thinking that if only that bird had a few feathers, Jimmy wouldn't have killed it."

"Why?" I asked, not sure of the point Karen was trying to make.

"Because then he would have seen that it was really a bird, not some ugly, scrawny creature with fuzz all over it."

"Oh," I said, "I guess it must have scared him. We all tend to destroy what scares us."

"You know, honey, I was convinced I could have saved

that bird if given a chance. It would have sprouted feathers and flown away."

"I have no doubt of that," I said, looking at Byron. I had my doubts about this little bird, though.

"For years I hated Jimmy for killing that bird. Funny thing is, I'm not sure I ever quite forgave him."

I did not know what to say to her. I knew it must have broken her heart to witness the death of that fallen bird, and I ached for her. Then I felt a sudden pang of guilt for having been so reluctant to look at Byron.

Maybe Jimmy smashed the bird so he wouldn't have to look at it suffering. Maybe I would have done the same thing. I needed to learn to be more like Karen, to be able to witness the suffering, take hold of it and turn it into a healthy life.

"I'm going to bed now," Karen said, giving me another good night kiss and patting Byron's head. "I love you, Mikey."

"I love you, too," I said.

She left the room, and some of the faint light seemed to go with her. The room seemed darker and suddenly chill. For the first time Byron and I were alone. I tried to feed him, but it was a struggle for both of us. He squirmed in discomfort, unable to get a good grasp on the nipple, which kept falling from his mouth. Each time the nipple fell out, I moved it in and out of his mouth until he began sucking again. It was a tiring, cumbersome process.

Then came the body tremors. I knew from reading the pamphlets that this was going to happen. Not knowing what else to do, I held little Birdie as close as I could while he shook uncontrollably, his little arms and legs jerking about like a marionette in the hands of a careless puppeteer.

Oh my God, I thought, *what did I get myself into?*

Byron began to make a little squeaking noise, as if something were caught in his throat. That made me panic big time. I wasn't a doctor or nurse. I had no training in drug withdrawal, except for those damn pamphlets. This kid did not belong with me. He belonged in a hospital.

Fear began to lay siege to my mind. What if the kid died? I'd be in the same boat as Jimmy: Karen would never forgive me. "Okay, okay, Mike," I said aloud. "Get a hold of yourself." There I was, doing it again—thinking of myself when I should have been thinking about Byron.

I knew the only way out of this mess, for the both of us, was for me to get in control of my fears. The only way to do this was to think of Birdie. I took a deep breath and readied myself to do battle with this hideous demon of addiction.

"I'll get you through this, little Birdie," I promised, clenching my teeth. "I won't let you down. You just hang on to me."

I wasn't sure how to help ease Byron's pain, but I started by placing him on my chest. I thought if he could hear my heart beating that would give him a place to focus, a sort of lifeline. I gently massaged his tiny back with my index finger. After a little while he stopped shaking, only to start again several minutes later. The poor kid must be exhausted, I thought.

On several occasions that night I thought Byron had fallen asleep, but it was hard to tell since his eyes were always closed. Once or twice I caught myself drifting off but managed to pull myself back into consciousness. A few times I almost gave in to the temptation to put Byron in his crib. The urge to crawl into my own comfortable warm bed and lay my head on my own soft pillow and dream about happy things was strong.

But more than I needed sleep, Birdie needed me.

During the long night I thought about many things. Some of my ideas were silly and nonsensical: I made up funny rhymes and said them over and over in my head. "Baby, baby on my chest. You're the bird and I'm the nest." Other times I thought about the print shop and scheduled an entire week's workload in my mind. I visualized new letterhead designs, business card layouts—anything to keep awake.

Once I glanced at a photo of my parents on the mantelpiece and remembered the first time Karen had gone to their house and met them. That was over fifteen years ago.

My mind drifted. I recalled what Karen had said to me later that evening, after the visit, when she was getting in my car so I could drive her home. "Those aren't the parents you described to me," Karen said.

"What?" I looked at her, startled. I had thought she'd had a pleasant evening at her prospective in-laws.

"You said you were a close family."

"Yes, and I meant it," I said. My family was always close, sometimes too close. One or the other of my parents was always around to take care of my wants and see to my needs.

"But a close family is one in which your folks are always there for you," she said.

For the life of me, based on that definition of "closeness," I could not understand how she could see my family being anything but close. My father worked at night so he could care for me during the day, and my mother worked days so she could care for me nights. Since I was an only child, I got pretty much everything I asked for, sometimes even when I didn't ask for anything. Once during a thunderstorm, I remembered, I had climbed into my parents bed, afraid of the noise. The very next day they bought me a puppy. "He'll protect you from the storms," they said.

"That's right, and we are close," I insisted. "Personally, I thought the evening worked out just fine."

"Oh, your parents are nice enough. That's not the issue. They're just not close to you in the ways that really matter," she answered. "It's nothing you can tell by watching. It's something I can sense. You and your parents—you're close in terms of proximity, but that's it. Your mom and dad were there with you when you were younger, but they weren't *there* for you."

The debate over whether or not I had a close family and exactly what the definition of a close family was caused an argument between us that lasted the full hour it took to drive her home. The more we talked, the more heated our words became.

"The problem is this," Karen said, losing patience with me. "You don't see any problem. When we have kids, what's going to keep you from repeating the same kind of 'close family' you had, where people wait on you hand and foot but don't come through where it counts?"

"What do you mean?" I asked. "You're so smart, you tell me what's missing. Why aren't we 'close' the way you mean? What is it that's supposed to count?"

"You'll figure it out someday," Karen said. Those were her final words and she never brought the issue up again.

Suddenly Byron, who had been sleeping peacefully, began to tremble like an aspen in a high wind. This time his tremors were much more violent than before and he was sweating like crazy. I was afraid that he was going into convulsions. I just kept holding on to him, telling him that everything would be better in the morning. It was just that that goddamn sun was sure slow in coming up.

At that moment, the only thing in the world that mattered to me was Birdie, and I was determined to pull him through this ordeal. If there were only some way I could have taken his pain into myself I would have.

Then a silly song by Herman's Hermits started running through my head and I started to sing to Byron: "Can't you hear the pounding of my heartbeat, 'cause you're the one I love, 'cause you're the one I love." Slowly his shuddering began to diminish and, after a few minutes, he once again lay still upon my chest.

In between Byron's fits I fed him formula, changed his diapers and cooled him down with a damp washcloth. I even said a few prayers. I figured someone up there had to be listening and I, as much as Byron, needed a lifeline.

As we entered the wee hours of the morning, I started to see myself as a medieval knight, strong and brave, and Byron as a new baby who would grow up to change the world. He had been entrusted to my care, and I vowed to faithfully protect him from all harm, even at the risk of my own life.

I smiled at the thought of me in a suit of armor. It wouldn't be bright and shining, of that I was certain. I had fought a lot of battles with former bosses, employees, vendors and fair-weather friends, and in the process had taken my share of hits. Furthermore, I had long since fallen off my white charger, so I had to rely on myself to get anywhere.

Who was I kidding? I was no knight, but maybe I was a good daddy. I was nearing thirty-seven and feeling the changes. I still had my hair, but it was thinning, and I was gray at the temples. But, old man or gallant knight, I was being true to my word: I remained wide awake as Byron rested on my chest, determined to fight off the invisible demons that tortured him.

After what seemed like an eternity, I noticed a glimmer of light and looked up through the patio doors; the horizon was beginning to turn red. The sun was rising. Glory, hallelujah! We had made it through our first night together.

I began crying as the sun climbed higher in the sky, the tears falling freely down my cheeks, tears of relief and strain. We had made it! We were home free! I knew that no matter how many nights Byron and I would fight this war, there would never be another so terrifying and dark.

"What's wrong?" I heard Karen's voice. I looked up at her through my tears.

"We made it." That was all that I could say. How could I explain that, after having three children, I finally realized what it meant to be a "close" family, that I had finally learned that to be a good father meant giving of myself, freely, without holding back or complaining. Nothing more. While I realized my parents had never been anything less than loving and caring to me, I now had a better idea of what Karen meant when she said "close."

Karen nodded. "You were there for him, Mike." She took the baby from me and stared at his face. "Look!" she said. Byron's eyes were open, the clear, pale eyes of a child who had survived a night in hell.

I took both Karen and Byron into my arms and began sobbing.

Two

THE EMPLOYEES AT THE print shop were well into their day by the time I arrived. Normally I was the first one there. I would make the coffee for the morning crew, deposit the receipts from the evening before, pay some bills, post the workload on the bulletin board and do whatever else needed to be done. I was the proud owner of Commercial Printing: Fast and Courteous Service For All Your Printing Needs.

I was feeling pretty chipper for having had only two hours of sleep, although from the stares I received from the shop employees I gathered I was not looking as good as I felt.

My pressman, Bill, who had been working for me since I started the business eight years ago, came striding into my office as I was pouring myself a second cup of coffee. "You look like hell," he said, getting straight to the point as he handed me a folder containing a list of jobs we had to complete before five that evening.

I rubbed my hand across my stubbly chin and decided, at the first opportunity, I would shave—and shower. How could I have forgotten to shower? At least I remembered to brush my teeth. At least, I thought I did.

I looked the workload over but there was nothing that appeared too complicated or out of the ordinary. "Doesn't look too bad," I said, replacing the separate sheets of paper in the folder and handing it back to Bill. "We'll probably be able to get this finished, oh say, half an hour before closing."

"Well, it is bad," he corrected me, handing back the folder. "You promised to have the lunch menus for Bowser's and The Grant Street Deli ready by ten-thirty, and the full menus for Soozie's and the Trattoria by ten forty-five. Plus we have two big brochure jobs that have to get out of here by noon."

"So what's the problem?" I asked, walking over to the corner table to inspect the box of Dunkin Donuts that I had noticed on the credenza.

"Last night one of the presses broke down, so we had to finish the rest of Blackenridge's job this morning," Bill explained, beating me to the donuts. He grabbed the only French cruller and bit into it. "M-m-m, this is good." He knew they were my favorite.

"I thought you'd be in at your regular time," he continued as he slowly munched on the donut, savoring each morsel. "I left a note for you on the bulletin board to get the press rolling, but you picked this morning to sleep in."

It was a good thing I was accustomed to Bill believing that he was the boss or I might have reacted a little more aggressively than I did. "I was up all night with one of the kids."

"Oh, no, which one's sick?" His burly tone of voice became soft and full of genuine concern. "I'll bet Connie's ear is acting up again. I knew when you got that swimming pool you'd have nothing but trouble with the ears. You should have called me. I could've come in early."

"It's none of *my* kids," I said, not wanting to get into a long conversation but knowing there would be no way of avoiding it. "It's Byron."

"Who the hell is Byron?" Bill asked in his usually charming manner.

"A foster kid."

"I thought his name was Adam."

I explained everything to Bill about how we got Byron and about our first night together.

"You're in deep, my man," he said, shaking his head, "and it's only been one day. I warned you about those people at CYS. You mark my words, they ain't gonna come and get that child. You're stuck with him now. I guess we better plan on you getting in here late for the next few weeks."

"A week," I corrected him. "Two weeks tops."

"Yeah, sure, don't worry about it," he said with a wave of his large, square hand. "I can take care of things around here. You help that little kid. He sounds like he needs you more than we do."

Bill took the folder from my desk. He ran his thick fingers through his massive mane of gray hair as he snorted like a raging bull. "Well, I don't know how we'll manage this," he said. "I don't know…"

I knew he had already figured out how we would get the work done, but he had a definite flair for dramatics.

"You call all the customers," he began, barking out orders. "Ask if they can pick up their jobs—that will save us a little time. I'll get Bobby, the new guy, on press two. After you're done charming the customers, meet me at the bindery."

"Okay, boss," I said, yawning. I was already beginning to feel the effects of the night before. "You're a lifesaver."

"Yeah, yeah," he said opening the door. Loud rumbling noises from the presses flooded the room, giving me a headache far worse than any hangover I had ever suffered in my earlier, more reckless years. "Save the sweet talk for your wife."

"But I like you better," I joked, raising my voice above the din.

Bill laughed, then stopped, closed the door and turned around. "You can mark my words," he warned, pointing his finger at me. "Those bastards at CYS are heartless sons of bitches. They're gonna screw you as sure as the day turns to night. You just ask my sister, Sally, what happened to her when she became a foster parent. She can tell ya a thing or two." He snorted again, as if to emphasize the truth of his words, and left.

Bill had already told me a little about what had happened to his sister. It seemed that Sally had wanted to adopt a little girl whom CYS had placed with her for four years. When Sally made the move to adopt, CYS came into the house, took the child and put her in another foster home. I remembered that a short legal battle had taken place, but Sally failed to get the little girl back.

I didn't know all the particulars, but I found it somewhat hard to understand that CYS would move a child if nothing was wrong with the family. Since I didn't know Sally except through brief phone conversations, I refrained from forming any opinion about who was at fault.

I gobbled down a couple of donuts, followed by a pint of chocolate milk. If Karen had only known the contents of what lay heavily at the bottom of my stomach, I would not have been allowed dessert for a week. Karen was always very careful about the family's diet. Especially mine. Although I never had a weight problem, she saw it as her duty to make sure I never would.

I joined the crew at the press and we worked nonstop through lunch. There was not a word of complaint from anyone as we pushed ourselves to meet the deadlines. Well, Bill did complain, but no one really paid him too much mind. We accepted his loud outbursts because every one of us knew he did the work of four men; complaints and the occasional curse were just his way of releasing tension.

As the day wore on, I wore down. I found it increasingly harder to concentrate, and often my mind would drift off to Byron. Was he eating? Were his eyes still open? Was he able to sleep? Sleep! I realized I had forgotten to tell Karen to rest him close to her heart.

"Bill," I called across the room where the pressman was busily stacking reams of paper on the shelves. "Take over the press, okay? I've got to make a quick phone call."

He waved in consent, and I hurried to my office and dialed the phone. "Hello, Connie," I said, "let me talk to your mom."

"Who is this?" she demanded.

"Your father. Remember me?"

"Yes," she giggled. "I know. I just wanted to see if you knew who you were."

Only Connie would think of such a thing to say.

"Here's Mom," she breathed into the receiver.

"Hi, Mike," Karen said. "How are things going at the shop?"

"Oh, fine," I answered. "I'm probably going to be an hour or two late, but considering the work we have around here, that's not too bad. How's Byron?"

"He's doing the best that can be expected," Karen answered. "But, Mike, he's so weak. The withdrawal is hitting him pretty hard today."

"Is he sleeping?" I asked. I felt as if I should just leave the shop and go home where I was really needed.

"Off and on."

"You need to put him next to your heart," I instructed her. "He needs to hear the sound of your heart beating."

"I'll try that," Karen promised.

I hung up the phone and returned to the press. I started the layout for a rush job and in my haste did something I have never done before: I accidentally turned the pages upside down and backwards. Fortunately, Bobby, our new hire, caught my mistakes before we began to print.

I praised him lavishly, and he gave me a shy smile. *How could I be so stupid?* I scolded myself. Of course, I knew the answer. I was dead tired, hungry as a dog and as smelly as a skunk, but I just couldn't stop. I had to keep pushing myself to get the work done. But even then there would be no rest for the weary. I did not have the slightest idea how I was going to function at work and still take the night shift with Byron. I thought about taking a few days off, just until Byron left, but that was out of the question. This was one of the busiest times for the shop and, although I knew I was not firing on all cylinders, I was still useful. Besides, Karen, who volunteered at the shop when she was needed, had more important business to attend to.

We finished the five o'clock job exactly at six ten. The customer did not care—much. I gave him a few tablets of note paper and a keychain stamped with the name of our company, then knocked a few dollars off the price. That kept him happy. He even gave me more work that was to be completed by closing the next day.

"Now, you'll have them done on time and you'll deliver them, right?"

"No problem," I assured him as I helped him load his car with the boxes of brochures, noticing that he was careful not to get too close to me. "Busy day," I explained. I was embarrassed that I had sunk so low in just one day. "It gets hot working the presses. It makes you sweat."

He smiled politely.

I went into the shop and helped Bill roll the carts, which were weighed down with a few tons of paper, into the storage area. "Thanks," I said to him, punching him lightly on the shoulder.

"For what?" he said, gruff as ever. "I'm charging you double for today. And you owe me two-twenty for the donuts."

He was always threatening to extract money from me, but he never did. In fact, whenever I offered to reimburse him for a snack, he refused my money. Whenever I gave him a raise, he would always worry that I could not afford it.

"Thanks for being a friend," I said.

"What?" he growled.

"I said, thanks for being a friend."

Bill grumbled something under his breath and walked away. He was not a very sentimental type.

I returned to my office to finish some paperwork that needed to be done, then called Karen to let her know I was on my way home.

"I'll call DiPietro's and order a pizza for us," she said. "You can pick it up on the way home. What do you want?"

"Hot peppers and mushrooms," I said, knowing I'd have at least half a pizza to myself. "I have to make a delivery downtown, so wait awhile before you call in the order." A squeaky voice in the background caught my attention. "Is that girl giving you any trouble?"

"No, not at all," said Karen. "Connie's been an angel all day. A real help. She's singing to Byron. Can you hear her?"

I listened carefully and heard Connie's shrill voice belting out a rock song: "De doo doo doo, de da da da...that's all I want to say to you..."

"A tender lullabye, eh?"

Karen chuckled, and we talked a little more before we hung up. I had almost forgotten about the delivery downtown and was about to lock the front door when I remembered. The Holstead Travel Agency down on Liberty Avenue needed the stationery we'd printed up for them.

Liberty was not a place I wanted to be too long after business hours. Although it was a bustling business area during the day, shortly after the shops hung their "closed" signs in the windows, that part of the city became home to a subculture of prostitutes, drug dealers, and homeless people.

I looked around the shop to see if anyone was available to accompany me to Holstead's, but Bill was busy checking the equipment for any potential problems and Bobby was nowhere in sight. I decided to make the delivery right away, all by myself, so I could get home before it got too late.

On the way to Holstead's I managed to hit every red light possible. The city was pretty much deserted and the street lights were just beginning to come on. As I drove down Penn Avenue, I saw a tired-looking man dressed in a blue pin-stripped suit, leaning against a bus stop sign. His tie was undone and his briefcase was propped against his leg. I sympathized with him. His family was probably missing him, too.

I liked it when the city was quiet like this, caught somewhere between the hustle and bustle of businesspeople and shoppers, and the night people who lurked in the doorways and alleys. I felt momentarily secure on its narrow streets lined with tall buildings, both new and old.

While I waited at my fourth red light on Forbes Avenue, I used the time to admire Pittsburgh's unique architecture, especially the old stone courthouse that looked almost like a medieval castle. When we'd first come to Pittsburgh from New Jersey ten years ago, Karen had been enchanted by the massive buildings with their carved friezes and huge granite steps.

Right smack-dab next to the courthouse was a brand-new office building, all glass and metal. The building was just one of the many changes that had taken place in the city since Karen and I had arrived. By the time we came, the steel mills and most of the large factories were closed. Nothing remained but the stories of a city where giant smokestacks loomed over the three rivers, bellowing black thunderclouds of smoke—the recollections of old men reminiscing over a bottle of Iron City beer at the local taverns. For most of the people, the mills and factories were fading from memory as Pittsburgh's new life as a service-oriented city began taking hold.

But, just as the mills and factories slowly faded, so had the city's friendly, provincial, small-town atmosphere. It used to be that passers-by would often stop to chat or help a stranger in the city; now they just barreled past each other without a word or a nod, as if other people didn't matter to them at all. I found that sad.

When the light turned green, I turned down a narrow side street. The shortcut would spare me at least two lights, which I felt sure would turn red the moment I approached them.

I turned on the radio and searched the stations for KDKA's news at seven. "Another suspected gang shooting leaves a pizza delivery man and father of three dead," announced the report, live from the North Side. "The suspects are two youths, fifteen and sixteen years old."

"Damn!" I said out loud. "Not another one." Pittsburgh was entering the big league, not only in jobs and funding for the arts, but also in violent crimes.

Ignoring the "authorized parking only" sign, I pulled in front of the Holstead Travel Agency and walked to the door. I found a note taped to the inside of the window addressed to "Mr. Printerman." The note read: "You're late. Go to back door and ring bell."

I got a cardboard carton packed with stationery boxes out of the back of the Land Cruiser, then walked around to the side of the building, searching for an entryway so I could carry out my instructions. I finally found an old, rickety iron gate, hanging precariously on one hinge, and nudged it open with my knee. I put the box on the step and rang the bell.

"Who is it?" I heard a voice call. It was deep and gruff and sounded a lot like Bill.

"The Printerman."

When the door swung open, I was surprised to see that the raspy, deep voice belonged to a rather attractive middle-aged lady. "Set it over there," she said, pointing to a beat-up desk.

As I turned to leave she stopped me. "Here," she said, removing the stationery boxes and handing me the empty carton. "You don't want to waste paper."

I accepted the box, thanked her for her conservation efforts, and promised that I'd put the box in the recycling bin at work.

The courtyard in back of Holstead's was filled with flowers and shrubs that someone had obviously tended with loving care. I stood near the open iron gate and leaned against the brick column to take a better look at the European-styled garden—a small concrete fountain, a wisteria-laden archway and a marble birdbath, tucked in the far corner, surrounded by red rose bushes. I was wondering how this design would look in my backyard when a man wearing a trench coat and wide-brimmed hat came by and tossed a dollar bill into my empty box.

I was stunned. He must have thought I was a homeless beggar. I was far too humiliated to correct the situation, so I tucked my head down and hurried past him to the Land Cruiser, waiting for this kind and generous stranger to pass. I thought if he saw me getting into my big car he might not make a donation to the next dirty, smelly guy he saw on the street who might actually need the money.

"Thank you, sir," I said as he walked by. He ignored me.

As I waited for him to turn the corner, I noticed three young women standing on the curb, as if they expected someone. The man who had just given me the dollar stopped and briefly spoke to the women, then shook his head and held up two fingers. A young black woman wearing tight jeans, a white halter top and red high heels nodded, then walked off with him. I assumed a deal had been struck.

One of the remaining women saw me and called out, "Hey, mister—you want some, too?" She turned and wiggled her buttocks at me.

"Forget him," the other one said. "He ain't got no money."

What a day! I said to myself as I hustled into my car. I wanted to get out of the city. *Now.*

I FORGOT TO PICK up the pizza.

When the kids and Karen learned of my blunder, I was forced back out into the car to drive another ten minutes to the pizza shop.

When I got back I checked on Byron, then sat down with Karen and the kids and ate some of the pizza with them. Afterwards I headed for the shower. The hot water felt good, and I lingered in the shower for as long as I could but not nearly as long as I wanted to. My shift was about to begin and, despite my exhaustion, I was looking forward to holding that little boy in my arms.

I put on my yellow pajamas that had pictures of Daffy Duck all over them—a Christmas gift from Connie. I think she was trying to tell me something. Although I looked pretty stupid in them, they felt comfortable and I had a long night ahead of me.

"You look cute," Karen said, entering the bedroom with Byron in an infant sack.

"When you're as good-looking as me," I said, staring into the mirror as I sucked in my stomach and puffed out my chest, "you can wear anything you want and look like a stud."

She burst out laughing. That was one thing I could always do—make Karen laugh.

"How's my pretty birdie doing today?" I asked, looking him over. His little dark eyes were wide-open and he did not appear nearly as dreadful as he did yesterday. But then, I may have been getting used to him. "I think there's been some improvement, don't you?"

"I hope so," Karen answered. Her voice sounded tired and stressed. "I held him all day in this carrier, next to my heart, like you suggested. I was afraid to put him down."

"I'll take over," I offered, reaching out for Byron.

"No, you get some sleep," Karen said, pulling back the bedspread. "I can manage for a bit longer. I'll wake you in a few hours."

I said good night to the kids and crawled into bed. It was nine o'clock. A few minutes later, Karen woke me up: It was midnight, time for my night rounds.

I went down to the kitchen and poured myself a cup of coffee and ate what remained of the pizza. Karen and I took a few minutes to share the events of our day: Chris had a new girlfriend who phoned him five times, though he refused each call. Connie had an earache; we thought it was because of the pool. Cameron's favorite red plastic fire truck got run over by the mailman, but at least he put the rest of his toys away.

I was glad to hear that part of our life was normal. Byron, on the other hand, had suffered greatly.

"I don't know if he's getting worse or what," Karen said. "At first I thought he was getting better. He wasn't twitching much and his little body didn't seem as contracted as it did yesterday. But then...I don't know what happened. When I was feeding him, he started throwing up and began having convulsions. For a minute I thought we were going to lose him. I called Dr. Watts—you know, the kids' pediatrician—and he said, considering what Byron was going through, he was doing pretty good."

"Do you want to admit him into the hospital?" I asked. "Maybe he'll do better there."

"I asked the doctor about that and he said that no hospital could give him the care we're giving him."

"I'm sure he was right." I hoped he was because we were doing the best we knew how to do.

Karen laid Byron on the bed for a moment while I put on my slippers. Even sound asleep, he looked tense and hurt. Most newborns sleep with one arm up and the other extended, like a fencer in the *en garde* position. But little Byron slept with his tiny hands clenched in front of his face, like a boxer warding off a blow. Man, I thought, what kind of mom would do this to her own kid? Then I remembered the women I had seen on Liberty Avenue earlier that day; I guess Byron's mother had had a pretty hard life. It was no excuse, but it was a reason.

Karen went to bed and once again Byron and I were left alone. I knew how our evening would unfold. I would hold him close to my chest so he could hear my heart beating. As the night wore on, I would stand vigil over him, I would sing to him, rub his back, feed him, change his diapers and dab the tiny beads of sweat from his little forehead.

Later, Karen and I would join a class offering information on caring for drug-addicted infants, but just then we were on our own. I prayed that Byron would become strong enough to cry; he had a hard fight ahead of him.

Three

"DID YOU PUT THE tray of cookies on the serving cart?" Karen asked, as she rearranged the tapestry throw pillows on the sofa for the third time in the last hour.

I glanced at the cart in the hallway, groaning under a plate full of orange pumpkin-faced cookies. It was hard to believe it was the middle of October already; three months—not just a week—had passed since little Birdie had flown into our house.

"Cookies present and accounted for, ma'am," I answered, snapping to attention. It was the third time in half an hour that she'd asked me the same question. Karen's normally high energy level had climbed a few points while we waited for our caseworker to arrive. The caseworker was running late, and I feared that she had forgotten about our appointment.

If she did, it would not have surprised me. We hadn't had much communication with her or anyone else from CYS for that matter since August. When we did speak, it was always by telephone. Even then, they never called us: We were the ones who had to take the initiative.

Karen normally would be the one to call with little updates on Byron's progress. We were happy and relieved when Byron cried for the first time, drank an entire bottle of formula without stopping, and slept through the night, and we wanted to share his success with someone. However, we were always disappointed that CYS lacked the same enthusiasm as we had over our little Birdie's milestones.

I collapsed in my recliner in the living room and thought about calling the CYS office to remind the caseworker. "Where the hell are you?" I'd ask. Not really, of course, but I did always seem to be the one calling with questions. *When are you going to place Byron? How much longer is he going to stay here? When are we going to get Adam?* But when I tried to get information from them regarding Byron's and Adam's future, the answers were always vague. After our conversations, I was left feeling confused and frustrated.

When we learned that Adam had been removed from the care of the good Sisters at Divine Providence, we demanded a meeting with our caseworker and insisted that she come to our home to witness for herself Byron's victory over drug addiction. And here we were. Waiting. My patience with CYS was wearing as thin as Connie's Halloween devil's mask.

I should have listened to Bill more closely. So far, he was right—CYS had not come back for Byron as they had promised. I was afraid that CYS might prove Chris' prediction correct, also, and wondered if we would ever get Adam.

As I waited for the caseworker, I hung up a few Halloween decorations in the window; one was a green-skinned, mean-eyed witch. I immediately thought of the caseworker. Now don't get ugly, Mike, I scolded myself, picking up a folder that contained a list of questions I had prepared for that evening. I had, over the months, jotted down queries and random thoughts about CYS's policies concerning the placement of a child: adoption procedures, follow-up procedures, and the number of children in the system.

One concern in particular nagged at me. Was CYS in the habit of "dumping" children—just dropping them off in the first likely home and forgetting about them until a permanent placement showed up? I could not help but feel that we had been duped into taking Byron so that the caseworker's workload was lightened. If this "dumping" were not against their policies then, at the very least, someone from CYS should have been more active in monitoring Byron's follow-up care once the child was placed. What if we were unscrupulous people who only wanted the child for extra income? The monthly check for sheltering a child was close to four hundred dollars. Since CYS allowed several foster kids in a family, a person could make a nice living off them.

My thoughts were interrupted by giggles. My children had trooped into the family room and begun to play with Byron, who was lying on his dinosaur blanket in the middle of the floor. Connie was shaking a bright yellow rattle in Byron's face while Chris danced around the baby, holding the musical bear. Cameron was telling little Birdie all about the Batman cartoon that was playing on the television. I felt myself fortunate to have such happy children.

As the kids' laughter intensified, so did the volume of the television set. The Joker's evil chuckling filled the room.

"Turn down that TV," Karen called from the living room. "You go settle them down, Mike. Tell them I don't want any problems from them this evening."

I rose and went into the family room to give the kids last-minute instructions about keeping the volume down when I caught Connie tugging on the back of Cameron's shirt.

"Stop it!" Cameron yelled, pulling away.

"Stop what?" Connie asked, looking at me. Her face was as innocent as a baby's.

"Listen, young lady," I said, my voice slow and deliberate. "You keep your hands to yourself. Understand?"

"But, Dad," she protested, "Cameron touched me first."

"I did not," he countered.

"Did too," Connie said, reaching out to grab his shirt again.

"That's it!" I interjected. As I was about to send Connie and Cameron to opposite sides of the room the doorbell rang.

"Mike, get the door," Karen called. "I'm in the kitchen getting the coffee ready."

"You two behave." I shook my finger in their faces and gave them my stern, fatherly look. "I mean it." Then I streaked down the hallway to the foyer, my heart thumping. "Okay, Mike," I said to myself, "calm down and smile."

I opened the door and a rush of the cool autumn air burst in. "Come in," I said, surprised to see another CYS agent accompanying Byron's caseworker, who looked just as disheveled as the first time I had met her.

The women, both carrying brown briefcases, walked into the entry just as another gust of wind caught the storm door, forcing it to open wide.

"You go in and have a seat," I said, stepping out on the porch to secure the door.

I was about to close the door when the wind picked up again, scattering the leaves I had raked into a neat pile earlier that evening. The full moon cast a gloomy shadow on the front lawn: Halloween was in the air. I could smell it. It smelled like dead leaves, woodsmoke and frost. I closed the door and shuddered. I had a terrible feeling that this year the ghosts and witches would be real.

I joined the CYS agents in the living room as Karen entered carrying a silver coffee service reserved for very special guests only. The platter full of cookies already rested on the table in front of the ladies.

"You have a beautiful home, Mr. Derzack," said the lady who I had not met yet. I watched her as she looked about the room. Her appearance was in sharp contrast with Byron's caseworker. Her dark, short hair was touched with gray at the front and, in spite of the wind that was blowing when she arrived, every strand of her hair was in place.

"Thank you," I said, placing the tray of cookies closer to her. "I don't believe we have met."

"I'm Diana Wagner, Linda's supervisor." She reached out her hand to shake mine and I could feel cookie crumbs on her hand. I could not help but notice the jewelry she was wearing, since it jangled whenever she moved. I quickly counted five rings and six gold bracelets. Pay must be good, I thought.

"Mrs. Wagner can answer your questions better than me, so I asked her to come along," Linda explained, spooning sugar into a cup of coffee, then handing it to her supervisor. "I'm really quite happy she was able to make it. She's a very busy person, you know. She doesn't often have the time to make a call like this.

"I'm sure she is very busy," I responded politely, though I was thinking, *Hey! That's no reason to be over an hour late!* I was feeling myself getting just a little irritated. It seem that Linda was using this opportunity to butter up her boss.

I reached for my folder, which I had labeled QUESTIONS in big, black letters.

"I see you are prepared," Mrs. Wagner said, sipping her coffee. "Oh, hazelnut! I love this flavor. Where do you buy coffee?" She turned to Karen, attempting to change the subject.

"A shop in the mall," Karen said, standing. "I forget the name. But before we get off the track, let me get Byron so you can see how well he's coming along."

We all watched Karen leave, and for a moment an awkward silence filled the room. "Linda, I think you'll be surprised at how different Byron looks now," I said at last. Although I knew I sounded cheerful enough, I certainly did not feel at ease with these two women in my home, though I couldn't quite figure out why. Maybe it was because of Mrs. Wagner's gold, which glittered like the contents of a jewelry store display window. I was sure glad Karen never wore such ostentatious jewelry.

Linda did not answer. Instead, she picked up the tray of cookies and handed it to Mrs. Wagner. For two well-dressed, obviously up-scale women, they sure were chowing down on the sweets. Even Cameron didn't gobble cookies with as much gusto as they did.

"The doctor says that his weight and height are pretty good, considering he was almost two months premature and born addicted. Of course, he's nowhere near normal for a four-month-old baby, but in time and with good care, he'll catch up. Anyway, that's what the doctor says." I smiled, rubbing my hands together nervously, but the women stared at me with a look somewhere between boredom and disdain, as if they had just come for snacks and no other reason.

"And he sleeps through the night sometimes," I continued, determined to keep away that wall of silence that waited just behind my words. "There are still a few nights when he doesn't rest easy, but for the most part, I think he has finally shuddered his way through the worst of his withdrawal."

"Well, Mr. Derzack," Mrs. Wagner said, reaching for a chocolate cookie, "that is really nice to hear. It must have been difficult for you."

For me? What was this woman thinking?

"I'd say it was awfully difficult for Byron," I pointed out, remembering what had happened the night before. Byron had begun squealing in the middle of the night, and I had picked him up. The poor thing was shaking as if he were freezing to death. His tremors lasted only for a few minutes, but I was not sure if they would return, so we spent the night together on the easy chair. I held him close to my heart, as I had done many times. I had long since learned how to catnap with Byron in my arms. His shakes did not return that evening, but what about tomorrow or the next day? Then a horrible thought shook my mind. What if Mrs. Wagner's visit had an ulterior motive? What if CYS took Byron and gave him to another foster family? Could they take as good care of him as Karen and I? Could CYS assure me that the next foster father would hold Byron close to his heart through the night if Byron suffered a relapse?

"Here he is," Karen announced, holding Byron up for everyone to see. "Isn't he a handsome little boy?"

"Is that the same child?" Linda gasped, putting down her coffee and walking over to look at him. "He certainly has gotten black."

Karen and I looked at each other. Of all the changes that Byron had gone through, his color was the least of the surprises. I made a mental note to file her observation of Byron in my mind. I wanted to think about her comment later and get some perspective on it.

"How do your other children interact with Byron?" Mrs. Wagner asked, sipping her coffee.

"They love him just like I do." That was the first time I said aloud what had been in my heart. I loved Byron as if he were my own son.

"I love him, too," Karen said, sitting down beside me. She gently took my hand in hers, and I felt tears beginning to blur my vision.

"So, what about Adam?" I asked, clearing my throat. "I understand that you have moved him out of the care of the Sisters at Divine Providence. Is that true?"

"Yes," Mrs. Wagner said, "and we're very happy to say that we have found him a permanent placement."

My mouth dropped open and I could not speak at all. Karen gave me a little poke in the ribs and I snapped my mouth shut. What the hell? I thought. Bill had been right.

"I thought we were going to be his permanent placement," Karen said, switching Byron to her other shoulder. "I don't understand."

I understood. CYS had indeed duped us into believing that we would get Adam if we cared for Byron, even though they never had any intentions of giving us Adam. Instead they had just proved Chris' intuition entirely correct.

"Listen, why don't you just keep Byron?" Mrs. Wagner said, patting Karen's knee. "We can't find anyone willing to take him, given his set of problems. And, being so dark, well, that's a problem, too."

"Why?" I asked, more curious than angry at this point.

"I don't know the exact answer to that question, Mike. May I call you Mike?"

I nodded.

"Well, Mike," she continued, "it's just that darker babies like Byron...well, even African-Americans are hesitant to give a permanent home to very dark children. I hate to say this, but light-skinned children are preferred."

I knew what Karen was going to say next so I beat her to it.

"We'll take him," I said. "But I don't want to be a foster care parent. I want to adopt Birdie." Karen and I had talked off and on about this possibility and one night decided that we could adopt both Byron and Adam, with some adjustment from all of us.

"We don't care what color he is or how dark he is," Karen chimed in. "All that matters is that we love him and we can give him a good, stable home."

"Who's Birdie?" Linda questioned, wrinkling her brow.

"Byron. Birdie is his nickname."

"How quaint," sniffed Mrs. Wagner, diving for a macaroon.

"We think it suits him really well." Karen's voice was getting that high-pitched quality and I knew she was losing patience with this evening's meeting. "Now let's talk about adoption. I don't want to lose Byron the same way we lost Adam."

Mrs. Wagner and Linda stared at each other for a few moments, then looked at Karen holding Byron. I noticed for the first time the sharp contrast between Karen's pale skin and Byron's blackness. It was shockingly beautiful and natural, like the stripes on a zebra or the foam on the ocean.

"Now, now, Mrs. Derzack," said Linda in a soothing voice. "I'm sure you are as happy as we are that Adam has a wonderful home."

"Adoption is something that I think is a very strong possibility in your and Byron's case," Mrs. Wagner said, sounding very dubious. "Are you sure you want to go through with it? After all, he's awfully dark."

"Of course," Karen and I answered together. I was beginning to take her insinuation that Byron's dark color was somehow a liability very personally.

"The black community often requests that African-Americans adopt African-Americans," Mrs. Wagner explained, still staring at Karen and Byron. "But you will be given top priority because of how well Byron has adjusted to you and you to him. The only real challenge probably could be from the mother herself, but she, as Linda may have mentioned, has a very serious drug problem. Unfortunately, that isn't her only problem. She's a prostitute too, you know. That's probably how she gets her money for the drugs. I would venture to say that we will never hear from her again. In fact, the judge has already started terminating her parental rights regarding Byron's sister, so I'm sure the judge would not have any problem terminating them regarding Byron." Mrs. Wagner reached for the briefcase and made an attempt to stand up.

I motioned for her to remain seated. "I realize that you're probably anxious to get home, but I have some questions that I would like to ask."

"Go ahead, Mike," Mrs. Wagner said with a smile, settling back into her chair and laying her briefcase on her lap. "We have plenty of time. What would you like to ask?" She stared at me, reminding me of my fifth grade teacher, Mrs. Locus, and for a moment my mind went blank. Everything regarding Byron and Adam had changed in the matter of fifteen minutes and I was not sure of which questions still applied.

"Do we have to be approved as foster care parents before we can start adoption proceedings?" I finally asked. "We still have not received documentation that we have been approved."

"Yes, Mike, that will be necessary," she answered.

"How long will that take?"

"Normally it takes a few weeks to a month and a half," she explained, tapping her fingers on the briefcase. She eyed the cookies but didn't reach for one. "I'm not sure what's taking your approval so long, but I'm sure it's just some small oversight. Linda will look into it first thing tomorrow morning."

Linda nodded as she poured herself more coffee.

"How long will the adoption procedure take?" Karen asked.

Mrs. Wagner explained the process to us. After we became approved foster parents, CYS would petition the judge to terminate the mother's parental rights. When the rights were terminated, then it was pretty much a matter of normal adoption proceedings, which Karen and I were both very familiar with.

I did not see much sense in discussing my concerns about how Byron came to us or questioning the placement of Adam, so I ended our meeting. Besides, I was anxious to talk with Karen about our new plans. I was sure that once the kids got through their initial disappointment about Adam, they would welcome their new baby brother with open arms.

The wind was howling when Mrs. Wagner and Linda left our home. They struggled against the night wind, holding their skirts down with their free hands. As Mrs. Wagner turned to wave good-bye, a dark gray cloud drifted over part of the moon; her shadow, distorted in the half-light, seemed to twist and squirm on the concrete driveway. I quickly closed the door.

*S   *S   *S

THE NEXT MORNING, AS I listened on the other phone, Karen contacted Jane Worley, the director of services for CYS, and told her that we wished to start the adoption proceeding for Byron without delay.

"That is wonderful news," Jane Worley said, sounding genuinely happy for us. "But I have a very full schedule right now. Give me, say, two—no, three weeks and I'll take care of everything for you. We'll have the ball rolling before Thanksgiving."

"Hi, I'm Mike Derzack," I interrupted, hastily introducing myself. "I have only one question: How do you feel about the mother? Do you think she'll come back for Byron?"

"I don't see that happening, Mr. Derzack," she assured me. "The mother has not responded to the formal papers regarding termination of one of her other children, so I don't think she's going to care much about this child."

"Thanks for your time, Jane," Karen said and hung up the phone. I waited until I heard a click on the other end. So, it was going to happen. Byron was to formally be my son.

"Now you have a new Mommy and Daddy," I said to Byron, giving him a hug. "What do you think of that?"

The children were called into the kitchen where Karen and I explained the situation. Chris was the first to express concern about Adam. I explained that Adam was given to another family and was doing very well. "I knew it," Chris mumbled, but he seemed to be satisfied and went out to play in the backyard as Cameron tagged along behind him.

Connie ran to the phone and called her girlfriend who lived next door. "We have a new brother," I heard her say as I headed out the door on my way to the shop. This morning I would be close to being on time.

I took a few deep breaths as I strolled down the sidewalk. The morning air was chilly and invigorating. Autumn was in its full glory. The maple and oak trees shimmered in gold, red and orange, and I promised myself to take Karen and the kids to Skyline Drive that weekend so we could enjoy the changing of the seasons as a family.

As I walked by the rose garden, I noticed that the yellow roses were drooping. A mild frost had attacked during the night. I always hated to see my flowers wither and turn brown, but this morning I wasn't going to let anything dampen my spirits. I was feeling happy and proud, just like a new father is supposed to feel.

On the way to the shop I stopped at the supermarket bakery and picked out a chocolate birthday cake decorated with large yellow roses. The lady waiting on me scribbled a message on the cake in blue icing: "It's a boy!"

I paid for the cake and waited for the woman to box it, then took it to the car and placed it carefully on the floor in front of the passenger seat. As I was driving down busy McKnight Road, a car in front of me slammed on its brakes and I slammed on mine. A box of stationery I had placed on the passenger's seat slid off and landed on top of the cake. I heard a sharp *crack!* as the plastic cover gave way, then a soft shearing sound as the box cut into the cake and smeared the lettering. Later, when I examined the damage, I found I could still make out the word 'boy.'

When I arrived, Bill was standing outside the shop, bundled in an old brown sweater, struggling to put the key in the lock. Suddenly the keyring slipped from his hand. His arthritis made it difficult for him to perform intricate movements with his fingers.

I eased out of the car so softly he didn't hear me. "Damn thing," I heard him say, as he stooped to pick up the fallen keyring. His old army dog tags slid from his neck and dangled in front of him.

I approached him silently. "Great morning?" I whispered into his ear.

He was so startled he dropped the keys again and his dog tags flipped up in his face. "You damn-near gave me a heart attack."

"Sorry," I said. I patted his tags. "Why wear these old things, Bill? They're falling apart. Heck, they're downright dangerous!" I touched his face where a tag had nicked the skin.

"Hell, a soldier's got to have his tags," grumbled Bill, brushing away my hand. "I served in Korea, you know. Now I serve in Pinegrove."

I was about to ask him what he meant when he beat me to the draw. "You look like you're in a good mood. What the hell are you so cheerful about?"

We went inside and over a cup of coffee and piece of squashed cake, I shared my joy with Bill.

"I'm happy for you," he said, slowly stirring his coffee with his spoon. He seemed hypnotized by the movement of the spoon. "I could show you things about the hell you saved that little boy from that would make your curly hair straight. I try to help out, but damn it! Things are bad in the projects."

"What things?" I asked. I was curious to know everything I could about what might have been Byron's life.

"Things you can't talk about," Bill said, gulping down his coffee. "You gotta see them. Hearin' about them just don't paint the proper picture."

I knew I had to see those things Bill couldn't put into words, those places where he still soldiered. I realized there would come a time that Byron would express an interest in his roots and ask the same questions that Chris and Connie had been asking lately: What was my mother like? Who was my father? Where do they live? Do I have brothers or sisters?

Karen and I were prepared so that, when the day came, we could supply the kids with the names of their parents and all the other information we had gathered about their biological families. In many ways we were relieved that, should either one of our children seek out their beginnings, they would find good people who had gotten themselves into a difficult situation. In the case of Chris' and Connie's birth parents, it wasn't that they did not want their children; they just were unable to care for them properly.

I always felt that it must have been very difficult to give your child up for adoption. How painful it must be to lose a part of yourself to virtual strangers. Never knowing how that child turned out must be the worst kind of hell.

"Take me to see that world," I said. "I have to know for Byron's sake."

"Pinegrove Terrace ain't like that world of yours at Fountain Valley," he said, looking into my eyes. An opaque veil covered his blue eyes, causing them to appear gray. Cataracts, I thought. How had he gotten so old without me noticing?

"There's no million-dollar houses," he continued, "no swimming pools, no Mercedes Benz, and hardly anyone to care for the kids."

"I want to go. I want to see it." If hell was where I had to go for Byron, I thought, then hell it would be.

Bill understood why I needed to know and agreed that, instead of having lunch, we would begin our descent into what he termed "the underworld."

The morning workload kept everyone busy and I hardly noticed that time was passing when Bill tapped me on the shoulder. "Come on."

Without thinking, I grabbed my car keys from my desk and followed Bill out the door. "What are you going to do with those?" he asked, pointing to the keys.

"I'll drive," I offered.

Bill laughed. "You're stupider than I thought. What, take your Land Cruiser into the bowels of hell? No, we'll take my car."

Bill's car was a rundown-looking, dark blue '78 Chevy Impala that had more than its share of dents and dings, but it ran like a dream. Bill had once shown me the engine, and it was as clean and shiny as if the car had just be driven off the showroom floor. The inside of the car was just as spotless.

As we drove down the Boulevard of the Allies toward Route 279, a plastic statue of Saint Christopher stood vigil on the dash, keeping watch on a string of rosary beads which swayed back and forth from the rearview mirror.

We turned off onto our exit, leaving the city behind us. I could see the dark red walls of Pinegrove Terrace in the distance. I had never visited that area of town before, but I knew that it was a development of project homes subsidized by the government.

I had seen pictures of the place on the evening news. Most recently a fire had swept through one of the apartments, killing a little boy. The fire chief blamed the fire on a smoldering cigarette; the community blamed the city fire department for not responding quickly enough to the blaze. Whether that was true or not, I did not know. However, the last time firefighters responded to that section of the city, they had been greeted with a crowd of angry people throwing stones and bottles at them, injuring a firefighter.

We followed a serpentine road up a steep hill, and there it was—narrow streets lined with row after row of red brick townhouses, blanketed with graffiti. The only pines in attendance were two spindly trees that guarded the entrance to the place. They rocked nervously in the breeze, as if they were on the verge of uprooting themselves and running away.

Bill and I drove past streets packed with houses, all of which looked exactly the same. Some of the homes were missing doors; other doors hung, bent and twisted, on their hinges. There were broken windows held together with duct tape and some that were missing the glass altogether. I couldn't see any lawn to speak of, just little patches of brown grass. Garbage lay on the ground and spilled out of dumpsters.

Behind several of the houses, shirts, underwear and socks were clothes-pinned to white ropes that had been hung between gray, weather-beaten posts. Toys, barbecue grills and lawn equipment lay strewn about the courtyards.

Other than looking unkempt and well-lived-in, though, the place seemed peaceful enough. Mothers sat on their steps, surrounded by young children, and groups of men huddled together in the shadows. Seven or eight kids, listening to music which blared from a black tape player, stood on the corner and waved to us as we drove by.

"Hey, Bill, how ya doin', man?" A young boy, maybe eleven or twelve, ran after the car and thumped his hand on the trunk.

"See anything strange about those kids?" Bill asked me. He stopped his car, rolled down his window and called to the boy.

I shook my head. I didn't see anything unusual. The kids, who were all black, appeared well-fed, healthy, and, in spite of their grungy-looking clothes (which Connie had explained to me were the height of fashion), were perfectly clean.

"It's a school day," Bill growled. He stopped the car, rolled down his window and called out to the boy who had followed the car. "Why aren't you in school, Charles?" Bill asked with all the concern of a worried father. I was touched by his genuine caring.

"Ain't no school today," the boy lied. "Who's that dude with you?" he asked, sticking his head in the window. "I ain't never seen him around here."

"I'm showing him around the place," Bill said, taking a packet of peanut butter crackers out of his glove compartment and handing it to the boy. "He's thinking about moving here."

"Thanks, man," Charles said, stuffing the crackers into the pocket of his Steelers jacket. I saw the logo on the zipper pull: Starter. Expensive make. "Got any more?"

"Go on," Bill snarled, shoving a small box of raisins into the child's outstretched hand. "Get out of here." We heard another thump on the car as we pulled away. Now I understood why the outside of Bill's car looked the way it did.

"Where are their parents?" I wondered out loud.

"Pick a night and I'll show you," he said, steering his way out of the development and onto the main highway. "'Course, it's not too safe here at night. All these people— they usually go no further than their own courtyards. Gangs, you know. Drive-by shootings. Charles was taking a big risk coming into the street after us.

"Anyway, we've gotta go. Got a lot of work to do back in the regular world."

As we drove back to the shop, I learned more about Bill's "soldiering" at Pinegrove and other dead-end places throughout the city. For years he had been volunteering his time at local churches, soup kitchens and wherever else he could lend a hand. Helping people was his real vocation.

I began to feel uneasy about my own degree of generosity. Bill, who had so little of life's luxuries, gave so much. I, who had a lot more than he did, needed to do more for my own community. I thanked Bill and God for the reminder.

THAT EVENING I JOGGED through the streets of my neighborhood, the cold air biting my face. I still was troubled over my tour of Pinegrove Terrace and needed to do some serious thinking.

My trip to the projects had opened my eyes about the results of government-supported housing programs. There wasn't any pride of ownership in that community. I was not so sure that I would feel any different about living than Charles did if I had to live in that squalid place. Just the thought of staying one night there caused me to run faster.

I passed block after block of groomed lawns and gardens carefully landscaped so that every season they burst forth with a colorful riot of flowers, bushes and hedges. Crocus, tulips, hyacinth and forthesia in the spring; foxglove, day lilies and roses in the summer; and neatly-trimmed green hedges and holly with red berries in the winter. Now the gardens were yellow and lavender with mums and dahlia blossoms. It was a well-planned spectacle of nature.

The swimming pools were all covered in preparation for the harsh Pennsylvania winter, but the fountains gracing the front yards were still spouting water into the air. Soon, they would be shut down for the winter, too.

I did not know how my neighbors had come by their

money, but Karen and I had worked hard for ours. Both Karen's and my parents were blue-collar workers, struggling like everyone else to put food on the table. They had given us love, support and a strong work ethic, but never much money.

I didn't feel guilty that I lived better than the people of Pinegrove. After all, I had been working over twenty years, mostly in blue collar jobs. Still, I was disappointed in myself for not having experienced the poorest part of the city sooner.

I stopped in front of the largest and by far the most impressive house in the plan. Rumor had it that almost everything in and around the house was imported from somewhere in Italy. The marble was from Rome, the gold bathroom fixtures came from Florence, and the stained glass was from a monastery in some village in Tuscany. The man who owned the home made his fortune selling security alarms. In a twisted sense, crime had been good to him.

Four

HE COUNTDOWN HAD BEGUN. It was twenty days until the arrival of Santa Claus. Still no call from Jane Worley about the Derzack's most coveted Christmas present.

One day we made arrangements to pick up the children early from Divine Providence, intending to take them to the mall for pictures with Santa and lots of Christmas shopping.

Karen dressed Byron in a modified red and white Santa suit (no black boots or belt) with a matching tassel cap. "All the kids wore this," was her defense of the outfit that I thought looked stupid. "It's a family tradition."

"Did Chris, Connie or Cameron think they looked cute when you showed them pictures of themselves looking like a miniature Mr. Claus?" I asked, remembering how embarrassed they got when Karen placed their pictures on the fireplace mantel each Christmas.

"Wait until they grow up," Karen argued. "They're too young to understand family tradition now, but they will when they have children of their own."

I was whispering my apologies to Byron for his mommy making him look silly when the phone rang.

Karen answered it.

"Mike," she said, covering the mouthpiece with her hand. "Pick up the phone. It's CYS." She turned back to the receiver. "My husband is on the other line," Karen informed the caller.

"Hello, Mr. Derzack. I'm Trixie Culvert." The woman's voice quivered slightly. "I have some good news."

Finally, I thought. It had been over a month since Karen last spoke with Jane Worley.

"We have found a pre-adoptive black family for Byron and we'll be picking him up in two weeks," she said.

"You what?" I asked. My heart tightened in my chest.

Trixie repeated her message in a firmer voice.

Stunned, I looked over at Karen. Her face was white and drawn: She was as devastated as I was. That heartless caseworker did not have the slightest idea that her words stripped from us every part of our being. I felt that I was floating, lost, like little Birdie must have felt on those long, dark nights months ago.

I glanced over at Byron who was lying on his Barney blanket. He looked like a forlorn little Santa. He was *not* going to leave me. I wasn't letting go of him.

"I don't understand," I said, trying desperately to remain civil. It seemed that every time I had any communications with CYS those were the first words out of my mouth.

"It's our policy to place black children with black families," said the caseworker, an arrogant tone replacing her earlier nervousness.

"I want to see that policy," Karen demanded. "You send it to me. No, never mind. I'm coming down to get a copy of it."

"That won't be necessary," said the woman, nervous again. "I'll make sure you get one." Then, without a good-bye, she hung up the phone.

Karen immediately called CYS back and demanded to speak with Byron's caseworker, Linda. She was not available. "Then let me speak with Mrs. Wagner," Karen yelled into the phone. The supervisor was in a meeting. "Then who is available?"

I took the phone from Karen. "This is Mr. Derzack. Put me through to Jane Worley."

"She's gone for the day," the voice said. I glanced at my watch. It was one o'clock in the afternoon.

"I know there must be someone I can speak to," I said, straining to keep my composure. "Unless you put me through to someone in authority, I'm going to come down there, and I won't leave until somebody answers my questions."

"We are open until four o'clock," the voice said sweetly. Then she, too, hung up without the courtesy of a farewell.

My emotions leaped from anger to frustration to sorrow all in a matter of moments. I could not believe that we had been betrayed by the very powers who had seemed so optimistic for us. What had gone wrong?

I tried to think, but I was frozen numb. I heard Karen sobbing and I came back to my senses. She was standing in the kitchen, holding Byron and rocking back and forth. Karen was only five feet tall, no more than ninety-five pounds, and she was often mistaken for the sister of our children instead of their mother. My heart was falling to pieces as I looked at this waiflike woman, tears streaming down her cheeks, clinging to our son. I had to be strong and smart if I was going to keep my family together.

I picked up the phone and called CYS. Again.

"Jane Worley, please," I said.

"Who's calling?"

"Joseph Smith," I lied. "I'm returning her call."

"I'll put you through."

"Jane Worley, may I help you?" Her voice was friendly.

"Jane, this is Mike Derzack," I said, wishing I were standing face to face with her.

There was a long pause.

"Oh yes, Mr. Derzack," she said softly. "What can I help you with?"

We talked for fifteen minutes about Byron. Throughout our conversation, Jane Worley was as pleasant as a warm summer day. "I understand your concern and I agree with you," she said. "Byron will not be moved until all your questions about his care, his placement and our trans-racial placement policy have been answered to your satisfaction. We owe you that, Mr. Derzack, for all the care you've given him."

I thanked her and hung up the phone. Thank God, I thought. I had at least bought some precious time. My attitude was now cautiously optimistic. At least I had the sympathies of the director of CYS.

Karen and I went about performing our holiday duties, enjoying them as much as we could. The children had their pictures taken with Santa, though Chris protested. At last he grudgingly gave in to Karen's insistence. "All right," he warned, "but this is my last year as a little kid." Karen agreed.

We had dinner at the food court in the mall. Our small table on the balcony overlooking the first level shops was filled with pepperoni pizza, French fries with melted cheese, hoagies and soft drinks. As we laughed and joked with the children, the grim possibility of Byron leaving us hung in the back of our minds.

The kids left to shop for gifts for Karen and me. Karen finished feeding Byron his bottle, then we walked around the mall, showing Byron the Christmas displays that adorned each shop window. He was as impressed as a five-month-old could be, but the colors all looked dim and dingy to me.

"I can't bear to think that they're going to take him away before Christmas," Karen said again and again.

Each time she spoke those words, I assured her that I would not let that happen. I did not know what my options were, but it just did not seem right that CYS could do such a thing. I wished Bill were around so I could have asked his opinion, although I was pretty sure he wouldn't have anything good to say about CYS.

SEVERAL DAYS HAD PASSED since I spoke with Jane Worley. Karen and I had gotten over our shock and our lives were returning to normal. Both of us believed the best way to approach the situation with CYS was to put our questions and concerns in writing.

One morning Karen brought Byron down to the shop so we could draft a letter to CYS. We were halfway through it when Bill interrupted us. "CYS is on the phone," he said, wrinkling his brow. "Those bastards."

Karen took the call. The conversation was short and one-sided. I could tell by the sullen expression on her face that the news was not good.

"They say they're coming to take Byron tomorrow at nine o'clock," Karen murmured, sounding as if all hope had just been drained out of her.

Bill grumbled something under his breath, then closed the door behind him and left us to figure out our problems alone.

"What are we going to do?" Karen asked, pacing the floor. "They sounded pretty no-nonsense."

"One thing I can promise you—come tomorrow they'll leave our home empty-handed." I picked up the phone book and looked up the telephone numbers for all the media in Pittsburgh. It took most of the afternoon, but one by one I told them my story. Everyone agreed to come to the house to report on the event.

As a final courtesy to CYS, I contacted the only person who cared to get on the phone with me at their office, the deputy director of CYS. I told her to be prepared for the media tomorrow morning. After a long pause, she replied,

"Well, just make sure you hide Byron's face, and don't give his last name." The battle had now to come to a head.

That evening I could not sleep. Karen did not even try. She stayed in the kitchen, cooking and baking, until dawn.

By eight-thirty in the morning most of the press had arrived. The cameras were being placed into position, tape recorders were being loaded with fresh batteries, pens were poised ready to write, and Karen and I were both silently praying.

Promptly at nine o'clock two female employees of CYS pulled into our driveway. We watched from our window as the cameras filmed them walking up our sidewalk and onto the porch. Before they had a chance to ring the doorbell, I opened the door and stepped out onto the porch. Karen stood close beside me holding Byron.

"We're here to get Byron," the older lady said, reaching out to take him from Karen's arms. Karen moved back slightly into the protection of the foyer.

"Where is your court order?" I asked.

They looked at each other, dumbfounded. They seemed like two robots who had just lost their programming.

"W-we don't have one," the younger caseworker said, shrugging. "But you must give us Byron."

"No," I said flatly. "I won't without a court order demanding that I do it."

They stood staring at me in silence for a full minute. Then, with the cameras still rolling, they simply stalked off, ashen-faced. The reporters crowded around us, asking questions, and we answered them as well as we could. It wasn't much of an interview, but it gave us an opportunity to inform the community how subversive CYS was.

As long as it took for the caseworkers to report back to their office empty-handed was as long as it took for Jane Worley to call us. "Listen, Mr. Derzack," Jane Worley said, her pretense of friendless gone. "I don't appreciate you embarrassing my people the way you did. Your behavior was rude and completely out of line. My job around here is hard enough without the likes of you. I'm sending the counselor and caseworker back out for that child, and I suggest you hand him over before things turn nasty. And, Mr. Derzack, be forewarned, I am rapidly losing my patience with you."

She was losing her patience with me?

"Jane," I reminded her, "you said that you would not take Byron until our questions were answered and I'm holding you to your word. My questions haven't been answered yet."

"There is something you don't understand, Mr. Derzack." Her voice grew louder. "I don't have to answer any of your questions. We have found a black family for a black child and that's the only answer you need and the only one you are going to get."

"Please give me some reason why you are taking Byron away from us other than him being black and us being white," I pleaded. "Did we do something wrong?"

"Mr. Derzack, I'll repeat this just one more time," she said, slowly sounding out each word. "We give blacks to black families."

I was prepared for that and fired off a stream of questions in quick succession. "Who is this family? How many children do they have? What does the father do for a living? Where do they live? Do they know about Byron's addiction? Do they know he needs special care? See? I have a lot of questions."

She clammed up completely. I realized that our conversation had ended and I said good-bye. She slammed the phone down. Doesn't anyone there know how to end a phone conversation? I thought.

Karen and I were nervous for the entire day. We were not certain how our plight would translate to the public when it aired on the six o'clock news. We had just brought to the community's attention that a white family was fighting to adopt a black child. How would that play in Pittsburgh? I wondered. What if the Klan got involved?

It wasn't all that long ago that the North Hills of Pittsburgh had witnessed a cross burning when a black and white couple moved into the neighborhood. And Mel Blount, a former Pittsburgh Steeler, was still experiencing problems with the Klan in his efforts to help black children. They had even threatened to burn down his youth home and kill him.

We all huddled around the television, ready to videotape our impromptu interview. We managed to catch the coverage on WPXI, KDKA and WTAE.

"You look very beautiful on TV," Chris complimented his mother. "And, Dad, you spoke very clearly." I guessed that was Chris' way of saying I did not photograph well.

"This is s...s...so embarrassing," Connie said, covering her eyes. "Dad, everyone's going to see your hair sticking up. You look like a wild man."

Cameron was the wisest of all. He had no comment.

Byron continued to cuddle with Karen, unaware that the match had been struck to ignite our world.

Shortly after our segment aired, the phone began to ring continuously. Caller after caller offered their support and encouragement. "God bless you," one lady said, crying. Karen and I were overwhelmed with the amount of compassion that poured through the telephone wires from people we had never met.

Those many phone calls renewed our hope and gave us courage to push onward. While I was engaged in a conversation with a black woman who was discussing the problems that face the black community, our call was interrupted by the operator who said there was an emergency call coming in.

I panicked. I felt that something awful had happened to my father. Karen saw me struggle to catch my breath and picked up the hall phone. Then, like the wicked witch from the Wizard of Oz, Jane Worley's voice came through the receiver. I was so relieved that it wasn't bad news about my father that I could not be angry with her for scaring me so.

"Mr. Derzack." Jane Worley was businesslike and abrupt. "You are to appear in court tomorrow. Judge Lerner's office at nine o'clock. And make sure you bring Byron." As I expected, she hung up the phone in her usual manner—with a crash.

"They mean business," Karen said, trembling.

I put my arm around her. "We'll get through this," I assured her. "They won't take Birdie from us."

I called a few attorneys and briefly explained our situation. Although all of them were sympathetic, only one had time to meet us at the courthouse the next morning. I felt somewhat relieved that we would have counsel present, even though he or she would only have a sketchy idea of what was going on.

After the kids were all in bed, Karen joined me in the kitchen. I had just eaten a ham and cheese sandwich, yet was still hungry. "Let's have a pizza delivered," I said, dialing DiPietro's Restaurant.

"None for me," Karen said, holding up her hand.

"A large with everything on it," I said. All day I had felt as if I were starving.

By the time the pizza had arrived I had already downed two Clark Bars and a glass of milk.

"What's your problem?" Karen asked, as she watched me gobble down the pizza. "I've never seen you eat like this before."

I didn't know. I was just hungry.

Neither Karen nor I could sleep so we passed the hours in the kitchen, reminiscing about our three failed adoptions. Our first attempt was the most painful.

A young mother with three small children found herself pregnant again. The husband's job did not pay enough to support the five of them, and another mouth to feed was simply out of the question. Teary-eyed, the mother approached us when she heard that we were trying to adopt.

We agreed that, by law, all we could pay for were the medical and legal expenses. Karen grew happier with every day that brought us closer to having a child to love and raise as our own.

Karen was present during the delivery. It was a baby girl, and Karen was the first to hold her. We were to pick the child up the following day, but when we arrived, both the natural mother and father were waiting to speak with us. We went to the maternity ward and entered the room amid the sounds of shouting and sobbing. I felt as though we were interrupting a fight. Tears were streaming down the face of Marie, the natural mother.

"Here's the deal," the father said, not wasting any time. "You get the child if you give us money to get to Texas, six months rent and ten thousand in cash. Then we'll bring back the kid to you."

I was speechless. He was selling his baby to us.

"Yeah, mister," he said, resting his foot on the bed. "If you don't pay it, someone else will." He was probably right.

I looked at Karen. "Well?"

"Marie, do you agree to this?" Karen asked, moving closer to her.

"I don't have any say-so." She lowered her head.

"Of course you do," Karen said, sitting down beside her. "This is your baby. Don't you want what's best for her?"

"I know what's best for the kid, and that's whatever's best for her old man," the husband said, standing up and moving in Karen's direction. "And lady, what's best for me is a ticket to Texas, rent money and ten thousand bucks."

"We can't agree to this," I said, still in shock over this father's callous treatment of his child. "It's against the law to sell babies."

"Then go call the police," the father laughed. "By the time they get here we'll be long gone."

They checked out of the hospital as we stood in the hallway and stepped into the elevator with the infant. As the elevator door closed, I knew a door had slammed shut for Karen and me. We both felt helpless and sad, realizing that some desperate couple would pay the asking price to have this little girl. We returned home in silence, only to be greeted by a party of friends and neighbors, who had prepared a celebration for our new baby. It was a depressing evening for all of us.

"But," Karen said, wrapping the last piece of pizza and placing it into the refrigerator, "That was then and this is now. We've gotten a little smarter and we know how to fight."

That was certainly true. Tomorrow would be our testimony of just how skilled we were in fighting for our children.

AROUND THREE-THIRTY IN the morning Karen and I decided that we would at least try to get a few hours of sleep. Despite my worry, I fell asleep as soon as my head hit the pillow, and my sleep was peaceful and absent of dreams. When Byron woke me up for his five o'clock feeding, I felt surprisingly refreshed and alert. Karen, on the other hand, was tossing and turning.

Later that morning, Karen fed Byron while I tended to the other three kids. I got Chris and Connie off to school and took Cameron over to a neighbor's house. I felt a constant flow of nervous energy pulsing through me, as if I were going on vacation for a week or about to interview for a fantastic job. I was in such a rush to get things done that I was sure I had forgotten something. We were hurrying out the door when the phone rang.

I told Karen to let it go, but she was worried that a phone call that early in the morning was important, so she answered it.

"Hurry up," Karen called excitedly from the hallway. "Congressman Ron Klink is on the phone. He wants to talk with both of us."

With Byron in my arms, I ran to the kitchen phone. A congressman wanted to speak with us?

"Congressman Klink," I said, "Mike Derzack."

"I won't take up much of your time," he began. "I know

you have a hearing this morning with Judge Lerner, but I think what I have to say will be of interest to you."

"I'm sure it will be, sir," I said, sitting down on a chair.

"Saw your story on TV," he continued. "Just want you to know I've had my share of dealing with Lerner when I tried to adopt my foster child, and I'm calling to warn you not to trust him, CYS or any of the child advocates. They're all in bed together."

"I understand," I said. The pieces of the puzzle were coming together for me. CYS was not in the business of helping kids; they were in business to do business. These kids were their bread and butter, and they would do whatever it would take to keep the children warehoused and ensure the survival of their agency and jobs. They'll say anything to the judge if they think he'll buy it. And keep in mind that the judge wouldn't have his position and neither would the child advocates if CYS was doing what served the best interests of the children in its care.

"One last bit of warning," he said. The concern I heard in his voice seemed to come from his heart. "Don't leave that courtroom without that child. If you do, you'll never see him again."

"Thank you for your call, Congressman," I said, holding Byron a little closer to my chest. I could not bear the thought of having his world turned upside down. "I don't have any intentions of letting them take my child until I am sure his best interests are being served."

"Let me ask you, Mike—what excuse did they give you for taking Byron?"

"We're not black and Byron is."

"I'm no lawyer, but that sounds like it's against the law," the congressman said. "If you need my help, call me. Good luck to both of you."

I hung up the phone more frightened than ever. I was also more confident than ever, and ready to make a stand. I knew there were forces at play that I was not aware of. I felt as if I were going into battle without armor and without a weapon to fight an enemy I could not see. But I was ready to take on the world if need be for Byron's and my family's sake.

I opened the door to leave and was greeted by a wave of media, lobbing questions at us left and right. Karen and I huddled close together, trying to protect Byron from this strange world. I only made one statement: "We will do what it takes through legal means to keep Byron with us."

WE HAD LITTLE TROUBLE locating Juvenile Court since it was across the street from Magee Women's Hospital, a place that was very familiar to Karen. The doctors there had performed countless tests on her, conducted five failed attempts at artificial insemination and gave her countless injections of fertility hormones. It was also the place where she had given birth to Cameron.

This was our first visit to Juvenile Court and I found the whole process very disturbing. A line of screaming kids and growling parents formed outside the entrance. I thought of the contrast between Magee and this hell hole, separated by just a street. The hospital did so much to bring children into the world and form a family. Juvenile Court was where all the failed families ended up.

Karen held Byron tightly as we waited in the chilly air. Dark snowclouds were forming on the horizon, and I hoped the winter storm the weathermen were calling for would not arrive ahead of schedule. The line moved very slowly, but we finally made it to the foyer, where hot air blasted at us from an overhead vent. I soon discovered what was holding us up: Each person had to go through a metal detector.

"Step over to the side," a hefty guard ordered a black woman holding a child in each arm as she and a young boy about twelve years old set off the security alarm. "Over here, Nancy," he called to a woman guard who stood off in the corner.

Nancy quickly frisked the young woman, the two small

children, and then the boy. "Here it is," said Nancy, pointing to a kitchen knife taped to the boy's leg under his jeans.

"I told you not to bring that thing," the woman said,
pushing him with her hip. "What's wrong with you, boy? I
should tell the judge that you're an evil child and let him
take you off to jail."

The boy said nothing. The knife was confiscated and the
woman and children were allowed to proceed to their
destination.

At first I was amazed. When I was that age, it would
never occur to me to smuggle a knife into a courtroom. Of
course, I realized a moment later, I hadn't grown up in a
place like Pinegrove Terrace. That boy was probably afraid
he'd have to protect himself and his family.

We walked through the metal detector and over to the
information table.

"Judge Lerner's chambers," I said to a gray-haired
woman who looked like she could be a grandmother to
world. "I have a nine…

"This floor straight back and to your left," she answered
without looking at me. "The judge is running late. Have a
seat in the hall and someone will come get you when your
case is being heard."

"Thank you," I said.

"Why, thank you," the woman said emphatically as she
looked up and smiled. "Those are words we don't hear too
often around here. This must be your first time."

"And hopefully our last," I said, wiping the sweat off my
forehead. I did not know if it was hot or I was just that
nervous.

"You're Mike and Karen Derzack, aren't you?" she said,
adjusting her silver-rimmed bifocals. "I saw you on the
news last evening. Good luck. You folks are pretty brave."

We walked up a couple of steps into a long hallway so
crowded with people that I couldn't breathe. The air was
stale and heavy with the stench of cheap cologne, body
odors and liquor. Karen and I pushed our way through the

throng of bodies to the front of Judge Lerner's chamber door. We stood quietly leaning against the tan-colored wall until a seat became available on one of the long black wooden benches scattered about the hallway.

"Do you know what our attorney looks like?" Karen asked, rising on tiptoe as she tried to peek over people's heads. "It's almost nine o'clock." She was so nervous she was almost jumping like a pogo stick.

"Relax, honey, she'll be here," I said, wishing that I had just one ounce of Karen's seemingly endless energy. "She said she'll recognize us from our newspaper picture."

The whole situation of being in Juvenile Court was weighing heavily on me. There were so many children with parents who appeared to be playing dress-up for the day. Men were wearing wrinkled, outdated suits that did not fit them very well, their ties crooked, their hair combed but dirty-looking. Most look of them looked tired and malnourished. The women wore everything from faded business suits to brightly-colored jumpsuits that looked wildly out of place in the somber halls.

These were people whose problems went far beyond bad hair days and ill-fitting clothing. When I looked closer into their faces, I saw fear and despair in their eyes. Their attempts to hide years of abusive behavior and neglect behind neckties and perfume were so futile and pathetic that I found it hard to look at them directly.

One little boy was crying and pounding his head against the wall. No one seemed to care. Once or twice the mother told him to stop, but that was the extent of it. I wondered if it would be appropriate to get a guard. I decided to tell the grandmotherly-looking person about the situation. She would know what to do.

"Oh, Mr. Derzack, you are a newcomer, aren't you?" she said with a smile, putting down her pen. "It's best you mind you own business. There's nothing you can do to help that child. If you try, you'll only cause trouble. And, Mr. Derzack, that's the last thing we need around here." The security alarm went off, putting an exclamation point on her comment. "See what I mean?"

I nodded and returned to my seat. The boy went on banging his head, and I really was beginning to consider trying to stop him myself when a voice called our name. "Here we are!" I shouted, jumping up and waving like some school kid answering a teacher's question.

A middle-aged guard with a belly that hung over his belt directed us to an empty courtroom and told us to make ourselves comfortable on the hard wooden seats. We waited and waited.

"Karen and Mike." A young lady who looked as if she were barely out of law school entered the room, a yellow legal pad tucked under her arm. "I'm Katie Johnson, your counsel. You'll have to bring me up to speed on what's happened to you."

We went through the whole story from the day Byron came to us through the phone call we received from Congressman Klink. "I don't think CYS has a leg to stand on," she said, smiling. "No judge in his right mind would take that child away from you.

She left the room, while Karen and I continued to wait. It was not until early that afternoon that we were summoned into another courtroom where our case was to be heard.

The room was surprisingly small and cozy. The judge's bench at the front of the room did not look as ominous as I had anticipated. Two young, attractive women in dark, conservative dresses sat on each side of the Judge's bench; one was the court stenographer, the other the bailiff. Five people were already sitting at the large semi-circular table directly in front of the judge's bench, and I recognized two of them: Linda, Byron's caseworker, and Mrs. Wagner. I assumed that one of the five was the attorney for CYS.

Katie instructed us to choose a seat among the row of benches at the back of the room where the "audience" sat. We took the last bench in case Byron started to fuss. As we were taking our seat, a light-skinned black woman, smartly dressed in a black skirt and white silk blouse, entered the room and quietly slipped into the bench across the aisle from us.

"She must be the lady who wants Byron," Karen whispered, drawing the baby closer to her.

"All rise," the bailiff announced, "Honorable Judge Lerner presiding."

We stood. I found myself hoping that, indeed, the judge was honorable.

"I don't trust him," Karen whispered.

Karen had an uncanny ability for making correct first impressions. In the many years I had known her, she was never wrong once when it came to "reading" people she had just met. I felt my heart sink a little lower.

The judge looked all right to me, though. He was somewhere in his earlier forties, average height and seemed a little on the thin side, though it was hard to tell for sure because of his flowing robes. His long narrow nose and narrow, deep-set eyes were accentuated by his slicked-back, dark brown hair that thinned at the top and curled at his shoulders. He looked more like a Latin tango dancer than an authority figure to me.

He spoke to my counsel for a few minutes. I strained to hear what they were saying but I could only make out a few unimportant words. He did not make eye contact with her, and that was a little disconcerting.

The court was brought to order. The CYS attorney requested that the judge remove Byron from our care, stating that we had not been formally accepted as foster parents and that CYS had found a black family willing to "consider" Byron for adoption.

"And, your Honor," the lawyer said, walking over to the judge with a newspaper in his hand, "the Derzacks, as you will see, refused to turn Byron over to CYS officials and went public. This is against CYS policy of the minor's right to privacy."

The judge took the newspaper, glanced at it, then put it

over to the side of his desk. I had guessed that he was aware of the recent media.

"Mrs. Wagner," the judge said, leaning forward in his chair, "can you tell me why you wish to remove the child?"

"Since Byron is an African-American, we have found a suitable black family for him, your Honor," she said, avoiding his eyes as much as he avoided hers.

"Who is this family?"

"A black mother who has full-time employment," she answered

"Is there a father in this household?" he continued, probing.

"No, there is not." Mrs. Wagner shifted her weight from one side to the other.

"Are there other children in the household?" From the weary sound of the judge's voice I could tell he was beginning to lose his patience.

"Yes."

"Are they playing Twenty Questions or what?" whispered Karen. I could only shrug in total ignorance.

"How many children, Mrs. Wagner?"

"Four, your Honor."

"Four children." He repeated. He sat back on his chair and ran his fingers through his hair. "When did you find this family?" he asked, staring up at the ceiling.

"Last week." Mrs. Wagner fidgeted with some papers and knocked them off the desk, scattering them on to the floor. She bent down to retrieve them, perhaps to escape Judge Lerner's questioning for a few minutes, but the judge was too fast for her.

"Leave them," he ordered.

Mrs. Wagner straightened herself in her chair, struggling to regain her composure.

"Now let's see...where were we?" The judge leaned forward and placed his elbows on the desk, resting his chin in his hands as if deep in thought. "Oh yes, you say you found this family a week ago. How?"

"The mother is an approved foster parent."

"How many of the four children in the household are foster care children?"

"Two, your Honor."

"Two," he repeated.

"Two, your Honor," Mrs. Wagner said nervously.

"I might bring to your Honor's attention that the Derzacks were contracted strictly for short-term shelter care. They understood that at the time," the CYS attorney said, taking the heat off of Mrs. Wagner, who took a deep breath and relaxed in her chair.

The judge nodded, as if this whole case were now making sense to him. Karen and I glanced at each other with a look that silently conveyed a single message: Things were not going in our favor. We had agreed to a short-term arrangement. We were sunk. I had the sudden feeling that they were going to take Byron from us before we left the courtroom. Our little boy had only a short time to remain in the security of our arms.

"And how long was that short-term shelter care supposed to be for?" the judge continued.

"I don't know, your Honor," the lawyer said, looking at Mrs. Wagner. The heat was on her again.

"Well, Mrs. Wagner, do you know?" The judge cocked his head to one side like some huge bird of prey which had just noticed a fieldmouse.

"Your Honor, it's hard to say how long a dependent like Byron will be in the care of a family, being drug addicted and all."

"How long did you tell the Derzacks that the child would be in their care?"

Mrs. Wagner coughed into a hanky. "A couple of days, maybe a week."

"And how long was he there?" This was worse than pulling teeth, I thought. I was glad I wasn't a judge, for I knew I did not have the patience to play this game every day of the week.

"Five months."

"If the Derzacks were approved foster parents, how long would they have had to have Byron in their care to earn entitlement to their questions regarding a new placement for him?" the Judge asked. I had a feeling that he already knew the answer.

"Six months," Mrs. Wagner answered, her shoulders slumping. "But, your Honor..."

"Does anyone from CYS care to give me any other reasons why this child should be removed from the care of the Derzacks other than his color?"

No one answered.

"Well, then I guess I've heard all there is to hear from CYS," the Judge said, abruptly swinging his chair to the left, then back again. "Next I'll hear from the Derzack's attorney."

Katie cleared her voice and stood up. "Your Honor, we are requesting that Byron remain in the Derzack's custody and that they be allowed to adopt said child." She sat back down.

That was it. One lousy statement. We were finished.

"And," Katie added, standing back up, "I ask that you give Mike and Karen Derzack an opportunity to address the court."

The judge raised his eyebrows and grinned. "Good thinking, Ms. Johnson. Although I already know what the outcome of this hearing is going to be, I'm still going to grant your request only as a courtesy. I know that the Derzacks' emotions are running high and I think that this court owes it to them to listen."

Karen was busy feeding Byron his bottle so I walked up to the witness stand took my seat before the Judge. I stared up at him. I was uncertain what to do next, so I waited, knowing that he was going to rule against us. I prayed that my words would change his mind.

"You may speak now," he whispered.

"Thank you, your Honor," I said, realizing that before

me sat not only a judge but a man who was probably a father himself. I decided to let all my defenses down and simply express my love for Byron. I told him everything from the moment Byron came into our lives, to the nights we spent together, to Byron's visit to the mall in his Santa suit.

"I was a good father before Byron came to us and I love all my children enough to die for them," I said, choking back tears. I closed my eyes and paused for a moment, fighting to collect my composure. "But Byron taught me a lot about myself."

I lifted my hands to my chest as if Byron were in them. "Your Honor, every night that I held my little Birdie made me understand more deeply what love was all about. I looked inside myself and, well, I had in my mind an image of myself, but Byron was like a little mirror reflecting back to me a man I did not recognize. At times I didn't like what I saw.

"Then Birdie would remind me of what I was capable of becoming. I let myself go, your Honor. I let myself love him. No questions asked. No conditions. This tiny, drug-addicted, homeless little black baby taught me that to be a good father I had to give of myself. The good with the bad. The whole thing.

"Birdie taught me..." I began to cry, but I kept on speaking through my tears. "He taught me to love the right way. Your Honor, we love him so much that if you can show me Birdie is better off without us, then I'm willing to let him go."

"Thank you, Mr. Derzack," said the judge. "You may join your wife now."

I walked back to Karen through a silent courtroom. A feeble smile crossed her lips and I could tell that she had been crying. I sat as close to Byron as I could get. Thank God he was asleep and would never have a memory of this horrible day. Goodbye, Birdie, I said to myself, I'll always love you.

The judge began his closing statements. He reiterated that not only was my testimony a courtesy but this whole hearing was a courtesy to Karen and myself. I felt as if my grip had been weakening and soon I would have no hope left to hold on to. My words of love had fallen upon deaf ears and cold uncaring hearts. The judge was going to force me to give up my son.

"It is the opinion of this court," the judge began, staring directly at the people in front of him. He paused and took a deep breath, as did everyone in the room. I held on to Karen's hand, crushed by the tension in the courtroom, which seemed strong enough to explode the place sky high. "...That the child's best interest is served by having him remain with his family, Mike and Karen Derzack."

"What...what did he say?" sputtered Karen. "Did he say...?

"We got 'im!" I gasped, and she collapsed into my arms. I held her so tight that I was surprised I did not hear a few ribs crack. We both cried with joy.

"Furthermore, since the father is deceased and the mother is unable to provide proper care for her child, I am instructing CYS to begin termination of the natural mother's parental rights. Also, I'm instructing CYS to assist the Derzack's in their adoption of Byron. If CYS decides not to assist in the adoption, the Derzacks have the means to do it by themselves." Judge Lerner turned toward the CYS attorney, his gaze as steady as a hawk's. "My strong suggestion is that you give them your support. Is that understood, counsel?"

"Yes, your Honor."

"Mrs. Wagner, do you understand?"

"Yes, your Honor."

"It is by order of the court that the child not be removed from the Derzack's home without prior order of court. Is that understood?"

"Yes, your Honor."

"Mr. and Mrs. Derzack, the best to you and your little boy." He went on to set a new hearing for February, then dismissed the court.

I looked over at the woman I thought was to be Byron's new mother. She seemed unaffected by the decision.

Katie ran over to us and joined us in a group hug. We had triumphed. The deputy director of CYS came over and joined in our hug. "I'm very happy for you," he said, offering me his hand. "Let's put this whole thing behind us and move on together to get this little boy adopted."

I shook his hand. At that moment, in the glow of victory, I believed he would stand by his words.

As we left the courtroom the media gathered all around us, snapping pictures and asking questions. When Byron woke with a start, crying, as the cameras flashed in his face, the sheriff's deputies pushed the media back down the hallway to give us some breathing room and protect us from the crowd.

"Mrs. Derzack, how do you feel about the judge's ruling?" shouted a young black reporter, standing on tiptoes.

"Christmas is already here for me," Karen answered, cuddling Byron. She began to cry. "The judge has given us our Christmas, and now we're going home."

"Mr. Derzack, any comments?" an unidentified voice called.

"I'm elated. Justice has worked on our behalf."

"What are you plans now?" another reporter screamed out.

"We have already scheduled a February court date to seek permanent custody of Byron. But for now, as my wife has said, we're going home."

As we passed by the crowd waiting in line to go through the metal detectors, a few people cheered and clapped.

"All right, Mother Derzack." A black boy around fourteen or fifteen stretched out his hand to give her a "low five."

Karen's arms were full, so I touched my hand against his.

"You want another child?" he asked. "I'll come home with you."

From out of the crowd came a face I had not seen in many years. "Jeanie, is that you?" I asked the young black woman.

"Yep, it's me, Mike. You're doing such a great thing. My mother and I just had to come down and be with you and Karen. We took the day off from work."

Jeanie had babysat our children on many occasions before we moved to Fountain Valley. I gave her a hug. It was so good to know that I had friends in my corner.

"Thanks, Jeanie," I said. "Merry Christmas to you and your family."

We were waiting to cross the busy street to the lot where our car was parked when I noticed the black woman from the courthouse talking to a flock of reporters. I had to find out who this woman was, whether she was the proposed foster mother or someone else. I tugged at Karen's coat and motioned for her to follow me. We walked over to the reporters and stood close enough to listen to the black woman as she was being interviewed, though I was careful that she did not see us.

"Black parents are best for a black child," she said, into the microphone. "A study commissioned by the National Association of Black Social Workers says that black children are better off with black families. Children in trans-racial homes are often deficient in self-esteem and feel alienated."

"Can you tell me more about this black woman who was considering adopting Byron?" said one reporter, motioning her to wait a minute as he thrust a new tape in the recorder.

"The black woman you are referring to is a loving, nurturing person. Black parents are best prepared to teach a black child about his heritage and to prepare him to deal with racism. Only someone who has been a participant rather than an observer is able to teach the black child about these issues. The only reason the Derzacks were selected to provide emergency care was that our agency has difficulty in finding black foster parents for black children and will place children temporarily in the homes of white families."

Our agency? I thought. All right, she wasn't the foster mother, but who was she? Why was she so important that she was being interviewed?

"Thank you, ma'am," the reporter said, shutting off his tape recorder. I watched as the woman walked across the street, and when she was out of earshot I approached the reporter.

"Excuse me," I called out to him. Karen was close behind me. "Can you tell me who that lady was you just interviewed?"

"Oh, that's Alice LaPort. She's a regional director for CYS," he replied, turning on his recorder again. "Did you hear Mrs. LaPort's interview?"

"Yes, we did," Karen answered, cradling Byron, who had fallen back asleep.

"What do you have to say about the cultural difference?"

"First of all, Byron is a part of our family," she said, calm and controlled. "We feel it is best for him to be with us. I have three children, two of whom are adopted, and together with them, Mike and I will work with Byron to help him learn about his black culture."

She turned to walk away, then turned back. "One more thing," Karen added. "You know, learning is not a one-way street. We'll learn from Byron and he'll learn from us."

"Mr. Derzack, your comments?"

"We love our little boy," I said. "Everyone else seems to notice the color of his skin more than we do. To us he's just a little baby in need of love and a home. We can provide him with that. Sure, we make our share of mistakes, but what parent doesn't? But we are good parents, and we will learn from our mistakes and move on."

The reporter turned off his recorder and put it in the pocket of his red parka. "Listen," he whispered, moving closer to Karen and me. "I probably shouldn't be telling you this, but you seem like good, honest folk. Watch out for LaPort. She's a member of the National Association of Black Social Workers. Are you familiar with them?"

"I never heard of them until today," I answered.

"Well, they're kind of right-wing. A bit radical, if you know what I mean. Strong fundamentalist Muslim ties.

They've been putting pressure on CYS for some time now to form a black division of CYS."

"I'm not sure I understand what you mean," I interrupted.

"Well, they want black kids to be sent to a division that is run entirely by black workers. They don't think whites can do the job right. They want all support services to also be run by blacks for blacks. They are a very vocal group and I wouldn't underestimate their power. They're pressuring the local powers that be, namely Commissioner Lefler, and right now I think their cry of racism is working. In my opinion, I don't think anyone at CYS knows what they're doing. It's one big money-making racket, and the black workers want their share."

I found this reporter's comments to be very strange, considering he was black. At first I did not know what to make of him, and I guess my confusion showed on my face.

"Listen," he said. "I love kids. I'm like you. I don't care what color they come in, but some people on both sides of the line do. Here's my card. If you need any help or information, off the record and on my own time, I'll help you."

I took the card and read it. "Thanks, Vernon Washington," I said, shaking his hand. I felt as if I had found a friend.

"I'm not saying you'll need my help, but nothing is as simple and easy as it seems. Be prepared."

As Karen and I drove home, the snow started to fall. The words of the reporter hung heavy in my mind, but at least for the moment our world was safe. We had won our first battle. I would face whatever I had to—tomorrow.

Five

THE HOLIDAYS ENDED IN a blur of shopping, gift-giving and visits from relatives. Then the in-laws left, the kids went back to school and the pace at the shop became fast and ferocious. If the economy had taken a turn for the worse, as the newspapers were reporting, then I had something to be extra grateful for. I found it necessary to hire a new person, since Karen had stopped volunteering at the shop almost entirely. Although Byron was growing stronger by the day, at times he would relapse, and we could not risk leaving him with a sitter.

One morning I was at the shop when Karen paid an unexpected but welcome visit. Byron was bundled in is blue snowsuit with only his big brown eyes peering out.

"Let me see how our boy is doing," Bill said, helping

Karen remove Byron's suit. "Just look at those chubby cheeks! And those hands! Why, they look they belong to a one-year-old. You've done a good job with him, Karen."

I cleared my throat.

"And you too, Dad," he added, rolling his eyes. "What a big baby."

Karen laughed half-heartedly and agreed with him. Obviously something was wrong. "Could you keep him a few minutes while I talk with Mike?" Karen asked Bill, handing Byron to him.

Bill took the baby in one hand and the tote bag filled with extra diapers, formula, baby wipes and clothes in the other and walked out the door. Normally I would have found humor in watching this rough, gruff man turn into jelly around Byron, but I knew Karen did not make a trip into town just to say hello.

"What's up?" I asked. "Before you answer, tell me: Should I sit down?"

She nodded as I seated myself and prepared to hear some bad news. "The February hearing has been canceled."

"Those things happen, they'll reschedule." I knew that Karen did not drive all the way from Wexford into town to deliver that message. I braced myself, wondering what was really the matter.

"They already did reschedule, for March 12th. But now we've got a very big problem." Karen hung her green wool coat on the clothes rack and sat down. She look tired and upset. "CYS just keeps acting stranger and stranger."

"Just tell me straight out, please," I said. "I can handle it," although truthfully I knew I had not yet recovered from CYS's last round of dirty tricks.

"Byron's mother wants him back."

I felt as if I had been smacked in the face with a wet sock. I had forgotten all about the mother, and I thought CYS had, too. I had never even considered the possibility of Byron's mother coming into his life again. For a moment my mind wandered in limbo, my emotions whirling in wild disarray.

"So what do we do now?" Karen asked, staring at me as if I had the magic answer, but of course I was just as confused and hurt as she was. How could a destitute drug addict have enough wits about her to ask for her child back? Did she contact CYS on her own? Why after all this time did she come forward?

"When did this happen?" I asked, flipping through the rolodex for our attorney's telephone number. I dialed the phone but the line was busy.

"I don't know." Karen sighed. "CYS just said that the mother is back in the picture."

"That's it?" I slammed down the receiver. "That's all CYS said, that she was back? What about her drug addiction?"

Karen shrugged. "They didn't mention that."

There was no way I was going to give my baby to a drug addict, no matter what CYS said. Plain and simple, I did not want to lose Byron. After I calmed myself down, I tried to look at this predicament from a different angle. If Byron's mother had beaten her habit and could now provide for him, it seemed only right and natural that she should have custody of him, especially since Byron was still young enough to bond with her. But was she well enough to bond with him?

I no longer trusted CYS nor their opinion of the mother. Perhaps they had lied about that, too. Perhaps she was not as bad off as they had led us to believe.

I dialed the phone for the second time. This time I got through to Katie, who told me that, for the mother to petition the court for her child, she would first have to be enrolled in a drug treatment center.

"You realize," Katie said, "the only way you will get to keep Byron is if the mother fails at her rehabilitation."

"What are the chances of her failing?" I asked, trying to remember the odds against a person overcoming a deep-seated drug addiction.

"They're very high. Only about three out of a hundred addicts stay off drugs after graduating from a rehabilitation program. But keep in mind that the courts will probably give her every opportunity to prove herself."

"I understand," I said. "What will happen to Byron while the mother is trying to get clean?"

"We'll asked the judge to allow you to retain custody of Byron until the mother stays off drugs for an appropriate time period—that is, if and when she does. I have a good friend who's a substance abuse counselor, and I want you to meet with him. I think you won't feel as panicky about this situation if you hear from him how difficult it is for someone to kick a drug habit, especially someone with a history like Lucy's."

"Then you believe CYS's earlier analysis of the mother, that she's a total loser who's abandoned her children in the past?"

"The court documents back them up."

I finished my conversation with Katie and called Byron's caseworker, who confirmed that the mother had recently entered Meadville Drug Detoxification Center, about fifty miles from Pittsburgh. Her stay was to last thirty days.

"I still don't understand how the mother could show up out of nowhere," Karen said, straightening some papers on my desk as I hung up the phone. "This whole thing just doesn't make sense to me. At first CYS told us she's a good-for-nothing who deserted her kids and that they had no idea where she is. Now all of a sudden she's a concerned mother who enrolled herself in a drug program so she can be reunited with her children. I'm not buying it. Something about this whole thing stinks."

I agreed. This new wrinkle in the case was not ringing true, but we could not do anything about it until the March 12th hearing, which was a month and a half away. Until then we could do little else but wait and worry.

I did not know how Karen and I would make it that long. I felt as if our hands were tied. She and I sat staring at each other without speaking a word. "That's it," I said, breaking the silence. "I can't stand it! I have to do something." I picked up the phone and dialed CYS. I wanted to know when and how the mother had come back on the scene, and I even thought it might be possible that CYS had searched her out and made some kind of deal with her—go into a rehab program and we'll get you out of prison. I would not put anything past Jane Worley.

After a few minutes of waiting, I got through to Byron's new caseworker, a Dorothy Bilensky.

"I'm so glad you called," she said. I was not expecting such a warm reception, and it threw me completely off guard. "I was just about to call you."

"Oh?" I said, certain that she had bad news for Karen and me; that seemed to me the pattern with CYS.

"Some of Byron's family members would like to begin visitation with him, so we will be sending a caseworker to your home tomorrow to take Byron to the meeting."

"Whoa," I said, "wait a minute. What family members? Where is this meeting taking place and for how long?" I was not going to allow CYS to take my child anywhere. I was afraid they would not give him back.

"The aunt," Dorothy explained. "Actually, Byron's great-aunt. We'll have the reunion here at CYS headquarters. I've already made arrangements to have Byron picked up at one-thirty and returned to you by five."

"We'll bring him down tomorrow ourselves," I said. I needed to see for myself what was going on.

"No, that won't be necessary," she responded, her voice firm. "It's our policy to take care of all the transportation arrangements in matters like this."

"I don't care what your policy is," I said flatly. "Karen and I will drop our child off tomorrow to meet his aunt, and we'd also like to be present at this meeting."

"Absolutely not." The caseworker's voice became sharper as she grew impatient. "The family wants private time to get to know their nephew. You will only be a hindrance."

Now I was beginning to become impatient with her. Karen and I were the only family Byron had known for the first eight months of his life…and now we were in the way? Where was the aunt when Byron was born? Where was she when he had gone into convulsions and needed comforting?

"I'm only going to say this one more time," I said, sounding as determined as I could sound. "I will bring my son down to meet his aunt. If she prefers that my wife and I not be there, I'll honor her wishes. But at the very least I would like to meet this woman."

"Out of the question," Dorothy said. "That is not an option."

"Why?" I asked. There'd better be a good reason, I told myself.

"We find it unproductive and distracting to have non-relatives present at these reunions. The aunt's wishes are to see her nephew, not you."

"Did she say that?"

"Yes."

I drummed my fingers against my desk in frustration. Was this person telling the truth? How could I know one way or the other? "Well, for the time being I'll take your word for it," I said. "However, I have a difficult time believing that Byron's aunt would not want to meet the people who having been caring for her nephew for eight months."

"Well, believe it, Mr. Derzack," Dorothy said. "We'll be there at one-thirty."

"You won't find anyone home." I could not believe this woman. I thought I had been perfectly clear about the driving arrangements, but I explained them to her again.

"Since the meeting has already been scheduled, I agree to it this time," she sniffed, "but in the future I must insist on other arrangements."

The conversation ended and I was furious. I couldn't believe that CYS expected me just to hand Byron over to them, no questions asked. Who did they think they were, the Gestapo?

Karen and I wanted to do the right thing by Byron, despite the deceptive behavior that CYS continually demonstrated. A child should know his aunt. Family, next to God in our mind, was the most important thing on this earth.

We stopped off on our way home from the shop and bought Byron a new outfit, a brown overall set. We wanted him to look good for his aunt, and we wanted her to be as proud of Byron as we were.

The next afternoon Karen and I arrived at CYS on time, just as we had said we would. Byron looked dapper in his brown corduroy overalls and white shirt, tan sweater and brown and tan cap, and he was giggling and squirming all over the place when we entered the sparsely decorated lobby. I checked in with the receptionist and was told to have a seat.

We waited for about ten minutes. I nervously glanced through an outdated *People* magazine while Karen fussed with Byron. Finally a caseworker came over and without a word took Byron and disappeared down the hallway.

"Mr. and Mrs. Derzack," the receptionist said, from across the room. "The caseworker has instructed me to tell you that you must leave the building before the aunt arrives."

That was an interesting bit of news. Without any argument I grabbed Karen's arm and led her out the door.

"What's your hurry?" she asked, attempting to stop.

"We're going across the street to wait until the aunt shows up," I whispered, escorting her out the door.

"Good idea," Karen whispered back. I felt like a spy, and I guess I was spying. But what else was a father to do? If CYS would not allow me to meet Byron's family, at least I could try to meet them on my own.

We stood in the freezing rain across the street from the CYS offices, refusing to give up our stakeout regardless of how bad the weather was and how cold we were getting. After at least twenty minutes, a white Chevy pulled up in front of the CYS building and a woman I recognized as Byron's old caseworker got out the driver's side. A stocky black woman, smoking a cigarette and wearing a wrinkled beige raincoat, got out of the passenger side. Her coarse hair was dyed dull red, and she made me think of those women at Juvenile Court who tried to hide their harshness under cosmetics.

I watched as the woman took a last drag from her cigarette, then blew the smoke out in a mighty puff in the direction of the caseworker. The black woman coughed and spat on the ground, then tossed the lit cigarette into the street.

I tried desperately not to judge her on appearances, but I could not help myself. All my senses told me to keep Byron away from her. She may have been his aunt, but...

"She looks a little tough, but she's probably a good woman," Karen said, reading my mind. "After all, she has been caring for Byron's three older brothers for years."

"Yeah, you're right," I said, feeling guilty that I had not been more readily accepting of this woman. After all, in a way, she was family.

Karen and I went to a café on Forbes Avenue for a snack. I finished my tuna on rye, then ate the French fries Karen had left on her plate and ordered a slice of cherry pie. "You'd better watch out," Karen warned. "You keep eating like this and I'll have to put you on a diet."

She was right; I was gaining weight. But it seemed like I was always hungry. Maybe it was nerves.

We returned for Byron on time. A caseworker holding him in the lobby handed him over to us without a word and walked away. Byron did not look any worse for wear, so I assumed the visit with his aunt had taken place without any problems.

When we arrived home a message from Mrs. Wagner was on the answering machine. I called her back at once.

"How nice to hear from you, Mr. Derzack," she answered, without conviction. "I've got good news for you." I laughed to myself; that would be the day, I thought. "Byron's mother is going to meet with him tomorrow. I'll send someone to pick him up around two o'clock."

"Wait a minute," I blurted out. "I don't understand why no one told us that Byron was scheduled to meet with his mother tomorrow."

"Why, Mr. Derzack," Mrs. Wagner answered sweetly, "we only just found out ourselves. I tried to let you know as soon as I could." Though I didn't believe her, I didn't see the point in saying so. Instead, the two of us got embroiled in the same argument I had had with Dorothy: Who was going to transport Byron to his family reunions? I stood firm. "I really insist on taking Byron ourselves, Mrs. Wagner," I said.

"Well, in this case it may be best," she seemed to capitulate. "His mother wants to meet you, you know. I think that's too generous of her, but that's just the sort of person she is." I felt my jaw slack open in surprise. His mom wanted to meet with us? I was so taken aback that I almost didn't notice the smarmy sarcasm in Mrs. Wagner's voice.

Karen and I were excited by this latest development. If we could establish a relationship with the mother, we thought, she would see her way to allow us, in some fashion, to remain a part of Byron's life.

A few hours after I talked with Mrs. Wagner, I received a phone call from Alice LaPort. The tone of her voice was cold and vindictive as she accused Karen and me of being uncooperative.

"I'm not sure why you think you should receive special treatment," LaPort said, not stopping to take a breath, "but people like you always do. That black child is under our care and we call the shots. Your behavior is both cruel and destructive to Byron's welfare."

Up until that moment I just let her speak. She was, in my opinion, an angry young black woman who hated whites. But I couldn't let her sit there and call me "cruel" to my own son.

"Now you wait one minute," I said, struggling to remain calm and focused. I did not see any reason to join in a discussion with this woman when she obviously had no intention of speaking in a civilized manner. "I don't understand why you called."

"I called to inform you and your wife that your failure to cooperate with the family requests to see Byron will not go unnoticed. I am going to file a compliant with the judge. You two are not going to get away with this." She paused an instant, and when she continued again, her voice wavered for a moment. "And, I'm calling to inform you that tomorrow's meeting has been canceled. No one should be exposed to your kind of behavior—especially Byron and his true family."

"Ms. LaPort," said Karen, who had been listening on the other line, "not only is your behavior rude, but you have been grossly misinformed. Byron had his very first meeting with family members yesterday, and we offered no resistance whatsoever. In fact, we dropped him off so they could meet him. Now, if you wish to cancel tomorrow's meeting, go right ahead. Good day, Ms. LaPort."

Karen hung up the phone at the same time I did. Surprisingly, I was not angry. LaPort resented Karen and me for no other reason than the color of our skin. More than anything, I pitied her. It's not easy carrying a heartful of hatred around with you. However, I was concerned that CYS allowed her to so openly express her negative attitude at the workplace.

"Well, I guess the meeting's off," said Karen.

"I don't know, I wouldn't bet the farm on it." I put my hand on her shoulder and gazed into her deep blue eyes, so wise but so full of strain. "Did you get a funny feeling from the sound of her voice, maybe as if she weren't telling the truth? It's hard for most people to lie, and this woman sounded as if she were lying. I think she's trying to set us up so that we won't come."

Karen's eyes grew large and round. "You're right, Mike! Her voice did sound strange, but I couldn't tell just why. Don't look now, but you're becoming awfully intuitive!"

The following afternoon we took Byron to his meeting at CYS. I had a feeling that LaPort was attempting to make us appear to be uncooperative, and I was right. When we arrived at CYS we were immediately escorted into a room where Byron's aunt and mother had been waiting.

"So this is my little boy," the mother said, taking him from Karen's arms. Karen graciously handed him over and began to tell the other mother about Byron's likes and dislikes, his favorites toys, his eating and sleeping patterns. I knew it must have been hard for Karen to step aside the way she did, but Karen could never act any way other than dignified.

"Thank you," the mother kept repeating. "Thank you for being so kind to my baby." She was a pretty young woman, stout, big-boned and round-faced, though the dark brown circles under her eyes indicated she hadn't been sleeping very well lately.

"What is your name?" Karen asked her.

"I'm Lucy," she said, and I remembered hearing that name before. One of the CYS people had mentioned it. At that moment a caseworker interrupted us and asked us to leave so that Byron could get reacquainted with his mother.

We did as she asked, but as we left the room, Byron started to cry. I had to turn a deaf ear to his wailing, or else I would have run back into the room and snatched up my little boy, proper protocol or not.

Lucy entered the drug rehabilitation program the following day and the visitations with family ended as quickly as they had started. Both Karen and I knew that one visit and a short stay at a detox center would not be enough for Lucy to prove that she was capable of caring for Byron, and we were sure the judge would feel the same way. We were frightened, though, since we both had a terrible feeling that CYS would not care one way or the other. Karen told me she was sure they would try to pull some shenanigans at the March hearing, and I had no reason to doubt her.

A few days after our visit with Lucy I was at the shop working the press when Karen ran into the room. The noise from the machines drowned out Karen's voice as she motioned for me to meet her in my office. Seeing Karen mouth the words, "It's important," I asked Bill to take over for me and dashed into my office.

"What's up?" I asked, wiping my brow with a towel that I wore draped around my neck.

"I've been down at the courthouse today doing some detective work of my own," Karen said, pulling out a sheet of paper from her coat pocket. "You won't believe what I found."

She handed me what amounted to a rap sheet on Lucy, and I read in amazement the criminal record of the woman who wanted to take my son away from me.

"See here?" Karen pointed to a date. "Lucy was in the Allegheny County Jail in November. There was a warrant out for her arrest for violating her parole. See? Right here," she repeated, punching the paper with her forefinger.

"All right, Karen," I said, pulling the paper away from her. "I can read. Prostitution, huh?"

"That's not the important thing," Karen said impatiently. "Look at the dates. Go on, look! I'll bet you that CYS had something to do with Lucy getting out of jail."

Slowly it all began to come together for me; what I had suspected earlier had been true. Up until November Lucy had dropped out of sight, probably doing her best to avoid the authorities. She was caught and imprisoned; the attempt to place Byron with a black foster mother fell through; CYS located Lucy and helped her petition the court for a stay of her sentence; then they helped her get into a rehab center. Damn it! I thought. They had made a deal with her...at Byron's expense. If only I had proof.

Bill knocked at the door and entered, carrying Byron. "Uncle Billy has something he wants to show Mommy and Daddy," Bill said grimly, throwing the morning newspaper onto my desk. "Front page. I can't believe it."

Karen and I both huddled together and read the headlines: CHILD FOUND DEAD...FATHER ARRESTED.

As we read on, Karen and I moaned aloud. My stomach did flip-flops. CYS had returned a sixteen-month-old boy to his drug-addicted parents, and a few days later the child was found bludgeoned to death under a car tire in the middle of a hillside. The responding officer said it was the worst thing he had seen in twenty years of being a cop. The baby's innocent face had made even him cry. The father was being charged with murder.

"Oh, my God," Karen cried. "I'm not giving Lucy our baby until I see proof that she's clean. I mean really clean."

That was my feeling, too. Although I felt sure that Lucy herself would not intentionally hurt Byron, she might just be spaced out enough to hand him over to some dangerous people. I only hoped that the judge agreed with us.

"I told you those people at CYS were SOBs," Bill said, nodding toward the newspaper. "Now they went and killed a little kid. But that won't change 'em. It will still be business as usual for them, those heartless ba…" Bill caught himself. Cursing in front of children, even babies, was something he never did.

Actually, I felt like finishing the word for him. Instead, I said, "Bozos, right?"

"Banana-brains," Bill grumbled.

"Telephone, Mike," Bobby called from the doorway. "It's for you or Karen…some lady, she wouldn't give me her name."

I nodded and picked up the phone. "Hello, Mike Derzack here," I said.

"Is this the Mike Derzack what's been in the paper?" The woman had a distinct Pittsburgh accent. "You don't know me but I have some information that you and your wife may be interested in hearing."

I whispered to Karen to pick up the other phone. "My wife is on the line, too," I said. "Go on."

"Hello, Mrs. Derzack, yinz two sure are good people," the lady whispered. "I can't talk long, see, I'm calling from a pay phone, so I'll make it quick. Byron's grandmother on his daddy's side has been arrested for selling cocaine to an undercover cop. She's also been takin' care of Georgia, Byron's big sister, but she shouldn't be. Tried to shoot a man not too long ago. You don't want Byron to get to know her."

"Please, won't you tell us your name?" pleaded Karen. "If you'd agree to provide the judge with this information, then maybe…"

The phone went dead. Karen looked up at me, tears in her eyes. "I scared her away," she murmured.

"It doesn't matter," I assured her, taking her into my arms. "At least now we know the truth." Some of the truth, I corrected myself. How much more truth we had yet to uncover I had no idea at all.

The morning of March 12th dawned dreary and gray. Karen and I were awakened at about six o'clock when the phone rang. It was Katie's secretary, Marge.

"Sorry to wake you up so early with bad news," she said.

Why not? Everyone else does, I thought. "What's the matter? Is Katie sick?"

"Worse than that, I'm afraid," Marge said. "She was mugged a few days ago, walking to her car in a public parking garage. She's out of the hospital, but there's no way she can represent you today. Worse yet, no one in the office can help you on such short notice, either. I hate to say it and I do want you to know how sorry she feels about it, but I guess you're on your own."

"Oh, great!" I said, immediately realizing I must have appeared pretty self-centered. "I'm sorry about Katie, but isn't there some way we can delay the hearing?"

"Yes, it's called a continuance," Marge replied. "Katie approached Judge Lerner for one, but he denied it, so the hearing is on as scheduled."

I shook my head in disbelief. If your attorney was mugged and landed in the hospital, and that *wasn't* a valid excuse for a continuance, then what the hell was? "Did he say why?"

Marge hesitated, and I swore I could hear her trying to remember. "I think Katie said he thought she wouldn't be needed, something like that."

We hung up a few minutes later, and I explained the

situation to Karen. "I wish I'd studied law instead of English Lit," she joked nervously, her voice trembling.

"We'll just have to do the best we can, honey," I told her, giving her a quick kiss. "We'd better get showered and dressed."

As Karen and I drove to Juvenile Court, a light drizzle was falling. Despite the gray clouds, spring was in the air and the streets smelled like black earth. I was growing anxious to work in my rose garden. I needed the distraction because during the last couple of months I had gained twenty pounds and my appetite was nearly out of control. Every day, since the threat of losing Byron began, I felt as if I were going to battle, not knowing when or if I would get a next meal.

Karen and I did not know what to expect at this hearing, and we constantly reminded each other how we wished Katie were with us. We figured that Lucy would be there to petition the court for her son. The courts, Katie had assured Karen and me earlier, would not give Byron back to the mother until she had successfully completed an intensive drug rehabilitation program and was living on her own for a good long period of time—drug free. That made sense to us, especially in light of the newspaper article the morning before.

As I pulled into Magee Woman's Hospital's parking lot (the courthouse had no parking facilities), the sun began shining through the clouds, and I took that as a good sign. As we crossed the street to the courthouse, I noticed Alice LaPort talking with reporters. At first I began to feel a little hot under the collar as I realized that her opinions of transracial adoptions held as much weight as they did. But, I reminded myself, everyone is entitled to her opinion.

Still, I could not help but wonder what the repercussions would be if a white woman were to say that African-Americans had no right to adopt a white baby because they would not be able to give him the white experience. I just shrugged my shoulders as I heard her refer to Karen and me as "white folk" and "kidnappers."

"Doesn't anyone care about Byron?" Karen did not bother to hide her disgust at LaPort's comments as she turned and stared at the back of the woman's head. If a stare could drill a hole, LaPort's head would have a cavity six inches wide and eight inches deep, right between the ears.

"Let it go," I whispered. "She's not worth your time."

"I know," Karen admitted.

A few reporters snapped our pictures and asked how we felt. Karen nodded to me to answer for us.

"It's very emotional," I said. "You have no idea what my family has been going through. My children are confused and upset. Not one day passes that one of them doesn't express the fear that Byron will leave us. Just the other day Karen found Cameron, our youngest, sleeping on the floor next to Byron's crib. When Karen asked him what he was doing there, he said he was worried that the police might steal Byron during the night while we slept."

I thanked the press for their continued interest in the story, then we hurried off to join the others in line.

Once through the line we were immediately ushered into an empty waiting room. Once again, we waited. I sneaked Hershey's kisses into my mouth to help ease the gnawing in my stomach, and Karen pretended not to notice.

"Good morning," said a well-dressed young man, passing us on our way into the courtroom. I recognized him as one of Katie's colleagues and wished he could go into the courtroom with us. "How is everyone today?"

"Not good," Karen answered, wiping Byron's dripping chin. "Last time we sat here for hours. It's hard on the baby."

"Well, that's the way the system works," the lawyer answered, wishing us good luck.

While we didn't have Katie, we did have the knowledge that she had helped us. We knew she had prepared and presented an extensive motion requesting the judge to allow Byron to remain in our custody and to make us a party in this hearing and future hearings. That meant we would have certain rights, including the right to access information.

"Do you know how long Lucy has to get herself clean before it's too late for her to reclaim Byron?" I asked Karen. She had been doing a lot of research in the University of Pittsburgh's law library recently, and I knew she had an excellent memory for tidbits of information. I feared that this custody battle Karen and I were waging could go on forever.

"There's no time limit," she sighed. "The law is very generous, too much so, on behalf of the biological parents. This custody battle between us and Lucy? It could go on forever."

I thought about her words for a moment as every inch of my being silently cried out that such "generosity" was wrong. Something had to be done to change the law. I decided that I would call my state representatives and push them to change the legislation. I knew Birdie was sent to us for a special purpose. Perhaps getting the law changed to prevent this situation from happening to other children was the reason we were suffering through all this turmoil. I felt that once I had accomplished this goal, God would allow Byron to stay with us.

Shortly after lunch, the courtroom filled up with people, and I was surprised to see Byron's aunt sitting next to Lucy. What was she doing there? I wondered. Her presence made me feel uneasy. Was CYS up to something that involved the aunt?

The courtroom fell silent when the judge entered the room. Then the circus began.

CYS gave a shining report on Lucy's stay at the Meadville and requested that Byron be returned to her immediately. The judge nodded and closed his eyes. For a moment I was afraid that he had fallen asleep.

"If your Honor does not return Byron to his mother," the council for CYS continued his plea, "then it is the mother's wish to have her aunt, who is caring for Lucy's three other children, care for Byron until Lucy is able to provide for Byron."

I looked over at the aunt who was nodding wildly in agreement with the lawyer. I half-expected her to stand up and yell "Hallelujah!" She took Lucy's hand and patted it.

I could not allow myself to believe for one second that the judge would turn Byron over to his aunt's care.

Lucy was the first to take the witness stand. She looked very respectable in a charcoal gray suit and ivory-colored blouse, but something wasn't quite right about the way she moved. She seemed to have trouble walking, and right before she took her seat she wavered. For a moment I thought she was going to faint, but she simply sat down and stared out at the courtroom, her hands clasped around her knees.

Judge Lerner asked her if she wanted to make a statement, and she did. "I want to thank the Derzacks for taking care of Byron," she said, her voice hardly louder than a whisper, despite a microphone. "But I did real well in Meadville, and I'll do anything to get my kids…"

Lucy seemed distracted. She looked around the room as if she were trying to figure out where she was. I could see a lot of Byron in her chunky face, and my heart went out to her. It was a shame that half of her twenty-three years were spent doing drugs, selling herself and having babies. She might have been a wonderful person.

"…And so I think I'm ready to take back my kids. I can't wait to be back with my family again." With that, the judge asked her to step down. She was done. That was it.

"I can't believe it!" Karen whispered to me fiercely. "Why didn't the judge ask her about what happened to Georgia? I mean, isn't this whole thing about whether Lucy is competent to take care of kids or not?"

I shrugged, unable to think of a good answer. I knew that Lucy's addiction had driven her to dangerously neglect her children. She had been homeless at the time Byron's siblings were taken away from her, and Georgia, Byron's sister, older than him by less than a year, was nearly dead when they found her, starving and dehydrated. The child was placed in the hospital, where she recovered and was handed over to Byron's paternal grandmother, who, if our mystery caller was to be believed, was hardly a model of virtue.

"I'll ask Katie about that," I promised Karen. "You'd think that would be important."

"You'd think," Karen muttered.

The judge did not permit Karen or me to speak. That was a shame, since I figured that would have been a good opportunity to set the record straight about Lucy. On the other hand, we really didn't have to say anything about our position: Everyone was well aware that we loved Byron and would fight for him.

After a few more statements from various people, the judge cleared his voice, then pounded his gavel. He paused for a minute, took a deep breath, then voiced his decision. "I will not give Byron's great-aunt custody of the child because I do not want another temporary home for Byron, on the possibility that someday he may live with his biological mother." The aunt started to cry and wail, but the judge continued. "Therefore, I have decided that Byron will remain with the Derzacks until Byron's mother has successfully completed her rehabilitation."

Karen and I were elated. We had won another battle. I felt that we were closer to keeping Byron for good.

Everyone started to talk at once, and the judge smacked his gavel, producing a noise that echoed off the walls of the courtroom. He wanted everyone's attention and he got it. "I'm not finished," he boomed. "If the biological mother wishes to be united with her children, she must enter a long-term program for substance abusers. Also, I am ordering that psychological testing be conducted on the biological mother, the aunt, all the children and the Derzacks. This testing will be done in time for an April 21st hearing."

The judge dismissed us and without a word we left the courtroom. I was absolutely aghast that CYS would try to unite Byron with people who could not possibly care for him. It was clear to me that the organization was determined to take Byron away from us and did not have the slightest regard for what was best for him.

I wondered where the law stood on this issue. Was

family reunification paramount, even if it was clearly not in the best interests of the child? That was another topic to discuss with my state legislators.

The press surrounded us as we pushed our way to the street corner, and I expressed my gratefulness at the judge's decision. "We're taking Byron home," Karen commented briefly. "At least until the next hearing." As the aunt approached the reporters, she began to cry and they ran over to her for her comment.

I stopped and followed the reporters, making no bones about my intention to eavesdrop on her interview. If this lady had a shot at taking Byron, I wanted to know everything about her.

"We'll have to go by the judge's decision," she said, sniffling. "We just have to hope that Lucy does what she has to do to keep her babies together. Byron is in good hands, but we wanted to take him home."

I watched her performance. She did not have me convinced that she was seeking custody of Byron for any reason other than that CYS had put her up to it. Where had she been the first eight months of Byron's life?

The media slowly drifted away from the aunt except for the man I recognized as Vernon Washington. The two of them spoke in whispers for a few minutes, and I was turning to walk away when I heard him ask, "Why do you want all these kids?"

I swung around to hear her answer. She held her left hand in the air and rubbed her thumb against her index finger. For the money.

That night I couldn't sleep. I kept having dreams about standing outside a decaying house, watching a little sparrow in a filthy cage in a dark, deserted room. Whenever I tried to enter the room and release the sparrow, the scene shifted, and I was outside the building again, watching the pathetic bird.

The next day I was a wreck at work, and even Bill stopped complaining and tried his best to help me through the day. "Want to take another ride to Pinegrove?" he asked during a coffee break.

I nodded. "Yes, yes I do, but this time at night."

Bill was quiet for a few moments as he sipped his coffee. "Okay," he said at last. "If you want to."

I couldn't get the image of the trapped bird out of my mind and I realized, if I ever was going to be at peace with myself, I'd have to face Pinegrove Terrace at night. Alone. "Can I borrow your car?" I asked. "I want to go there alone."

Bill nearly choked on his Maxwell House. "Are you nuts?" he cried.

"Yes, I'm nuts," I muttered. "I'm nuts about that little boy. I'm being driven crazy by a system that seems to care about itself a lot more than it cares about him. I'm a maniac, because I don't understand how giving my son to people who can't take care of him or don't really want him is better than giving him to us, when we love him so desperately."

Bill was silent for several minutes, and I thought he might not have heard me. "Come by tonight about eleven," he whispered at last. "I'll make sure the Chevy's got a full tank."

When I arrived at Bill's house late that night, he tried to talk me into taking him with me, but I refused. I needed to go alone. This was my descent into hell and I had no right asking someone else to accompany me.

From Route 279, the main artery into the city from the north, I could see lights shining up on the top of a hill. That was Pinegrove Terrace. I had passed it every day for five years and never paid it much attention. Now it was very important to me, for I could not discount the possibility of my son living there one day.

The back of my neck was dripping with sweat as I drove into the complex. In the daylight with Bill it had appeared harmless enough, but now it seemed full of shadows and harsh lights, sinister and forbidding. I felt like a coward as I struggled with myself to continue my journey.

I caught a whiff of marijuana as I passed by a well-lit, fenced-off courtyard, but I couldn't see anyone. I parked the car by the side of the court and waited. From somewhere in the shadows I heard a repetitive whacking sound—someone dribbling a basketball? I squinted, but still I saw no one. A high-pitched laugh rang out, then stopped abruptly. I smelled tobacco smoke and a sweet scent I couldn't identify.

All the disembodied smells and sounds were beginning to get to me, so I decided to drive on, away, and fast. "Left onto Tenth street," I said out loud, making a mental map as I negotiated a turn. I did not want to get lost. Tenth was dead quiet, so I turned onto Eleventh Street. As my headlights cut through the darkness, I thought I saw several dark shapes dart across the street and melt into the surrounding buildings. Big cockroaches, I joked with myself, but it wasn't funny.

From nearby I heard the smash of breaking glass and stopped the car in the middle of the street, but no one appeared and the night soon fell silent again.

Again I smelled the sickly tang of marijuana, and then the smell of frying bacon. I picked up new smells from street to street as I drove, but the strange smell I couldn't identify followed me everywhere. It wasn't sweat and it wasn't decay and it wasn't smoke and it wasn't alcohol…but it was something like all of those smells combined and flattened out. Whatever it was, I was beginning to hate it.

As I turned onto Robin Avenue, I heard a thump on the hood of my car. I looked in the rearview window, saw several boys running at the rear of the car and slammed my foot on the brakes as the youths surrounded the Chevy. Then through my window I saw a familiar face: It was Bill's young friend, Charles. I searched for a button to open the window, then remembered that the Impala's windows had to be rolled down. I located the handle, and when the window was half-open the boy popped his head through the opening and looked around.

"Hey, man, whatcha doing driving Bill's old wreck?" he asked, as another youth rocked the car. I felt my heart pounding in my chest.

"My car's broken down," I answered, fumbling around to open the glove compartment. I searched around with my hand until I found what felt like a package of crackers. "Here." I reached out my hand. "Bill said if I ran into you, I was to give you these."

"Batteries?" he asked, holding the package in his open hand.

I looked in his palm. I had given him a package of AA Eveready batteries. "Yeah, for your boom box." Good recovery.

"Well, this ain't the right size," he said, stuffing them into his pocket. "But tell Bill I said thanks, okay, man?

"It's cool," Charles said to the rest of the boys, motioning for them to move away from the car. "He's Bill's friend." The others began to make their way across the street, and Charles turned toward me. "You move in yet?"

I shook my head. "I thought I'd check the place out at night before I made a decision."

"Well, if I were you, I'd move to the 'burbs with the other white folk," Charles advised. For a few seconds his laughter filled my ears, then he thumped the roof of the car and started to follow the others.

"Wait," I called. "Tell me how you know Bill."

"He's my dad...kinda." Charles returned and leaned against the car door. "I got caught stealing some chicken from old man Greeley's store on Fifth Avenue. The old man was threatening to call the cops until Bill talked with him and made it right. Now I can't shake Bill. I guess he feels responsible for me. He makes sure I have food, some spending money, clothes. Bitches at me for missing school and stayin' out late. You know the stuff that fathers do. I don't listen much, though."

"Where's your real dad?" I pried.

"Ain't got one," he answered, looking about to see where the others had gone.

"Your mom?"

"Ain't got one of those either," he answered, "but I do all

right." I wanted to take him home with me, but I knew this child could not be repaired, no matter how much care Karen and I gave him. The damage was too extensive.

I fished a twenty dollar bill out of my shirt pocket. "Here's twenty bucks. It's for you." Charles eyed the money, hesitating. "Bill said I was to give it to you so you could buy a new pair of jeans. Go on." The young man nabbed the money and disappeared into the night.

It was now one o'clock in the morning. I was tired and my mind was filled with fear and anger. I retraced my route and headed back toward the main highway. As soon as I drove past the pathetic pine trees, the smell which had been so strong in the streets faded and disappeared. What was that stuff?

In another thirty minutes I would be safely in bed, but what about Charles? Where would he be? Would he find a haven for the night or would he continue to wander the streets? Just like my dream sparrow, Charles was trapped so tightly I could never free him.

I pulled into my driveway and parked the old Chevy behind my Land Cruiser. As I got out, I ran my hands over the dented top and sides. The Chevy was nothing but a heap of rusting, twisted metal held together with good intentions, and it looked hopelessly out of place in front of my suburban house.

Although the night was warm, I began shivering. I knew how it felt to be out of place.

I took a deep breath of air, cold and clean with the last bit of winter's breath in it. It felt good to be living and to be out of Pinegrove. Suddenly I knew what the smell had been: It was not a smell that I was used to, for I had never had any wants, had never known tremendous lacks of things—of food, of promise, of hope. That smell was the smell of despair, a smell that Byron might soon be all too familiar with.

Six

S EVERAL DAYS AFTER MY visit to Pinegrove Terrace, Bill noticed the batteries were missing from his glove compartment. It was driving him crazy trying to figure out where he had misplaced them, so I finally broke down and told him about my encounter with "his son." He gave a hearty laugh.

I laughed with him, but I soon realized I had little to be happy about. Just the next day Jane Worley called to inform us that Lucy had entered Sojourner House, a live-in drug rehabilitation center in the city. While we were happy for Lucy, I knew that Sojourner had a waiting list a mile long. "Gee, it's sure lucky that she got in so quickly," I told Jane Worley.

She agreed and immediately began bragging about how

she had been instrumental in establishing Sojourner House. I figured she used her influence to move Lucy up to the top of the list. CYS's power seemed to be very far-reaching.

"I suppose you give preference to women who need help to get them reunited with their children," I said innocently.

Suddenly Jane Worley had another call waiting; she didn't have time to answer my question. However, she did have time to inform me that Lucy's visits with Byron would be increased to every Tuesday and Thursday, starting the following week. "We'll pick him up and take him to Sojourner House," she said.

There was no way that I was going to give in to that demand and I told her so. "I don't think it's good for Byron to take him into that kind of surroundings."

"We don't have the time to argue this point. Just have him ready at nine A.M. next Tuesday."

"No," I said, not even sure she was still on the line. I waited for a response. When I did not get one I hung up the phone. That woman was my worst nightmare.

I tried to forget about Jane Worley by burying myself in work, but throughout the day she kept creeping into my thoughts. Who was this woman? What was her experience? How did she get so much control over people's lives? I decided to make a few phone calls about her so I could try to understand what kind of individual I was dealing with.

That evening Karen and I made some calls to a few friends and acquaintances, among them Sally, Bill's sister. I learned that Jane Worley had worked for the Butler County CYS and I was not a bit surprised when I found out the she had married her boss, then was promoted to Allegheny County. I wondered how much of the taxpayers' money went into developing that relationship. "She's as heartless as a stone statue. All she cares about is money," one of my sources informed me. That bit of information was nothing new.

The next morning I was telling Bill about Jane Worley when Katie stopped by the office. She appeared to have recovered from her ordeal, though she didn't want to talk about it. She also didn't smile as much as she used to. "Good news," she said. "I got you an appointment with Dr. Lipinsky, the psychologist and drug counselor I told you about. He'll meet with you and Karen tonight. No charge. He knows all about you and said it would be a honor to meet with you."

I called Karen about the meeting and she had just enough time to find a babysitter for the kids and drive into town. She picked me up in front of the shop and we drove over to Oakland, the section of the city that's home to the University of Pittsburgh, Carnegie Mellon University, two colleges and several major hospitals.

Karen cautiously negotiated the Land Cruiser down Forbes Avenue through the middle of heavy rush hour traffic. I knew better than to disturb Karen's concentration, so I gazed out my window at the sea of university students who were lost in their own world of academic life.

Suddenly, I yelled for Karen to stop as a young man who had been standing on the street corner swinging a khaki backpack from his hand took a step into the road. Karen slammed on the brakes and we came to a screeching halt just inches away from the man. He strutted in front of our car, flashing us a toothy grin as Karen tapped her fingers on the steering wheel and muttered something under her breath.

I delighted in the student's "the world must wait for me" attitude, and I tolerated it with pleasure. I chuckled to myself to think of the major attitude adjustment this kid was in for. In a few short years college would be a fading memory and he would be at his first job selling hamburgers at McDonald's.

"Were we like that?" Karen asked, scrunching up her freckled nose.

"I was," I answered, remembering a time when nothing or no one could stop me, including a four-ton truck. I was invincible. I would live forever. Just then I realized that I was growing old. The twenty years that separated me and that young man might as well have been a hundred. For a brief moment I wanted my youth and innocence back. I wanted to run away to the Cayman Islands, buy a boat and sail in the warm blue waters for the rest of my life.

"Well, I wasn't," Karen said, parking the Land Cruiser in between a silver van and a black sportscar with such precision that I was impressed. "Why would someone want to risk his life by walking out in front of a car?"

"He doesn't realize he can die," I said, searching my pockets for a couple of quarters as I opened the car door. I slipped the quarters into the parking meter, then Karen and I made our way down Atwood Street, looking for number 113.

We found Dr. Lipinsky's building in short order and opened the massive oak doors of the old brownstone building. In the lobby we were greeted by a receptionist who buzzed us through to the doctor's office.

Dr. Lipinsky met us with outstretched arms and threw a flurry of compliments at us before ushering us into his office. "I'm so glad to meet you two," he said, running his hands through his mop of gray hair. I watched entranced as his nostrils flared in rhythm with every word he spoke.

We followed the doctor into what he referred to as his dungeon. "Please have a seat," Doctor Lipinsky said, opening the door of a small white refrigerator that was well stocked with red and white cans of Classic Coke. He took a can, handed one to each of us, popped the tab on his and took a long gulp. Karen and I sat down in front of the doctor's desk and waited for him to begin the meeting.

"Refreshing," he said, wiping his lips on his shirt sleeve. I felt as if I were in the middle of shooting a commercial.

The doctor lumbered over to his red leather chair and plopped down in it. His ruddy face glistened with sweat, which he sopped up in a Kleenex. "How do you know when a drug addict is lying?"

Karen and I looked at each other and shrugged our shoulders. I did not know what to make of this man. Was he asking me a real question or was he about to tell a joke? The pictures on his walls looked as if they had come out of *Mad*

Magazine: Sigmund Freud with his mother; a portrait of Carl Jung which was actually a jigsaw puzzle with a piece missing; a dog ringing a doorbell with his snout as a woman rushed to let him in. With nothing more to go on, I guessed that the doc was about to deliver a punchline.

"Every time he opens his mouth," he deadpanned. The doctor took another drink of Coke, then opened his desk and pulled out a silver foil bag of Snyder's potato chips. "I didn't have anything to eat today," he explained, extending the open bag of chips to Karen and me.

Karen politely refused and glared at me with murder in her eyes as I took a huge handful from the bag. My food consumption had become a major stumbling point in our marriage. In the past two months I had gained well over twenty pounds and Karen showed little or no tolerance for my problem.

"Drug addiction is like a cancer eating away at every fiber of a person," Dr. Lipinsky continued, shoving a few more potato chips into his mouth. "The addict has no sense of morality, ethics, right or wrong. His actions are driven solely by getting that next fix. Nothing else, and no one else, matters."

Karen and I listened to Dr. Lipinsky's gloomy prognosis for recovery. As he spoke, passion—as well as a few crumbs of potato chips—issued from him. Every so often he would stop his lecture, swivel his chair around and stare out the window to the row of shops that lined the street, as if questioning why he was in this crazy line of business.

"What are Lucy's chances?" I asked. "Will she make it?"

"No." His quick, blunt response made me shudder. "It's hard enough for a person who enters a program such as Sojourner House of their own accord to succeed. But from the sound of things, your Lucy cut a deal. This wasn't something she wanted, it was a way to get out of jail. In my opinion, it won't work out."

"Is there anything we can do to make it work?" I asked, explaining that my little Birdie was about to become a part of Lucy's recovery program every Tuesday and Thursday. I did not want Byron subjected to any part of Lucy's withdrawal or unpredictable behavior.

"No, I don't think there's anything you two can do to help. But," the doctor reassured us, "so as long as the mother is being watched, Byron will be okay. Sojourner's is claiming to have a fifty percent success rate. That's forty-seven percent above the national average. However, they've only been in business a couple of years. Statistically, it's kind of like a rookie baseball player getting a hit in his first at bat. Suddenly, he's batting 1.000, but by the end of the season, he's hitting .200. Time will tell."

I told him about CYS and how underhanded and deceitful they had been up to this point. What if Lucy were failing the program? Would they cover that up, too?

The doctor gave a grunt. "From here on out, I advise you not to trust anyone. You've got a little boy's life at risk here, so get proof of everything. Don't settle for anything less than the actual drug test results. Of course, they'll claim confidentiality. Tell 'em to screw the mother's privacy. She's lost, anyway. It's the child that counts now."

That was not the answer I wanted to hear. I wanted him to say that everything would be all right, that Lucy would recover and that Byron would have a loving, caring mother and a secure home.

"Did anyone explain Sojourner's program to you?" the doctor asked, standing up and walking to the refrigerator. He offered us another Coke. Karen declined, I accepted. "You don't have to answer; I know they didn't. Why should they? You two only have your hearts and souls invested in Lucy's outcome."

He sat back down and patiently explained the four phases of the program. "At first the residents are not allowed to leave the premises. They are under strict supervision. I doubt whether Byron will be allowed many visits during this stage of the game. Lucy will be having too much to contend with and her pain will be great. When the residents successfully complete that phase, they are allowed occasional supervised furloughs. If that goes well, then gradually they earn more freedom and can come and go pretty much as they please, but they have to sign in and out. The last phase is to prepare them to live on their own. For the most part, they are unsupervised, and that's where the trouble begins. Maybe they'll get your Lucy into PennFree."

"I'm not familiar with PennFree," I said, trying to absorb as much as I could about the fate that awaited "our" Lucy.

"It's a program that offers housing for the recovering addict and her family. It's a strict program, and if the recovering addict messes around with the rules, she's booted out."

As the doctor spoke, it began to dawn on me that I had a boatload of research ahead of me. I wanted to learn everything I could about the programs Pittsburgh had to offer. In my heart of hearts I wanted Lucy to succeed, yet I knew her chances were next to none. Maybe I could find some way to show her our support.

"What if Karen and I kind of make Lucy a part of our family?" I asked, thinking that our support would ease her burden, thus giving Byron a better shot at a stable family should the case go in her favor.

The doctor scratched his head and fluffed up his graying hair. "You haven't been listening, Mike, have you? You still think Lucy can be saved. I'm telling you, if you give this woman anything out of the ordinary, one day you'll find her at your doorstep asking for money. And you know where that money will go, don't you? You better write her off and put all your efforts into keeping your child away from her. It's sad, I know, but that's the cruel truth."

My head spun like a top. Keep Byron from seeing his mom? Now that was a crazy thought! It would be impossible for me to prevent Byron from seeing Lucy. The court had made its decision, and I had to obey the law. I did not know what else to do.

"There is a remote possibility that Lucy could recover.

Just do your best to prevent Byron from being given to her custody until she has been out on her own, drug-free, for at least a year's time." The doctor's warning was very clear. I hoped that when the time came, the judge making the decision would understand the risks and give Lucy the time and space to heal properly.

We thanked the doctor for his generosity and expertise. During the long walk to the car, my mind was flooded with thoughts of doom. Lucy's stay at Sojourner was going to take one year...then add another year to prove she was capable of staying off drugs. Byron would be almost three by then! To give him up after all that time would be cruel, but it would be even worse to give him to a mother who, at any time, could slip back into the nightmarish hell of drug addiction and take Byron with her.

All of us—Karen, Byron, Lucy, the judge, CYS, and now the Sojourner House—were becoming so enmeshed that I doubted if we would ever separate ourselves from each other. Perhaps it was fate, I told myself. Perhaps it was just plain bad luck.

THE REST OF THE week was quiet, almost normal. There were no meetings, no reporters, no television cameras, and I was caught up on the jobs down at the shop. For the first time in months we had the appearance of being just another average family.

Much to Karen's delight, my appetite also was returning to what it had been before the battle to keep Byron began. I even lost a few pounds and my jeans were fitting much better, though they were still much too tight. I was anxious to drop off the extra pounds, not only so I would feel better, but so I could cope with summer clothing. The temperatures were nearly spring-like now, and the thought of me in shorts and a t-shirt made me feel embarrassed.

One morning Karen and I sat down to a breakfast of cold cereal at the kitchen table before starting our day. Karen was in the process of bribing all three kids with a trip to the

Science Center if they helped clean out the collection of toys, tools and clothes that had accumulated in the garage over the winter months. I loved these family moments: negotiating a deal with our kids to do something that, when we were kids, we would have done just because our parents told us to. But there were times when we did not want to be like our parents, so we did things our way.

"Okay, Mom, how about this?" Connie bargained. "If you throw in that Guess jacket I saw at Kaufmann's last week, I'll do an extra special job of cleaning up."

"If she gets a jacket I want a..." Chris stopped for a moment to think of something he would like to have.

"I want something too," Cameron chimed in.

"Forget it," I interceded. "You'll clean the garage and get nothing but a pat on the head and like it." So much for not sounding like my father. It worked, though. Both Connie and Chris agreed that a trip to the Science Center was payment enough. Cameron left the table to play with Byron, who was cooing and gurgling in his highchair.

We were busy discussing the details of their after-school cleaning spree when CYS interrupted our family moment to remind Karen and me that Byron was scheduled to meet with his "real" mother that afternoon. Then and there we had the same go-around we always had about CYS transporting Byron to Sojourner House. "You are only causing problems for yourself, Byron and Byron's mother," the caseworker said, trying to make us feel like we were not cooperating with the rules. But I was not going to permit some stranger to take Byron on a half-hour drive to and from the city. The trauma of being left with strangers at Sojourner House for two hours was enough for him, and I said so.

Karen and I hung up the phone, disgusted with CYS's growing hostility. "Those people are..." Karen said, stopping herself mid-sentence. I felt a stillness in the room, like the dead quiet before a storm. We glanced at the children and saw all three of them staring at us, their mouths open, fear shining in their eyes. Karen and I had both noticed that the kids grew uneasy whenever we had an encounter with CYS.

Connie gulped, her eyes flaring even wider with anger. "Why don't you just do what they say?" she screamed, knocking over her chair as she stood up. "What difference does it make who drives Byron? They're going to take him away from us anyway."

Connie ran from the table and Karen followed her upstairs. "If you don't listen to them they might take us away, too!" Connie cried. Then the bedroom door slammed shut.

For a moment I searched for the words to tell Chris and Cameron how sorry I was that I did not pay closer attention to their feelings. I had made a mistake.

"Dad, you know, this has been pretty rough on us," Chris said. I pulled my chair closer to his and put my arms around him. "I'm not sure how much more of this we can take."

I felt my heart rip in two as I held him closer to me. I wished to God that I could take all of his pain and make it my own. "Of course you're scared," I said, stroking his blond hair. "Sometimes I'm frightened, too. I wish I could explain to you why adults do what they do, but this thing with CYS is beyond normal reasoning. I can promise you this, no one will ever take any of you away from us. And, if they tried we would fight them until every ounce of our strength was gone, just the way we're fighting for Byron."

"But what if my 'real' mom or dad came looking for me?" He spilled out his fears. "Will CYS try to take me away from you and give me to them? I don't want to leave you and Mom. Connie doesn't want to either. She doesn't mean it when she threatens to run away and find a real parent. She only says that because she gets upset sometimes when she doesn't get her way."

Tears filled Chris' green eyes and slid down his cheeks. I tried to wipe them away, but they kept on falling. "Why don't we sell the house and move somewhere where they can't find us?" he whimpered. "Even if we don't see our friends again, we'll be okay, right, Cammie?"

Cameron did not turn his attention away from Byron. I watched the back of his head as he nodded. "I don't want to see my friend Jeff anyway," he muttered. "He hit me on purpose, so I don't like him anymore."

On the surface Chris' suggestion sounded like a good one. If only it were that easy, I would move us all to the Cayman Islands, buy that sailboat I had been talking about for years and make a living taking tourists on cruises.

"We can't do that," I said, breaking away from my dream of tropical winds and waters. "It would be wrong."

"I knew you would say that." Chris forced a smile. "I guess we have to do what's right, huh?"

"Always," I said.

"But CYS is wrong, aren't they? Why don't they have to do what's right? Can someone make them do the right thing?"

I thought how strange the adult world must look to a child. I was at a loss to explain why laws don't protect our children very efficiently and why the interests of self-serving bureaucrats are put before the best interests of our future.

"First you have to make sure that you are doing what in your heart you know is right," I answered, like some ten-cent philosopher standing on a street corner soapbox. "I know it sounds corny, but with truth comes dignity and strength. Then use them to fight for what you know to be right. That is what your mother and I are doing."

But what was my truth? I knew it was the right thing for Byron to stay with me, but it was also right to help Lucy. But if I helped Lucy, I could lose Byron. For a moment I was confused. It appeared that I was in the proverbial damned-if-I-do, damned-if-I-don't situation.

Cameron turned to face me. "You know what I think?" he said, offering a five-year-old's wisdom. "I think you should tell God what CYS is doing to Byron and let Him take care of them. The sisters at school tell God everything and no one hurts them."

Could the answer be that simple? I was afraid to look too deeply for the answer. I was afraid that I would find I no longer had a faith, so pure and innocent, like Cameron's. I promised myself that one day soon I would check in with God.

"That was a wonderful suggestion, Cammie," Karen said, entering into the kitchen with her arm around Connie. Karen leaned over and gave Cameron a kiss on the forehead.

"You are a smart little boy," Connie praised her brother.

Cameron beamed. He had an answer that eluded most adults and even his snotty sister.

"Everything all right?" I asked as I motioned for Connie to sit on my lap.

Connie snuggled up to me like she did when she was a small child. "Yes," she said, pushing Chris away from me. It was good to see that Connie was herself again.

I sat with the children while Karen went upstairs to pack a "care package" for Byron. She returned moments later weighted down with a bag full of the essentials needed to make Byron's visit comfortable. I looked into the bag and was amazed at how much Karen had squeezed in there: New undershirts, bottles, rash medication, diapers, toys, a change of clothes, baby food, special shampoo and a comb were just a few of the numerous items.

Chris and Connie left for school feeling much better, having shared their feelings with us. Cameron watched his allotted ten minutes of morning television, then took off to visit with his friend, Tommy, who lived three houses down from us.

I puttered around in the garage, arranging the tools on the peg board. I was admiring my handiwork when I realized how temporary the order would be. Within a week the tools would be scattered all over the house, and I would not be able to find so much as a wood screw when I needed one. But for the moment, I knew where everything was.

"Go get showered up," Karen said, entering the garage, Byron in her arms. She walked over to my workbench and rearranged the row of socket wrenches. "They were out of order," she explained.

I showered, shaved and within half an hour we were on our way to Sojourner House. I felt somewhat upset that I had to leave my son at a rehabilitation center with a woman neither he nor I knew very well. But when I saw Lucy standing in front of Sojourner House, pacing back and forth as if in anticipation of seeing Byron, my misgivings eased a bit.

"Hello, Lucy," I called as we crossed the street.

She waved back.

"She looks tired," Karen observed. "But she's been going through a lot. Maybe seeing Byron will lift her spirits."

As we approached Lucy, I realized that she was very nervous about the meeting. An aide from Sojourner House stood beside her, watching as Karen handed Lucy our little Birdie. At first Byron began to whine and cry, fussing and twisting to get free of his mother and back into the arms of Karen.

"Everything's all right, honey," Karen soothed him. "Mommy will be right back." Realizing what she had just called herself, Karen quickly diverted Lucy's attention to the bag full of goodies.

"Thank you," Lucy said, genuinely happy at Karen's generosity and concern. "They don't have much here for kids."

"Come on, Lucy," the caseworker said, taking her by the arm. "It's time to go inside."

I watched my little boy disappear through the glass doors, his eyes turned toward mine until the very last moment, and I thought of Dante watching his world gradually vanish as he descended into Hell. No torment could be greater than what I was feeling just then; I was dying inch by inch.

🐦   🐦   🐦

WE HAD THREE SUBSEQUENT meetings which, for the most part, were the same as the first. Lucy was growing increasingly comfortable with Karen and me and was spending more and more time talking to us about Byron. Every once in a while the aide would remind Lucy that she needed to go inside, but Lucy would pretend not to hear her. Byron no longer tried to free himself from Lucy's grasp, making the transfer from one mother to the other much less difficult.

We had opened the channels of communication between us, and I was glad that we were at last all working together to support each other through this difficult period.

Lucy had moments when she would flare up over something trivial like a spilled bottle or a stain on her blouse, but she would always calm herself, "for Byron's sake." I thought her irritability was understandable, in the face of what she must have been going through. However, on the third visit, Lucy seemed extremely high-strung and very agitated, so much so that the aide took Byron instead of Lucy. She began accusing us of spying on her and blaming the aide for stealing her cigarettes. Byron began to cry. At that moment the first red flag went up in my mind, telling us that something was not going right.

We were a little nervous about the next meeting, but it went off perfectly. Lucy seemed to have forgotten the tension of the previous visit, and we were all friends again.

Karen and I were surprised how quiet CYS had been during our visits with Lucy. I felt that they were noticing that our little talks with Lucy were doing her good. Karen was not as optimistic as I was, however.

We were on our way to the fifth visit at Sojourner House when Karen had a feeling that something was very wrong with Lucy. "I don't know what it is," she said, showing me the goose bumps on her arms. "Something isn't right about today's meeting. I hope Lucy isn't sick."

"If she were, CYS would have canceled the meeting," I said, turning into the parking garage. A crash of thunder sounded, startling Byron, and he started to cry.

"See?" Karen said, taking him out of his car seat. "He feels it, too."

"The thunder scared him, Karen, that's all," I said, grabbing a paper bag filled with Byron's essentials, and noticed a few gifts for Lucy: Toothpaste, deodorant, nail polish and chocolate candy. Karen's thoughtfulness never ceased to amaze me.

We were standing on Penn Avenue across from Sojourner House, waiting for the light to turn green, when we were intercepted by a blonde, heavy-set woman who identified herself as Ms. Clarke, a caseworker for CYS.

"Stay where you're at," she demanded, pointing her finger at us. "Don't go over to Sojourner House. Your presence there is not welcomed."

"Excuse me?" Karen answered. "I don't know what you're talking about."

"Listen, lady, don't you dare give me any trouble," said Ms. Clarke, taking a step toward Karen. Her teeth were clenched, as if she were straining to keep her temper.

Karen stepped back and almost tripped over the edge of the sidewalk. I placed myself between her and the threatening woman.

"Hold on one minute," I interrupted, only to be drowned out by her demands.

"I have orders to take Byron to his mother and you're standing in my way," she barked, her hooked nose twitching up and down.

"Whose orders might they be?" I asked, half-expecting her to answer that her orders came from *Der Fuhrer*.

"You really thought you could pull it off, didn't you?" she asked, attempting another step toward Karen.

"Pull what off?" I asked, not allowing her to pass. A few bystanders stopped to watch the encounter.

"Everyone knows what you're up to," she said accusingly. "You two are doing your best to get in good with Lucy, then you're going to undermine her chances of recovery so you can keep her child. Well, I've got news for you, it isn't going to work. You've been found out."

"Hold on one minute," I tried, getting in a word, but the woman was determined to speak her mind.

"You think that bringing things for the baby is going to show what wonderful parents you are. Well, we don't need your stuff. We will supply whatever Byron needs."

"Are you saying that Byron does not need his formula or diapers?"

"You heard me right. But if it makes you feel better to bring them, then bring them. We won't use them, though."

"I have something I would like to say," I said, attempting to get control of the situation, but the woman was not to be stopped.

"Now give me Byron and I'll take him over to his mother." Ms. Clarke reached out for Birdie. Karen backed away and Byron started to scream.

"I have no idea who you are and who gave you the authority to take Byron from us." Karen held tightly onto Byron. "How do I know you're not some crazy person who's going to steal our child?"

"Does Jane Worley's name ring a bell?" Ms. Clarke said, sidestepping me and grabbing Byron's arm. "Now give me the child or else I'll call the police. You can watch from here where I'm taking him."

Byron cries grew even louder and he kicked his tiny feet against the woman's arms.

"Lucy doesn't want to see you anymore," the woman whispered, staring into Karen's face. "You are hindering her progress."

"Go on, honey, give her Byron," I said as a light spring rain began to fall. It was evident that Byron's welfare meant nothing to the bullying woman. The only way to end her show of force was to give into it. I did not want Ms. Clarke's rude, hostile outburst to affect Byron more than it already had.

Ms. Clarke carried Byron, thrashing and screaming, across the street. As I listened to him cry and watched him struggle to free himself, I promised him that Ms. Clarke would pay dearly for my Birdie's anguish, even if I had to go to the corners of the world to make it happen.

I was furious. I could feel my blood pressure rising, turning my face as hot as a furnace. The hunger that had been gnawing away at the pit of my stomach weeks ago had returned.

"What now? What now?" cried Karen, as tears of anger and frustration coursed down her cheeks and mingled with the rainfall.

I managed to steer us back to the car, where I called Katie on the car phone. When I had relayed to her the event that had just taken place, she was almost as angry as I was. "I'll take care of this," she promised. "This is unheard-of behavior."

The next day I received a copy of a letter that Katie had sent to Jane Worley. She blasted CYS for the "outrageous treatment" and "indefensible insensitivity" we had received from Ms. Clarke.

For the next ten days I waited patiently for Jane Worley's response. In the meantime, we continued to surrender Byron to a CYS caseworker for his visits with Lucy. When at last a letter did arrive, via our attorney, I was somewhat surprised that CYS still had the ability to shock me with their underhanded tactics.

The letter didn't come from Jane Worley but from the deputy director. The deputy director claimed that Worley was out of the office for the next two weeks and was unavailable for comment. He, however, had plenty of comments, and I grew livid as I read his accusations against us.

...related to the Derzack's alleged rude treatment, I suspect that this perception may be related to a lack of understanding of the nature of the work at Sojourner House. This program serves clients who for a variety of reasons have a high need for safety and confidentiality. The Derzacks have both crafted and attracted considerable media attention and public recognition. It does not serve the larger interests of Byron, his mother, the other clients and staff of Sojourner House to have their confidentiality and presence compromised...

...I would ask mediation from you with the Derzacks in order to minimize unnecessary friction and/or an adversarial climate that is counter-productive to Byron's care and all of his relationships...

This was turning into an uphill battle. Now the deputy director was distorting facts. If the media had been in contact with Sojourner House, neither Karen nor I had any knowledge of it, although Katie had told us someone from the media was investigating Byron's case. Karen and I had been relieved to hear that: If only someone would look deeper into CYS, we were sure, they would find a basket full of dirty laundry.

I finished reading the letter and was about to file it away in my desk drawer when I noticed the letterhead named the Board of County Commissioners. I decided to contact them about the problems we where experiencing with CYS.

I called the chairman first. He did not take my call but within five minutes after I hung up I received a phone call from Jane Worley. The conversation was brief and to the point.

"Stop calling Commissioner Lefler. He will not take your calls."

I felt like I had entered the Twilight Zone. Was there anyone of importance in Allegheny County who wasn't in bed with CYS?

All right, I told myself. Think this thing out. Why was CYS so important? It did not take me long to figure out that the answer was plain old filthy lucre. Every child caught in the system brought in so many dollars, and the more kids the more money.

I felt a surge of disgust rise within me. How could any agency, especially one charged with helping children, use kids the way CYS did? The child welfare system was little more than a set of warehouses bulging at the seams with faceless children.

I realized that I had to go out of Allegheny County with my concerns, so I contacted Senator Hart, our state official in Harrisburg. I poured out my heart to her and begged her to do something, anything to stop this nightmare.

The senator listened patiently to my rambling, then spoke in a calm, soft voice. "I hear what you're saying," she said. "Now let's start doing something about this mess. Can you send me any information documenting your story?" I was elated to find that I had finally found a sympathetic ear and agreed to send her a history of the events that had taken place since the day Byron entered our lives.

"Senator, don't you think we need to get some kind of legislation in place to ensure that the interests of the child are being met? I mean, we could limit the amount of time a biological parent has for claiming a child that she had abandoned or cannot properly care for," I said, blundering my way through ideas I had spent many months forming.

"I agree," she said, sounding very committed to the cause. "You know, there are laws dealing with the treatment of abandoned babies," she went on. "I would say that Byron is a good case in point that the existing laws about abandoning babies are not working very well, are they?"

"They sure aren't," I paused, still not believing that I was actually making some headway.

"Mr. Derzack," the senator asked, "what do you think is a reasonable time limit for the biological parents to seek custody?"

"Six months," I answered without hesitation. Any more time, I knew, and it would be very difficult for the baby to bond with his parents.

"I agree," she said firmly. "I'm going to be at my office in Cranberry in two weeks. I'd like to meet you and your wife in person. And," she added, "bring Byron."

We ended our conversation and I felt as though I had been sent an angel. In all of this mess, I had finally found someone who cared for the children. I drafted a letter to her, made copies and sent them to all the media, and overnighted hers. I felt sure that Senator Hart would make things rock and roll.

Excited about the positive talk with Senator Hart, I called Karen to share the good news with her.

"That's great," she said, not sounding as joyful as I had hoped for.

"What's wrong now?" I asked. Why was it that every time I had good news, she offset it with bad tidings which usually involved CYS.

"The psychological testing is to begin tomorrow. Guess who's doing the testing."

"Dr. Lipinsky?"

"I wish."

I almost rammed my head into the wall when Karen told me who was chosen to perform the tests: Lanni Komma, a court-appointed psychologist whose services were frequently employed by CYS.

"Pretty unbelievable, huh?" Karen sighed into the phone. "We don't stand a snowball's chance in Hades. How much would you like to bet that that psychologist will deduce that Lucy is a normal mother and I am a dangerous psychotic?"

I had had my fill of CYS intervention and I did not trust anyone who in any way worked for them, just as Dr. Lipinsky had suggested. I agreed with Karen that both of us were a hop, skip and jump away from the insane asylum if CYS had their psychologist evaluate us. I knew, down to the marrow in my bones, that this doctor would find Lucy to be a fit mother and request that Byron be returned to her permanently. And wouldn't that make CYS happy? We would be out of the picture, Lucy would be released from the program, she would fail and they would have Byron back on their books, making more money for them.

I wanted an independent source to test us.

"I'm calling Jane Worley," I said, getting ready to hang up the phone.

"Wait...Wait..." I heard Karen yell. "I already called her."

"And what did she say?"

"She said we have no choice. It's by order of the court that we are to submit to be tested by a court-approved psychologist. We are to be at the psychologist's office tomorrow at ten, and if we don't go, we'll end up in jail for violating a court order. Then they'll take Byron away from us."

"What about independent testing?"

Karen had suggested to Jane Worley that all parties get independent testing by a more impartial psychologist. She did not like the idea, but told us to go right ahead and find someone to test Karen and me. However, only their psychologist's reports were going to be presented to the judge.

I felt our ship sinking a little deeper into the murky waters of CYS. With a CYS-appointed psychologist calling the shots, we were as good as capsized before we even entered the fray.

I called Katie, but she couldn't give us any help and agreed that there was little we could do. I was disappointed that she would not at least attempt to force the judge into allowing outside testing. She feared that we would only antagonize the judge if we made an issue out of Dr. Komma's testing. "After all," Katie said, "Judge Lerner probably appointed her in the first place, and you really don't want to question this particular judge. He doesn't like his decisions questioned."

"What do you mean by that?"

She tried to toss it off as unimportant but I was not going to let her off the hook. I had the right to know everything I could about a man who had the power to take Birdie away from me.

"He's a little, well…unstable at times," she stammered. "I really shouldn't be talking about this."

"What do you mean, unstable?" I insisted. I felt the hairs at the back of my neck stand on end.

"Okay, I'll try to explain. There was a time when Judge Lerner was hearing a dispute about the assets in a divorce case. The attorneys involved could not agree on anything and were arguing back and forth. The judge stood up, threw his pencil into the air, said that the case was beyond him and walked out of the courtroom. When the judge didn't come back in fifteen minutes, the bailiff dismissed everyone."

"What?" I'd never heard of such a thing. "Maybe he was having a bad day," I reasoned. "Or maybe he was sick. It could happen to anyone."

"That's only one example," Katie continued. "He has a reputation for doing things like that. It's common knowledge among his peers that he has a problem making decisions, too. I don't think he trusts himself very much. He relies heavily on outside opinions, especially from the other judges. Unfortunately, Judge Lerner has managed to intimidate just about every juvenile lawyer in the city. I don't know how else to say it other than the judge holds grudges. If you make him mad, the next time you're in front of him—you lose."

I rubbed my forehead, as if by that action I could somehow understand the crazy situation Katie was outlining for me. "That doesn't sound legal," I said, remembering Karen's first impression of the judge. I realized she had been right all along.

"Hey, it's his courtroom," Katie said, matter-of-factly. "You know, Mike, you're missing something in all of this."

"Go on," I encouraged her.

"CYS, the advocates, the juvenile judges…they're all a tight group. They rely on each other for their jobs. The more kids in trouble, the longer they can drag out cases and the more security they have. Sad, isn't it?"

More than sad, I thought. It's immoral. And if the judge couldn't be counted on for justice, then what would happen to Birdie?

Seven

R. KOMMA WAS VERY different from what I had expected. She certainly was nothing like Dr. Lipinsky. The bright orange color of her loose-fitting African clothing made her light brown skin glow. She wore a stone medallion etched with a map of the African continent. Her braided hair, beaded jewelry and oval-shaped eyes gave her the appearance of a wise, spiritual tribal leader.

She spoke with Karen and me for few a few minutes together, going over the procedures that she would be following. Her words were well chosen and scholarly. "Initially I'd like to speak with you, Mr. Derzack," she said, her voice calm and reassuring.

Karen retired to the waiting room, and Dr. Komma and

I chatted about the hot weather we were having as I followed her into one of CYS's sparsely decorated offices. I seated myself on a vinyl covered chair and waited for the doctor to get comfortable behind the gray steelcase desk. I noticed the words "this work sucks" scratched on the top of the well-worn desk.

Doctor Komma looked very much out of place behind that drab desk. I pictured her own office tastefully decorated in soothing earth tones, African artwork bedecking the walls and shelves.

I found myself charmed by her and wanting to trust her, but Dr. Lipinsky's warning kept sounding off like a siren inside my head every five minutes: "Don't trust anyone."

His words and my feelings were in conflict, even though I knew that once again CYS had stacked the deck against me. Dr. Komma was, in a way, their psychologist; she was black, and obviously a learned person who was proud of her African heritage.

And well she should be, I reasoned. I was proud to be of Slovak descent, and Karen was proud of her Spanish background. Of course, that did not mean we thought kids of Slovak heritage were better off in Slovak homes or Spanish kids with Spanish families. Kids just needed love. Any psychologist knew that. And they knew about drug addiction and how destructive it can be. I had nothing to worry about.

"I'm going to be real honest with you, doctor," I confessed. "I had my doubts about the outcome of today's meeting." I waited for her reaction. It was just as orderly and neat as her words had been.

"Oh?" she questioned, placing her opened notebook on the table. She looked at me for a couple of seconds, then continued to search her briefcase for something. "What makes you say that?"

"I wanted to be evaluated by someone independent of CYS's influence. I was afraid since CYS is paying you, you'll give them the recommendation they're looking for."

"And what is CYS looking for?" She closed her briefcase and gave me her full attention. I felt like a laboratory rat being sized up for testing some new food additive.

"They want you to give Byron back to Lucy."

"We all would like to see mother and son reunited," she said, placing her hands together. "And, Mr. Derzack, that is what CYS and the court is aiming to accomplish. I was called in to give my opinion as to when Lucy can best care for her children."

"What if it is not a matter of when, but if, Lucy can give Byron the kind of stability and love that he is getting from us?" I asked. "What then?"

"Ah, Mr. Derzack." She smiled reassuringly. "No one is going to place Byron where he will not get adequate care. If Lucy is found incapable, then Byron will be placed where the courts see fit."

"Do you think black children should be placed with black parents?" I asked point-blank.

"Oh, my," she laughed. The gusto in her laughter, which was almost contagious, surprised me a bit. "What I personally think isn't the issue here. What matters is Byron's welfare. Now let's get on with our interview."

I was not comfortable with her sidetracking the first question, but I was pleased that she was thinking about Byron's best interests; she was among the few who did.

She gave me a questionnaire which was relatively simple and straightforward—name, address, medical history. I completed it in just a few minutes. When I handed it back to her, she studied it for a short while, then placed it in a blue folder.

"Tell me about your relationship with Byron," the doctor directed me. "Start anywhere you like and feel free to say anything you wish."

I talked for about a half-hour while Dr. Komma occasionally punctuated my more emotional moments with a sympathetic nodding of her head.

As I brought my story to an end, I fired one last bit of concern at the doctor. "If Lucy's given enough time to heal—you know, a year at Sojourner, a year living clean on her own—won't Byron be too old to bond with her?"

"Well, Mr. Derzack, if that would really be the case, I would say yes," the doctor answered, gathering up her notes and placing them in the same blue folder. "But it isn't. Sojourner is designed to keep mothers and children together through the rehabilitation program. They not only help patients through their withdrawal, but they teach them acceptable parenting skills."

"Isn't it hard enough to go through drug recovery without taking care of, in Lucy's case, a one-year-old and a two-year-old?"

"She'll have plenty of support," the doctor answered. She stood up, walked to the door and opened it. It was my cue that our interview was over.

We exchanged polite thank-yous and I left the room as Karen entered. I could tell by her taut expression that she saw this meeting as a battle.

"She's all right," I whispered reassuringly. At least I hoped she was. My judgment of people was always too generous. Considering all the setbacks, stabs in the back and disappointments that I had experienced by the bushelfuls, I was often surprised at my own innocence when it came to evaluating other people's character. Karen forced a smile, walked into the room and closed the door behind her. I sat down in the tiny lounge, pulled an action-adventure novel out of my jacket pocket and began reading.

An hour passed. The hero in my novel was about to square off against an international crime lord and Karen was still talking with Dr. Komma. I did not know if this was good or bad. It did not surprise me, because Karen was very thorough and wanted to make sure she understood each topic before going on to the next. It was very much against her accountant-like nature not to have the sum of the parts add up.

Karen would go over and over an issue until every stone was unturned, and I knew that, as polite and courteous as

Karen was, her probing could drive some people to distraction. I was nervous that Karen's strong sense of right and wrong might be triggered by some passing comment or incomplete answer the doctor would give regarding Byron, causing Karen to flare up like a stick of dynamite. Without a doubt, Karen was the embodiment of protectiveness—a real mother lion.

I was thinking how our basic temperaments differed. Karen often complained that people mistook a passive attitude for being friendly and balanced. So when Karen got hot on an issue and stirred up the waters, she looked like a shrew or a troublemaker. I appeared calm, which made me look as if I were in control. Actually, when Karen is on a mission, I'm as scared as hell that I will not be able to keep up with her passion and commitment.

I admired Karen for a lot of reasons—her constant search for the truth, the gentle nurturing she gave her children, her undying loyalty to friends and family. Karen simply was incapable of lying or stretching the truth. I never lied, but I had a talent for sugarcoating the truth to make it more palatable. Karen did not have that gift.

Finally Karen came to the door and I heard her and the doctor laughing about something. I saw the doctor lightly pat Karen on the shoulder, as if to signal that everything would be all right. I was relieved that the meeting had gone so well.

Karen joined me in the room and motioned for me to get our coats. She was smiling and I thought she was pleased with her meeting. Then I saw her right eye twitching. Oh no, I thought. Something isn't right.

We made our way down the long gray hallways of CYS. It was a long walk past social workers, secretaries and receptionists, and my mind had plenty of time to conjure up every conceivable nightmare. What had happened in that room? I looked at Karen; her face was red. She walked with her eyes focused directly ahead of her, avoiding conversation with me.

Finally we reached the lobby. I waved good-bye to the receptionist at the front desk, opened the heavy glass doors and walked out onto the street. The morning air was vibrating with the screech of car horns and the roar of traffic.

"We're in big, big, trouble," Karen announced rather loudly. Her face was now white with hopelessness, though her cheeks still burned red.

"What happened?" I asked but I really did not want to know.

"What happened?" she exploded. "Don't you see it? Don't you understand what is going on here?"

I shook my head. I had no idea what she was talking about.

"Mike," she said, with the same inflection my mother used when I'd track mud on the freshly scrubbed kitchen floor. "This doctor has been bought and paid for by CYS."

"I thought you liked her. You seemed to be getting along just fine."

"Strangely enough, I do like her, but nevertheless, she has been bought," Karen said, as we walked into the parking garage.

"Mike, I had to tell her about my troubles at ALCOA."

I sighed and shrugged. "That might not look too good," I agreed.

Eight years ago Karen had had a very high-pressure job, and it had taken its toll on her: She'd been under a lot of stress and often worked late and on weekends. The company doctor had prescribed a tranquilizer for her, but the medication caused her to become depressed and lose weight. She had become so ill she had been hospitalized. Karen, ever the fighter, had struggled back from the illness, however, and had suffered no lasting effects.

"I'm sure it will all work out, though," I tried to comfort her.

"You wait and see. She's going to recommend that Byron be returned immediately to Lucy. Oh, my God, Mike..." Karen began to weep. "They're going to put my little boy into a drug rehab center."

We stood in the A level of Kaufmann's Parking Garage, and as cars passed us in search of a parking space, I pulled Karen close to me. I did not see or feel what Karen was experiencing. I wished I could. From where I stood, I believed the doctor would find Lucy incapable at this time to care for anyone, including herself. Maybe Karen was just overreacting. She was high-strung, a fact she herself admitted.

"No one is taking Birdie away from us," I whispered. I had made that promise before and I had kept it. This time would be no different.

Karen swallowed hard. The determined look of a boxer stepping into the ring spread across her face. "If they take Byron away from us, I will not rest until I know, beyond a shadow of a doubt, that Byron is safe and well taken care of. If I have to take on the psychologist, every single person at CYS and the judge himself, single-handed, I will." I believed her.

I forgot where I parked the car. I had been growing more and more absent-minded with every meeting that CYS had scheduled. I wondered if I would even have one clear thought left in my head by the time my involvement with the system was over.

After a good fifteen minutes, Karen spotted the car parked near the entrance to the garage. We had walked right passed it. We laughed at our folly, and I was glad to see Karen's spirits rise a little. She needed a distraction as much as I did.

When we got in the car I leaned over and gave her a kiss.

"What was that for?" she asked, buckling her seat belt.

"What do you mean?" I said, giving her another kiss. "You're my wife and I've missed you." Karen and I were spending precious little time together alone. When we finally found a few minutes to ourselves, we were either too mentally or emotionally upset to share an intimate moment.

"I've missed you, too," Karen said, sounding a little sad.

I went to give her another kiss when a driver that had been waiting for our parking space beeped his horn. I waved to him, then pulled out of the space.

We had a couple of hours before the kids would be home from school, and Byron was being cared for by our next-door neighbors who did not expect us home soon, so Karen suggested that we go to the shop. I had a ton of work waiting for me—bills that needed to be paid, letters written and invoices mailed. But Karen needed attention, too.

"Let's play hooky for the day," I suggested, turning onto 279 North. "We'll pick up a sandwich at the Post Office Deli and some of their pumpkin rolls and have a picnic a longside the pool. Just the two of us. What do you say?"

"Oh, all right," Karen said, as if I were asking her to get all of her teeth pulled. "There's just so much to do and…"

"Relax, Karen," I interrupted. "You're allowed to indulge yourself every once in a while."

She agreed. I knew it would be a struggle for Karen to kick back and put her feet up, but she needed to feel the sun and enjoy a cool refreshing dip in the pool.

We stopped at the deli and ordered two chicken salad sandwiches, but Karen did not allow me any dessert. If I wanted a pumpkin roll I would have to sneak out and get it later…which I made my mind up to do at the very first chance.

When we arrived home, George, our neighbor, was splashing in the deep end of the pool, while his wife Paula sat on the steps at the shallow end, playing with Byron. So much for lunch and a quiet swim with my wife. Byron was kicking the water with his tiny feet and slapping his hand onto the surface, splashing water into his and Paula's face. His joyous giggles filled the air.

"He's beautiful," Karen said, standing on the deck, looking down at Byron playing in the water. "Do you think George or Paula see black when they look at him?"

"No," I answered, watching the happy trio. "I think they see a happy, chubby little boy."

"That's what I think, too," Karen said, opening the patio doors.

"Hello, down there!" I called. "Want some lunch?"

George nodded eagerly and did a flip in the water, like a trained dolphin about to be awarded with a tasty fish.

Karen cut the sandwiches up into quarters as I grabbed the hamburger and buns out of the refrigerator and threw them into the picnic basket that was already filled with paper plates and cups. I went upstairs and changed into my new red and white swimming trunks, which were tight around the waist. I picked up the wrong size, I thought, tugging at the back of the trunks. I twisted the waistband to get a look at the size. "Yikes!" I said aloud. They were two sizes bigger than last year's trunks.

I put on a large t-shirt in an effort to conceal some of my newly-acquired bulk. No more candy, pizza, cookies or cake, I promised myself. And forget that pumpkin roll.

Karen was still in the kitchen when I grabbed the picnic basket and headed poolside.

"Hurry up," I called to her as I disappeared from the house.

"Put on a few pounds, hey, Mike?" George greeted me, as I jumped into the pool with my t-shirt still on.

"Still losing hair, I see," I retorted, diving to the bottom of the pool to retrieve one of Cameron's toy cars.

Karen came outside carrying a platter of salad and slices of cheese and raw vegetables—more food for our impromptu picnic. I got out of the pool and tended to my duties as chief hamburger griller.

While we were eating, George remembered that his boss had given him some tickets for the evening performance at Heinz Hall. "It's a ballet, *Gizelle*," said George, reaching for the ketchup. "Pretty good, too. Paula and I already saw it yesterday. Why don't you and Karen enjoy a night out? We'll watch the kids."

"What night are they for?" I asked, thinking what a welcome change it would be for Karen and me to sneak out on a date.

"Tonight," he answered.

"Well, what saith my fair damsel, the lovely Lady Karen? Care for a night out with your charming knight?"

Karen giggled, faking a girlish look as though she had just been asked out on her first date.

I took that for a yes.

When the kids came home a little later, we fed them an early dinner and sent them over to George and Paula. Then we took our time getting showered and dressed in our best clothes. Karen looked stunning in her black strapless evening dress, and I thought I looked pretty good in my new light-weight wool suit. I felt as if this was my first date with Karen as I watched her walk down the driveway, her hips swaying slightly in the tight dress. I opened the car door for her and helped her into the front seat.

"I love you," I said, kissing the back of her neck as she turned to find the seat belt.

The cares of the day were a million miles away from us as we drove back into town. The city lights sparkled off the rivers and romance was in the air. I reached for Karen's hand. I was blessed to have found her. She gave a direction to my life. Actually, she had threatened to leave me early in our relationship, saying that she did not want to have anything to do with a man who did not carry his own weight. And she meant that figuratively.

Back then I was deciding whether or not to stay with Johnson and Johnson Labs, doing research, or quit to go to their sales department or just do nothing until I figured out what I wanted out of life. When Karen gave me her ultimatum, I quickly made up my mind to go into sales so I could make enough money to support a family. I had decided fairly early in our relationship that I wanted to marry Karen, and if she were going to be my wife, then I was determined that she'd never lack for anything.

We parked across the street from Heinz Hall in a mammoth parking garage. As we crossed the street, we held hands, and only for a moment did I relinquish her hand as

I searched my pockets for the tickets. I found them and handed them to the usher, and hand in hand once again, we entered the lavishly decorated marble building, brilliant in gold leaf and red draperies.

The ballet was beautiful, but I was distracted throughout the performance. All I could think of was Karen—not the mother, not the wife, but the woman whom I loved and was very attracted to.

She sensed my ardor and became coy. Sometimes she'd squeeze my hand, sometimes she'd sit with her hands in her lap. She rested her hand on my thigh once, and just as I was about to take her hand, she drew it away. It was all part of a "dating game" that married people play.

After the ballet whirled to a finish, I did not want the evening to end, so I suggested that we go to Froggy's Restaurant for a light midnight snack. Froggy's was close, just a few blocks from Heinz Hall and kitty-corner from the shop. In our excitement about our "date" we had forgotten to get dinner for ourselves.

I had wanted to walk to Froggy's and feel the city surround us, but I knew better than to do such a thing. Pittsburgh was not as safe as it once was, so I drove the short distance to the restaurant.

As we passed our shop I noticed a light emanating from the pressroom. Was someone working late? I drove around the block and stopped in front of the shop to get a better look at what was going on.

"I hope someone hasn't broke in," Karen said, stretching to take a better look.

"Maybe Bill forgot to shut the light off," I said, not really believing that Bill would be so careless. He was meticulous when it came to having everything in order before he left the shop. "Or maybe Bill was sick and had to leave and someone else closed up."

"Or maybe one of the employees is doing a little work of their own on the side," Karen said. That sounded like it was nearer the truth.

I parked the car and told Karen to wait for me, which she refused to do. "We're in this together, Sir Knight," she said.

I quietly opened the door, hoping to hear the familiar warning signal of the alarm system, but the alarm had already been disarmed. I could see a shadowy figure in the back room.

I motioned for Karen to stay put as I reached for the baseball bat I kept hidden behind the front counter. I held the bat firmly in my hand and without taking a breath flung open the door.

Bobby jumped back in surprise as I entered the room, bat poised to strike.

"Whoa," he yelled, shielding his face with his hands.

"For Christ's sake," I said, lowering my humble weapon. My heart was pounding and my forehead was dripping with sweat. "What are you doing here?"

"Gee, man you scared me," he said, making a feeble attempt to regain his composure. "Bill had an appointment and had to leave early today, so I stayed to finish some work."

Bill never left early unless he were practically dying, I thought. Something was wrong here.

"Let me see what you're working on," Karen demanded. By the tone of her voice I knew that she had already pronounced him guilty of wrongdoing.

"It's just some brochures, that's all," he said, covering the plates with his hands. "It's no big deal. What, don't you trust me?"

"No." Karen's answer was about as honest as they come.

Reluctantly Bobby stepped aside while Karen inspected the plates. "Oh sweet Jesus," she sighed in disbelief. I felt my fingers encircle the bat even tighter as Karen cried, "Twenty dollar bills!"

I don't know who was more astounded, me or Karen, to find hundreds of twenty dollar bills that Bobby had counterfeited using our low-tech printing equipment. I inspected the bills myself. They sure did look real.

"I'm sorry," Bobby said over and over again between

fits of tears. He was a mighty scared twenty-five-year-old. "This wasn't my idea."

"Then whose idea was it?" I asked. I felt as though my life were totally out of control, and I blamed myself for being away from the shop so much.

"I can't say or they'll kill me," he answered, lifting his hands to his face. "I'm so ashamed. Please don't tell the cops, please. I have a family to feed. Just fire me and I'll go away. I'm sorry. I really, really am."

I felt bad for the kid. It seemed that he had gotten himself into a pretty deep hole, so I did not press him to give me the name of his accomplices. I did not want the responsibility of knowing.

"Okay," I said, easing my grip on the bat. "We have to talk about this in the morning, but if you are not here first thing, I will call the cops."

"I'll be here," he promised.

"You better be," Karen threatened, in a high, squeaky voice. She sounded like a mouse attempting to bully an elephant.

"I'll be here, Mrs. Derzack, first thing."

"You better be," she repeated. "Now get out of here."

Bobby left the shop in a hurry and I ran to the window and watched him run to the street. Satisfied that he was gone, I turned to Karen. "What do you think we should do?"

"There's only one thing to do—call the police."

"But I promised I wouldn't."

"No, you didn't," she insisted. "You just said you'd talk to him in the morning."

I dialed 911, explained the situation and was told to call the FBI. The FBI told me to call the Secret Service. After several attempts I got through. I was scared. I didn't want the Secret Service to think I had anything to do with this counterfeiting ring and I certainly did not want it to be made public. People might get the wrong idea.

"Stay where you're at and don't touch anything," the voice on the other end instructed me. "Someone will arrive shortly to investigate."

I handed Karen the car keys and told her to go home. It was a sad ending to our romantic evening, but Karen wanted to check on Byron, and the kids would need help in the morning getting ready for school. I knew I was in for a long, tiring night.

After Karen left, I occupied myself with adjusting the working schedule, now that I had lost one of my best employees. That meant I wouldn't be playing hooky again for a while.

I was on my way to the break room when I noticed a large box in the middle of the printer room floor. I shoved it with my foot to get it out of the way, but it did not budge, so I lifted the lid and looked inside. It was filled with stacks and stacks of twenties. I picked up a bundle and counted them: two thousand dollars. There had to be over ten thousand dollars sitting on my floor. Nervously I tossed the bills back into the box and put on the lid, wondering just how much money Bobby had made while he was working for me.

I heard a tapping on the front window and saw four men dressed in long overcoats standing outside. One was peering in the window, the other three were looking about the street. "Secret Service," said the tallest man, holding his badge up to the window. I was sure that this was a bad dream, or else I was caught up in some B-grade movie. I actually pinched myself. It hurt, so I was definitely awake. I felt like searching the room for cameras but instead I unlocked the door.

Agent Heilman asked me questions while the others combed the shop.

"Heilman, come here," one of the men called. I followed Agent Heilman into the storage room. The man pointed to several opened boxes all filled with twenty dollar bills.

"Some operation." Heilman sounded thrilled over the find. "You shouldn't have let him go," he said, admonishing me.

I lowered my eyes and didn't say anything. What did he expect me to do? Hold him at bat point?

"He probably won't show in the morning," the agent continued, "but in case he does, I want you to wear a wire. Tell him unless he tells you everything you are going to call the police."

I was uncomfortable with all the subterfuge. Me, wearing a wire, drilling a counterfeiter for information, was as farfetched as me donning a spacesuit and going to Mars.

"I think he'll know something's up," I protested. "I'm not a very good actor and I'm as scared as they come."

"Naw, you'll be fine," Agent Heilman said, trying to reassure me. I finally agreed, against my better judgment.

Heilman instructed me about what to ask Bobby while the other two agents, Harry and Lee, taped the microphone to my chest. "Listen to this guy's heart beating," Lee laughed, placing one side of the earphones to Harry's ear. He chuckled. I guess I did appear pretty ridiculous, and I'm sure my poor heart was rattling like a snare drum. I don't know if it was the absurdity of the situation or my lack of sleep that made me join in the laughter.

It was approaching seven in the morning. Although the sun did not shine much on the streets of the city, it was getting lighter outside. The agents locked themselves in the storage room while I waited alone in my office. I heard the door unlock and glanced out of my office window. It was Bill. I greeted him at the door and told him that I had no time to explain but that I wanted him to leave right away and have breakfast at the corner deli. I shoved ten dollars into his hand and shooed him out the door.

"If you're cheating on Karen, I'll kill ya," he growled.

"Not a chance," I shot back at him. "Just get out of here."

I hurried back to my office. A few minutes later Bobby entered the shop. I tried to look as if it were business as usual as I fumbled through some mail that had been left on my desk.

"Hi," Bobby said, standing in the doorway. "Can we talk?"

I motioned him into the office, where he sat down on the most comfortable chair. We talked about his earlier life on the streets, his wife, his kids, his eventual involvement with a man who enticed him with promises of big dollars, a new car and fancy houses in the suburbs.

Unfortunately, Bobby bought this line of crap. He was a good kid and a hard worker, but he had just not learned that there was no such thing as easy money. I could not in good conscience go on deceiving him, so I decided to play it straight with him and hope for the best.

"Bobby," I said, "let me level with you. The Secret Service is in the other room. They have heard everything that we've said. Your only chance to get out of this thing with your skin is to tell them everything they want to know."

I half-expected him to make a dash for the door, but he did not. Instead he started crying as all four agents appeared in the doorway.

"I'll tell you whatever you want to know," Bobby said, looking up through his tears. He was shaking violently, as if he were lost in a snowstorm.

The Secret Service escorted him out the door.

"You took a big chance," Agent Heilman said, picking up the morning newspaper from the step and tossing it to me. "Sometimes chances pay off. But be more careful next time."

Next time? I wasn't going to have a next time. I slumped down in my chair. What was going on? Whatever happened to my safe, predictable life? How did all this evil enter my boring, ordinary existence?

A bird chirped outside the building, and I thought of Pinegrove Terrace. Just the thought of those dark, looming buildings and hopeless people made me shiver. I felt as if I had entered into a different reality where everything was turned upside down and on its ear. Could it be that, when I visited Pinegrove, I took the demon of the night back home with me?

I spread out the newspaper on the desk in front of me, determined to distract myself. Then I caught the headlines: TODDLER GIRL MURDERED, FATHER SUSPECT.

While my heart rose to my throat, I quickly scanned the article. CYS had, against the pleas of the police and family members, given custody of a two-year-old girl to her father. This man had, just days earlier, held his girlfriend and her family at gun point, threatening to kill them. But CYS said that they were unaware of the incident. As soon as he could, the father checked into a motel, where the child's battered body was discovered by the maid a few days later.

CYS denied that this travesty was their fault, stating that the police had failed to inform them of the father's record. The police basically answered that CYS was full of shit, although of course they didn't say that in the paper.

I took a deep breath. I was remarkably calm. I had gained an instant understanding of this whole twisted nightmare with CYS. I was in a whole new reality, one which almost made sense, given the nightmare of Pinegrove Terrace and the corruption of the system. I was participating in a warped world where deception and lies were accepted as the truth.

My attorney was mugged, my employee was a counterfeiter, CYS were liars, a drug-addicted prostitute was a competent mother, my child might be spending a part of his childhood in a drug rehabilitation center—what next? Dark was light, I understood that now. But what was I to do with that understanding?

I walked about the shop like a zombie searching for a way back to life. Where was my world? Whatever happened to truth and honesty, doing the right thing? Why did little babies have to die? "I want to go home!" I screamed, searching the room for something to throw. I was lost, frustrated, angry and scared. I felt a volcano of despair bubbling inside of me.

I stumbled into the storage room, my eyes stinging with fright. Oh God, I pleaded, help me.

Before me was a newly installed plasterboard wall, separating the room into smaller compartments. I stared at its blank whiteness, as if the answers to this madness were written on its smooth surface. Then I balled up my hand and sent my fist ripping through the wall. I heard the crunching of plaster as I tore open a hole the size of a cannonball.

My arm plunged inside the wall up to my elbow and I paused a second before withdrawing my hand. I had never done anything like this before. I pulled out my hand and inspected the wall with a degree of fascination. I looked at my hand. Only a few scratches. Surprisingly, I felt good. I stood back, balled up my other hand, and made another hole. This time it hurt.

"That will be enough, young man," I heard a voice behind me and I whirled around, expecting to see my father standing in the doorway. I could feel the wildness in my eyes and the contempt in my heart as I glared at...Bill. I held up my hand. It was bleeding.

"I'm going mad," I said, half-making a statement, half-asking a question. We both stood, watching the blood drip from my hand and fall onto the floor.

"No, you're not, that would be too easy," Bill's voice lacked any sympathy. "You're in training. Now straighten up or they'll beat you."

He led me to my office, handed me a towel, then left the room. I wrapped it around my hand. I felt embarrassed at my weakness, especially in front of Bill, whose strength I admired so much.

The employees began to file into the shop. The smell of brewing coffee, donuts and aftershave filled the room. Everyone was busy preparing for the full workload. I could hear someone ask about the wall.

I sat in my chair, tending to my aching hand, when Bill entered, closing the door behind him. He poured us both a cup of coffee, and we drank without a word between us.

"I know about Bobby," he said, downing the last gulp of coffee. "He's a good kid. I talked to his wife a little while ago. They've been pretty hard up for money, what with three kids and all. She blames herself for their troubles."

I rubbed my eyes. What was I supposed to do about

Bobby's wife and kids? "Maybe I shouldn't have turned him in," I finally said.

"You did right," Bill said, arching his eyebrows. He seemed lost in thought for a moment. "Yeah, I would have done the same thing in your circumstances."

I poured more coffee into our cups and once again felt a cold silence fall between us. Bill's head was bowed as he studied the coffee cup he held between his opened knees. I felt as though we were in mourning for a dead friend.

"My life is turning to shit," I declared. There was not much more I needed to say.

"Yeah, I know," Bill agreed, still staring at the coffee. That did not make me feel any better. Where was the pep talk? The rally behind ol' Mike?

"Well?" I asked, staring at the gray-haired old codger. "You have nothing else to offer, except 'yeah, I know'?"

"Mike," he said, now looking at me eye to eye, "every man walks down his own road. You mapped out a journey to hell for Byron's sake, and I know you didn't expect it to be easy. Come on. Hell isn't found during a midnight ride to Pinegrove. It's inside here," he said, thumping on his chest. "You gotta figure out real quick what it is that you are going to do, boy. You've only got two choices...how hard can it be?"

Two choices? I waited for the answer.

"Didn't your daddy teach you nothing?" Bill asked, with a full head of steam. "You either take the dark into your light or take your light into the dark."

"Well, that makes it perfectly clear," I said sarcastically. I had no idea what Bill meant by that little bit of philosophical wisdom. It seemed like it was six of one and half a dozen of the other to me.

"You're a smart boy, you'll figure it out." Bill placed the coffee cup on the desk with a thud, then stood up and yawned. His long arms nearly touched the ceiling as he stretched. "Great morning, ain't it? Now stop feeling sorry for yourself and get to work," Bill grumbled, walking to the door. "We've wasted enough time."

I went to work. It helped clear my mind, but not my heart. I was still furious. Another child had been murdered. How was I to know but that my child might be next?

Eight

I TOOK ME A week to adjust my attitude. After a bit of soul-searching, I was able to put the events of the past few weeks into perspective. The death of the little girl still haunted me. I knew, from what Jane Worley had told me when we tried to introduce Lucy's criminal history in court, that criminal records are not taken into account when reuniting a child with his family. This made no sense to me, but it somehow made perfect sense to Jane Worley.

What it had come down to, apparently, was this: risking a child's death rather than exposing a criminal record. CYS chose a dead child. In Jane Worley's world, inviting the devil out to dine made sense. Both CYS and the judge in the case claimed they had not known about the father's criminal background. The police claimed that CYS was not telling the truth, but in the end CYS did not take any heat from the press; the judge did.

When I complained to Bill that none of this made any sense to me, he replied, "Who said life makes sense?" It was just a shame, I told him, that a child had to die to prove that point.

Our June 9th hearing regarding Doctor Komma's psychological report was postponed until the twenty-third. I was accustomed to delays within the courts and in a way I welcomed this one. If Karen's apprehensions regarding Doctor Komma proved to be true, we would have a real problem on our hands. But, since I had pulled myself together and was in a positive frame of mind, I believed that Byron would not be taken away from us. That was a reality I created for myself, and I did not want it disturbed. So when Vernon Washington walked back into my life I was not prepared to deal with the sad but eye-opening news he delivered.

Bill and I were in the front of the shop, talking about finding a replacement for Bobby, when Vernon walked in the door.

"Vernon, what brings you to my humble shop?" I walked over to him and shook his hand. I was genuinely happy to see him. He felt like an old familiar friend, even though I had only had one brief conversation with him.

"Bill, come over here," I called over my shoulder. "I want you to meet Vernon Washington. He's a reporter I met last year."

When they saw each other, Bill and Vernon stood frozen, wide-eyed, mouths agape, staring at each other. A smile spread across Vernon's face and seemed to engulf his entire head. Bill, flashing only a faint smile, blinked his eyes, as if waking up from a dream.

"Bill? Bill the Grump Wilson? You old son-of-a-gun," Vernon laughed, leaping toward him. "Let me take a look at you."

Bill's ruddy face turned scarlet.

"Man, you're as ugly as ever," Vernon exclaimed, grabbing Bill's forearm and pulling him next to him. Vernon locked Bill in an embrace, and rough-and-tumble Bill did not appear to mind this overt display of emotion. "How ya been, old man?" Vernon asked, not letting go of Bill. "I heard you died, but I guess that isn't completely true."

"You know each other?" I asked, though it was obvious they did. I felt guilty for disturbing a Hallmark moment, but I had to know how these two fit into each other's life.

"Know each other?" Vernon choked. "This guy is practically my father. Shoot, man, it's so damn good to see you."

"Well, you proved me wrong, you did," Bill said, wiggling loose of Vernon's tight grip. He stood back and gave Vernon a good looking-over. "I thought by now you'd be rotting in some prison or found dead in some alley."

"Aw, come on, you old sourpuss," Vernon said, capturing Bill in another embrace. "You wouldn't waste your time on no hopeless little nigger boy. Who you tryin' to kid, anyway? You always knew I was special. Hell, you even fell in love with me. Am I right?"

Bill would never admit that he loved someone, I thought. Not in a million years.

"If the truth be known, I'd say you were right," Bill answered, lowering his head. He pulled a handkerchief out his back pocket and gave his nose a mighty blow.

"This man saved me from hell," Vernon said, turning to me, pretending to not notice Bill dabbing his eyes. "If it weren't for him, I wouldn't be reporting on crime, I'd be doing it. At least as long as it took for me to get my brains blown out."

"Naw," Bill scowled. "You were always a good kid. You're the one that turned your own life around."

"You're the one that gave me the chance." Vernon turned to me again. "He can never take a compliment, have you noticed that?"

That was true. Bill seemed to have a positive effect on

everyone he came in contact with, but he never accepted a thank-you without a debate.

Vernon explained his first encounter with Bill, who he said, was bigger and meaner back then. The story was very similar to Charles'. I wondered how many more "Charleses" were out there whose lives had been touched by Bill. I felt uneasy as I remembered writing Charles off as lost and damaged beyond hope.

I left Bill and Vernon alone to reminisce. As I was filling out some work sheets, both men reappeared in my office. Bill closed the door behind them. "Go on, tell 'im," Bill said, pointing at me. "One more turd added to his pile ain't going to make much difference."

"Well, I don't want to send up any red flags, but I think you're headed for some dangerous waters." Vernon paused for a moment before sitting down, trying to wipe off some old ink stains that had long found their way into the fabric upholstered chairs.

"It's dry," I said, not blaming him for not wanting to sit down. His double-breasted silk suit, which probably cost him a month's salary, did not come off the rack at a department store.

"I really hate to be the one to tell you this," he said, closing his eyes as he sat down. I knew he was imagining a big red stain soaking into the seat of his pants. "But like I said before, when it comes to kids, well, I'm colorblind."

"Cut to the quick, Vern," Bill said, fidgeting in his seat. "We got work to do."

"Reverend Johns just called you 'crazy' in front of what well may be the world," he blurted out, flashing a hard look at Bill.

"Excuse me?" I had lost him somewhere. "Slow down and back up. Someone said I was crazy?"

"I was taping a press conference over at Mission Church in the Hill." Vern's Adam's apple bobbed up and down as he stopped to clear his throat. "The community leaders who are in support of Mel Blount's announcement to take his youth home private all had their chance to give a little speech.

"In most cases their rhetoric was more political than anything else. No one was paying them much attention, me included, when Reverend Johns gets up and refers to a white couple fighting to adopt a black child as crazy. He didn't use your name, but everyone who was listening knew he was talking about you and your wife."

I did not know what to make out of this information, but from the look on Vernon's face, I knew that it was important.

"He doesn't get it," Bill said, rolling his eyes. "You'll have to explain it."

"Reverend Johns is what you might call a separatist," Vernon began, spelling things out for me. "He's the president of the Pittsburgh chapter of the NAACP and has his own church. He has just taken a public stand on the issue of you adopting Byron. He has thrown his hat in the ring, so to speak. Now, I'm willing to bet that if he doesn't yet have the support of the national chapter of the NAACP, he soon will."

Christ, I thought. It was bad enough that the newspapers were picking up on the black-white issue, thanks to the likes of LaPort. But if the NAACP took an official stand against us...I didn't want to even think about how ugly things would get. Especially in the press.

"It gets even worse. Whatever Reverend Johns believes, he will solicit his congregation to believe the same thing. And it wouldn't take much effort, because black folks are true to their church. It's the center of life for most of us.

"He might also try and persuade the other pastors in the black community over to his side. They'll follow him, too, especially if the national chapter supports him. Then they'll convince their congregations that blacks and whites shouldn't mix."

"Oh, I see." I thought for a moment. "Wait a minute. I thought the NAACP was working for integration. Hell, I demonstrated for school busing. Has something changed since the sixties?"

"Man, Bill was right." Vernon was shaking his head in disbelief. "You really don't know what's going on."

"Listen to me carefully," he said looking over his shoulder, as if expecting some unwanted guest to be listening. "It isn't often that the Klan and the NAACP agree on things, but I'm afraid that not wanting whites adopting blacks is common ground for both of them. The Klan is afraid of racial impurity and the blacks are afraid they'll lose the black culture. Hey, go figure."

I picked up a pencil and began tapping it on my desk. I needed to think. A group as important and powerful as the NAACP couldn't possibly endorse such a biased attitude. It was only a few renegades talking out their own fears and anger that placed color before the best interests of a child. And busing was a good thing. So was integration.

"Hey, I got the whole thing on tape," he said, reading the disbelief on my face. "If you ever need a copy, let me know."

"Yeah, I might want to take a look…someday."

"Come on, Vern, let's get out of here," said Bill, tugging on the reporter's arm. He and Vernon walked to the front door, their arms around each other's shoulders. They talked for a few minutes, then Vernon reached in his pocket and shoved a wad of money into Bill's hand. Bill shook his head and attempted to give the money back. "For the kids, man," Vernon said, before stepping out into the sweltering heat.

With Reverend Johns still on my mind, I hurried through the remaining things to do on my list and rushed home to watch the six o'clock news. No reference to Reverend Johns' comments was reported either on television or in the newspaper. But then, the news wasn't about me and my problems with CYS. It was about Mel Blount and his problems with the CYS.

I did not want Vernon's information to be correct, but I knew it would be.

Since Byron was carried into my home, weak and sick, by some uncaring stranger, life had become different for me and my family. Everything seemed to tilt to one side like the floor of a carnival funhouse, and it was all I could do to get my bearings and continue on, deeper into the chaos.

Karen accepted Vernon's assessment at face value. She was a little upset that a man of the collar made an inference that she was crazy, but she soon forgot her indignation. We had an immediate obstacle to overcome—the unveiling of the psychological tests.

KAREN AND I RUSHED to get the kids off to daycamp and Byron fed and dressed so we could arrive early at the courthouse to wait several hours before the judge heard our case. We were all getting to be old hands at preparing for these events.

Connie made breakfast for Chris and Cameron, while Chris packed Cameron's Aladdin gym bag with a change of clothes, a peanut butter and jelly sandwich and an X-Men superhero figure.

Cameron played with Byron while Karen prepared his breakfast cereal: formula mixed with dried oats, a concoction which resembled wallpaper paste. We were a smooth-operating machine. Since our talk, the three kids had been very cooperative in matters that concerned their brother Byron.

We dropped the kids off at their daycamps and drove through rush hour traffic to Juvenile Court. Once inside the courthouse we waited our turn, glancing at each other nervously from time to time. Finally, after two hours, we were ushered into the courtroom. I was happy that this time Katie was with us.

We sat at the back of the courtroom with Byron. The place was becoming too familiar, and I wished I would never need to see it again. I could smell the Murphy's Oil used to clean the wooden benches, which was a relief from the cheap perfume and aftershave filling up the crammed hallways outside the heavy swinging doors. We rose as Judge Lerner entered the room and remained standing until he called the court into order. The judge was looking particularly happy that morning and actually joked around with the lawyers who sat in front of him.

"Okay, troops let's get this show on the road," the judge said, tapping the gavel lightly against the wooden block.

A CYS representative did not waste any time reading from the psychologist's report. "As the judge knows, the first and primary question was if the mother could maintain her treatment and recovery from her substance abuse. The second question was which of her five children should be placed with her in the program. A third and secondary question was, if Byron is not returned to the mother, should he be placed with his great-maternal aunt. The final and also secondary question was if the foster parents have met Byron's needs and if they have been sympathetic and dedicated to exposing Byron to issues of his birth culture and race."

I listened to the hour-long reading and debate of the psychological report. I was highly disturbed at the troubled nature of Lucy's other children. The three oldest all were experiencing emotional difficulties in varying degrees, and all of them were receiving therapy for acting out aggressive behaviors. It sickened me to learn that one was acting out sexual behaviors, even though he was just six years old.

There was little reaction from Karen as she held on to Byron. It was if she wasn't listening to the words being spoken. I figured she was remaining calm so as not to disturb our sleeping Birdie.

"In summary," the CYS worker said, still reading from the report. Finally, I thought. "It is the recommendation of the psychologist that the three oldest children not be placed with the mother at this time. Their emotional and behavioral difficulties, their level of neediness, their involvement in supportive services as well as the inherent problems in separating them would at this point in their development be detrimental. Doctor Komma does recommend, however, that the two younger children, Byron and his sister, Georgia, be returned to the mother and that the process of reunification for both children begin immediately."

I pressed my fingers into my temple and rubbed my aching forehead. How in the hell could any doctor in her right mind place two small children with a drug-addicted parent in a drug rehabilitation center, knowing what a mess the other siblings turned out to be? The world was crazy; I had learned that months ago, but this was unconscionable.

Karen still did not react. "Did you hear what they said?" I asked. "Hello in there." I tapped on Karen's head.

"Stop it," she grumbled, pushing my hand away. "You didn't expect anything different, did you? Let's wait to hear from the judge."

The judge was sitting quietly, twiddling his thumbs. He appeared to be as dumbfounded as me. I could not but get the feeling that his strategy did not work out. Instead of proving Lucy unfit to be a mother, the psychological reports had blown up in his face.

"No," he said, still rolling his thumbs, one over the other. "I disagree. The recommendation is denied. Byron is going to stay where he is. If any of you have a problem with that decision, file a motion. Everyone is free to go."

"But Judge Lerner," the attorney for CYS spoke up. "At least consider issuing a gag order to prevent the Derzacks from speaking to the media."

"Does the Derzacks' attorney agree to the implementation of a gag order?"

"No, your Honor, we emphatically do not," Katie said.

"Then court is dismissed."

I sat dumbfounded, frozen to my seat. That was it? It was that simple? The problem of custody seemed to have vanished into thin air. A wave of the judge's gavel and we got our wish. Byron was coming home with us.

Hope against hope, I wished that CYS would just give up. It had to be costing them a bundle of money to keep this case going, including the costs of keeping Lucy in rehab and paying a staff dedicated to thwarting our efforts to gain access to information. Certainly Jane Worley would welcome never hearing from me or Karen again.

Katie gave us the thumbs up and hurried out of the courtroom for a domestic case she was handling. Since her encounter with the mugger, Katie had lost some of her innocent laughter. The mugger had stolen more than Katie's purse; he had taken a part of her childlike joy with him.

THE DAYS THAT FOLLOWED were uneventful. Everything at the shop was going well and our three big kids were enjoying the last weeks of their summer vacation mode. Dressed in shorts, t-shirts and sandals, they staged elaborate squirt-gun battles with water pistols the size of my arm, capable of firing a stream of water into my neighbors' windows. The pool was nearly always filled with friends and neighborhood kids.

I had just stepped in the door, returning from an emergency run to the supermarket for bread, milk, steaks, hotdogs and hamburgers (I was to be master chef at Mike's Poolside Grill for a few guests), when Karen delivered the good news.

"Lucy called while you were out." Karen looked like the cat that swallowed the canary. "We talked for a long while and she told me things you would not believe."

"For instance?" I asked, separating the groceries according to what stayed in the house and what I needed to carry down to the pool.

"Well, she says she never signed Byron over to CYS. When she came back to the hospital to get him, they told her that he had been moved to a group home."

"Go on!" I acted shocked as I propped the door open and stepped out onto the deck. "CYS wouldn't lie."

"It gets better," Karen continued, following close behind me with a pitcher of freshly squeezed lemonade. "When the great-aunt wanted to know where Byron was, they wouldn't tell her. When she threatened to cause a problem, they told her Byron was in a group home and that she could not visit him."

"Not to take the side of CYS or anything, but remember what Doctor Lipinsky said about a drug addict?"

"I don't know, Mike." Karen walked carefully down the steps and swung open the pool gate with her foot. "I kinda believe her. Why would she lie about such a thing?"

I did not know why, but I felt Lucy was capable of making up stories on a whim. Perhaps she knew she would get Karen's attention by making up dirt about CYS.

Chris started down the steps, wearing his black and hot pink swimming trunks and talking on the portable phone. His discovery of girls had seemed to take place about a week ago, and since then the phone had become an extension of his ear.

"Go get me a pen and paper," Karen called to him. He heard Karen but continued down the steps. "Now," she ordered. "And hang up that phone."

Chris returned minus the phone and handed Karen a pen and a sheet of paper.

"Who are you writing to?" I asked, looking over her shoulder.

"Lucy," she said, covering the paper with her hand. "Go away. I'll give it to you when I'm done. We had such a good talk. I want to let her know we are thinking about her. And maybe this would be a good time to update her on Byron's needs."

I joined Chris in the pool and we played a round of pool basketball. I let Chris win, or at least I thought I did. I was a little out of breath as I lifted myself out of the pool.

"Here." Karen handed me the letter and I began reading.

Dear Lucy,

Hi. Thanks for calling back. I just wanted to drop you a note from all of us. Mike and I do often think about your family. We know that it is not easy for any of you, and we are praying for you. Also, as I mentioned to you over the phone, you and/or your family are always welcome to call or visit us.

If there is any way for you to come to our home, we would love to have you join in celebrating Byron's birthday. His first year checkup is July 15th at 3:45. Maybe you would like to go with us. And we are going to have to address getting Byron's hair cut. Please let me know what you think about this.

We are planning a trip to Disney World in the beginning of August. We plan on staying one week. This small vacation is going to interrupt the visitation schedule, but if it would be agreeable to you, we could add an extra visitation day to the weeks before and later. Is that acceptable?

Regarding baptism, we feel we should work together to get Byron baptized. Our family is Roman Catholic, but we have no problem, if it were your desire, to arrange a service in a domination of your choice.

Once again, thanks for calling. I'll be talking with you shortly.

"Are you going to mail this?" I asked, waving the letter.

"Yes," Karen answered, puzzled. "Why?"

"Because it will be intercepted."

"So what if it is?" said Karen. "It's a harmless little letter. What evil could they possibly read into that?"

"Just don't be surprised," I answered.

The next morning I mailed the letter to Lucy just as Karen had instructed, and sure enough, a few days letter we received a letter from Sojourner House—a neatly typed, grammatically perfect letter. Although it bore Lucy's signature, it did not sound a bit like her.

Dear Mr. and Mrs. Derzack:

I'm writing this letter in response to your questions concerning Byron's hair, baptism, and trip to Florida.

It is the custom of our family to not have our children's hair cut until they reach the age of two, and at which time my younger brother traditionally cuts all the younger boys' hair.

Baptism is a very special family occasion and is not performed until the children are age 4 or older. The entire family is looking forward to sharing this special occasion with Byron at that time.

Also, a very significant time for celebration in our family is the first birthday of our children. The past experience and memories of my other children's birthdays are very important to our family and, as with the baptism, we are looking forward to sharing this experience with Byron within his own family.

Being present as a guest at my own son's first birthday celebration would be an uncomfortable experience at this time due to our present conflict. However, I appreciate your invitation to attend.

I'm sure your trip to Florida is very important to you and your family; however, the regular scheduled visits with my son and daughter are very special to me and any disruption in our visits at this time may further hinder our bonding process. Also, not having my son nearby worries me and no amount of assurance from you or CYS will encourage me to believe that my son would be okay flying from Pittsburgh to Florida.

I would be more than willing and happy to have Byron stay at Sojourner House with me while you and your family take your vacation.

Lastly, I feel that in the best interests of all involved, any further questions or concerns regarding my son should be directed in writing to the appropriate staff members at CYS and Family Services. This should help avoid any miscommunications, so that we may all work together to ensure that Byron has what is best for him.

Sincerely,
Lucy

I started to laugh. For CYS or the staff of Sojourner House to actually think I would believe Lucy wrote that letter was like convincing me that Connie could keep her mouth shut for five minutes. I had my doubts that Karen's letter ever made it to Lucy. Now I was convinced that it had not.

The decision to have Byron go on a family vacation to meet Mickey Mouse would now have to be placed before the judge.

I called Katie at her home and read the letter to her. She found it amusing but not beyond the scope of CYS's cruel tricks.

"We better get clarification on the judge's ruling," Katie

said, her voice sounding tried. "And while I'm filing that motion, I'll file another requesting that you be granted permission to temporarily leave Allegheny county's jurisdiction with Byron so he can get his vacation to Disney World. What a crazy world this is, huh?"

Katie filed the motion the following morning and a court date was set for September 8th, which was quickly canceled at the request of Lucy's new attorney, Larrence Franklin. It was rescheduled for September 13th.

Fortunately, after a lot of delays, expense and rigmarole, we did get to take Byron and the other kids to Disney World, but not under the best of circumstances. Because the decision took so long, our plane reservations were canceled and we had to drive the whole crew of excited offspring from Pittsburgh to Orlando and back. That cut the trip mighty short and it left us with a Land Cruiser full of spilled potato chips, melted ice cream and lost toy parts, but in spite of it all we had a fun vacation. At least Karen and I were able to forget our worries about Byron, if just for a week.

I'll never forget when we got to the Magic Kingdom and crossed the drawbridge into Sleeping Beauty's Castle. There stood Mickey Mouse and Pluto—or at least very good, costumed facsimiles of them. Byron stared straight into their big fabric eyes…and burst into tears. I suppose a giant mouse can be rather overwhelming when you're barely a year old.

Mickey and Pluto knew what they were doing. They backed off, holding their hands to their faces as if startled and worried by Byron's wailing. At last Byron worked up the courage to tweak Mickey's nose, and Chris snapped a photo of it. It was an enchanted moment; the little boy who could not stop convulsing eight months ago had touched something magic.

The magic didn't last very long. By the time the hearing was supposed to take place, the kids had already been in school for a week and we were settling into our regular routine. Karen was enjoying the extra time alone with Byron, and he soaked up all the attention like a sponge.

I hoped there would be other vacations, but Lucy's lawyer was busy filing motions right and left to prevent us from taking Byron outside of Allegheny County again. To top it all off, the ruling met with several delays, and the hearing was rescheduled. Still, I was glad Byron had had a chance to see Mickey and Pluto.

Finally the day of the hearing arrived. On the way to Juvenile Court, Karen updated me with reports from Connie's and Chris' teachers. So far so good. However, I was sure that once Connie had become comfortable with her new class, we would be getting a call from the principal. It wasn't that she was a troublemaker; it was just that her teachers were continually worried that she talked in class so much she couldn't "apply herself" properly to her studies. Of course I knew she talked in class so much the poor teachers couldn't think.

Cammie was beginning kindergarten. Karen and I had made the hard decision to hold him back a year as his birthday was right on the borderline. Cammie's height was below normal, and we wanted to give him a chance to grow so the other kids would accept him more readily. The doctor had told us that hormonal treatments weren't necessary and nothing seemed out of the ordinary, but we still were very concerned. Karen, who did not believe in wonder drugs, would not have allowed these treatments anyway, unless it was life threatening.

When we arrived at the courtroom a guard at the door informed us that we were to wait out in the hallway. This time we did not receive any special treatment. We filed past the hordes of people lingering in the hallway and observed the typical scene: kids crying, adults ignoring their pleas, an occasional alarm going off.

I noticed Katie plowing her way through the mob, her appearance less than cheerful. She looked frazzled and disheveled, much like Byron's caseworker. Either the workload was getting to her or the mugging was taking a bigger toll than I had realized.

"Listen," Katie explained in a hurry. She made a feeble

attempt at placing a stray strand of brown hair back into the hairband she was wearing, just to have it flop back into her eyes. "You and Mike are not allowed in the courtroom. I'm sure that Attorney Franklin has something to do with this, but by rights this is a hearing of a minor and it *is* closed to the public. Obviously he has successfully persuaded the judge that you are the public. Why don't you just go home and I'll call you after it's over."

"I can't do that," Karen answered. Both she and I knew she would be hopping around like a Mexican jumping bean waiting for Katie to call. It would be bad enough sitting in Juvenile Court with her under these circumstances, but I didn't want to be locked in a car with her for twenty miles listening to her freak out over the court's position of reducing us to the "public." Every day Karen lost more patience with all the lies, and I was left taking the brunt of her frustrations.

"We'll wait here," I agreed with Karen, sitting down on a hard wooden bench. At least if Karen got too overwrought, I could escape to the bathroom.

"Don't let them put a gag order on us," Karen warned, following Katie as she hurried down the hall.

While Karen fed Byron, I entertained myself by guessing the kind of trouble my fellow hallmates were in. I recognized a few of them and actually struck up an interesting conversation with a black woman who was sipping whiskey from a flask she had smuggled past the guards.

"You know what the problem is?" she said, waving her arms as if blessing the masses. "It's this welfare thing. It strips all your dignity. Yessir, once you get used to making a living without putting in a hard day's work, you fall into the hands of the devil. And he don't care if you got no pride, neither. Just makes things a little easier for him, that's all." She stopped long enough to take another swig. "What's your name, son?"

"Mike Derzack," I said, holding out my hand to shake hers.

"Ain't you that man who's trying to take Baby Byron from his mamma?"

"That's what some folks believe," I said, withdrawing my hand.

"Well, you gonna need this more than I do," she said, offering me her bottle of liquor.

We both had a hearty laugh.

Karen and I waited for over an hour when an officer of the court explained that Katie was late for another hearing. We were to go home and wait for her call.

Karen's eyes grew wild with anger. The drive home was long and Karen struggled to keep her voice in check so as not to upset Byron. The more upset Karen became, the higher her voice went. "They're weaning us away from Byron," Karen whined. "It won't be long now before they take him away."

"That's it, Karen!" I screamed at her. I slammed on the brakes and pulled off to the side of the road. "I will not listen to your negative attitude," I said, gripping the steering wheel tightly in my hands. "It's hard enough for me to keep the faith. I can't do it for both of us."

Byron started crying.

"Now look what you've done!" cried Karen. She flung open the car door, stepped out and rushed into the backseat with Byron. "That's okay, sweetie, Dad's just a little upset." I felt as though I had just been kicked in the stomach. I wasn't the one who was supposed to lose his temper. I was steady, reliable Mike, the calm, logical guy you could rely on in a crisis. What the hell was happening to me?

"I'm sorry…" I began to apologize. I looked in the rearview mirror at Karen.

"Just take us home."

The rest of the way home, Karen played with Byron and he giggled at her antics. He had already forgotten about my outburst; I knew that Karen had not.

While we waited for Katie to call, Karen busied herself with a few household chores and I holed up in my study. I tried to read, but while I saw the words and turned the pages, I couldn't remember what I was reading. Finally I put the book down and called Katie. There was no answer at her home or office. I left a message on both answering machines, but she did not return my call.

Karen was upset, but she refused to be demonstrative about it. That was a major feat for Karen. Everyone always knew when Karen was happy and when she was not, and she rarely tried to hide her feelings from me. But today she did not want to share any part of herself with me.

I understood just why she was so upset. Karen always relied on my complete acceptance of her, and I was sure my outburst both confused and hurt her. Eventually, I hoped, she would put my actions in proper perspective. She would understand and adjust to the stress I was feeling. But that might take some time.

By bedtime Karen still was not talking to me, and I was growing more furious at her for not being able to understand my feelings. We went to bed breaking a promise that we had made to each other long ago: Never let the sun set on our anger.

As the night wore on I could hear Karen tossing and turning. Good, I thought. If I couldn't sleep, neither should she. As I lay in the dark, listening to the crickets calling outside our bedroom window, I suddenly had an odd experience. The image of Gwendolyn Clarke, an eighth grade classmate, popped into my mind.

I could see her pale face, soft blue eyes and wavy red hair, as if she were standing in front of me. She had died over the Christmas holidays, along with her two sisters and mother; she was only thirteen. A fire had swept through their old farmhouse as they slept. Only the father survived...barely. No one talked about it, except for a few whispers at recess.

At the end of the school year I was given the task of gathering up all the textbooks, checking for scribble marks and writing down the name of the kid that used the book. I was adding Johnny Peachtree's name to the list of offenders when I noticed a piece of yellowing, lined paper lying on the floor.

To Whom It May Concern: I want to grow up to be a dancer. But God has other plans for me. Dance for me...please. Signed, Gwendolyn Marie Clarke, age 13.

I felt as if I had been visited by a ghost! I ran out of the cloakroom, screaming my head off. And who was to say that I was not being visited by a ghost, right that instant, twenty-five years later?

"Karen...Karen," I whispered excitedly. I knew she wasn't sleeping although she yawned and rubbed her eyes.

"What? Is Byron crying?"

I jumped out of bed and pulled her to her feet. I put my arms around her and stumbled about the dark room, humming "Old Lump of Coal."

"What are you doing?"

"I feel like dancing. Don't you?"

Karen joined me, a little confused and a lot delighted. The romance was still alive between us. I could feel it, as bright and electric as a bolt of lightning. "I might be an old lump of coal, Lord," she sang under her breath, "but I'm gonna be a diamond some day."

I awoke early the next morning, holding Karen in my arms. I smoothed her hair into place and softly kissed her forehead. She was everything to me.

I had to find a better way to negotiate these terrifying waters. Losing my cool and lashing out at Karen would serve no good purpose and only destroy both of us.

I showered and shaved, threw on my jeans and sweatshirt and headed for the shop. I arrived just as a fax from Katie was coming through, and I watched the slow jerking movements of the paper as it inched through the machine. I felt the urge to pull on the paper to get it to print faster, but I managed to restrain myself. When the first page of her letter broke free, I picked it up and hurriedly read it.

Dear Mike and Karen:

Because you were not present in the Courtroom for the presentation of Motions by Larrence Franklin, Esquire, I want to review with you what transpired.

Mr. Franklin first presented the Motion which he had

forwarded to me the day before the hearing. He told the judge that they were seeking (1) immediate return of Byron or (2) the make-up of four visits missed due to the mother's illness.

Mr. Franklin then presented a second Motion, of which he had never given any of the parties notice. The second motion requested an injunction forbidding us to speak to the media. It was the same as the Injunction he had earlier presented to the Superior Court, which was denied.

I first advised Judge Lerner that the parties seeking the injunction had called the media on Thursday. I then reviewed the harassing and vexatious nature of the conduct of Attorney Franklin for presenting frivolous petitions to the Superior Court in an attempt to "judge shop" in Juvenile Court. I also noted that you are the only parties paying counsel fees in this litigation.

I further advised the judge that make-up visits were not only burdensome to you but upsetting to Byron.

The judge gave me a full opportunity to be heard, then he ruled that four consecutive visits on Saturday be granted to Lucy. Regarding the injunction: I argued that it was uncon-stitutional. The judge did not sign that order, but said that he did not want any of the parties talking to the media. I believe that it is crucial that we honor the judge's oral request until after the December 15th ruling.

As to the return of Byron, the judge did state that nothing that occurred at the hearing meant that he was necessarily granting the order of permanent return of Byron to his natural mother.

There was another page, but it didn't add anything new.

I was pleased with the outcome, and that meant that Karen would not be. She would find some darker meaning in the proceedings. The scary thing was that she was nearly always right.

I called Karen with and read the letter to her.

"What does Katie mean that we are the only ones paying attorney's fees? Who's paying for Lucy's?" Karen asked. "I'll bet it's CYS," she answered herself immediately.

No, I didn't think so, I told her. But who could it be?

After I hung up with Karen, I searched my desk drawers for Vernon's card and found it in the bottom of the top drawer under a heap of pencils, colored pencils and markers. It was bent and tattered but I could still make out the number.

I called him at once. "Vernon, it's Mike Derzack," I practically shouted into the receiver as he answered.

"How ya doin', man?" He sounded as if I had awakened him.

"I've got a favor to ask."

"Anything. Go ahead." I could imagine him sitting on the edge of the bed, shaking the cobwebs out of his head.

"Can you find out who's paying for Lucy's attorney, Larrence Franklin?"

"Are you kidding? That's an easy one. It's the NAACP. Man, everyone knows that. It was in the *Courier*." He paused for a moment, then added, "Oh, that's a black paper. You probably don't subscribe to that."

"Thanks," I mumbled. "I owe you one."

I held the phone in my hand until an obnoxious beeping sound told me I was taking too long to hang up. The NAACP? I wondered how many Lucys they were helping to defend. And why? Was it because I was white and my Birdie was black? If that were the reason, then maybe I was the target of racism. And it would be Byron who would suffer the most.

Nine

I T NEVER RAINS BUT it turns into a hurricane. I thought things were going pretty badly, but I had no idea of just how bad they were going to get.

The first thing that seemed to imply that our lives were going from bad to worse was a strange piece of news about—not Byron—but Adam, the little boy we had tried to adopt earlier. Thanks to one of the Sisters of Divine Providence, I learned that Adam had been removed from the care of the good sisters in July, almost a year after CYS had found an adoptive family for him.

This was contrary to what I had been told by CYS, a situation I had come to expect. Nevertheless, I arranged a meeting with Sister Mary Francis to discuss with her the events surrounding Adam's placement. What on earth had taken so long?

I drove up the long winding road to the convent's main building, a large red brick house framed by giant oak trees. It was well into fall now, and their leaves where bursting with bright yellows, oranges and reds.

I remembered back last year at this time when we were a much happier and "normal" family on our way to Skyline Drive to enjoy the delights of autumn. This year there would be no family outing. Between taking Byron to visit Lucy two and three times a week; my midnight rides to Pinegrove Terrace; my involvement in getting the Abandoned Babies Adoption Act into legislation; caring for the kids and going to work (which I was missing more and more of), there was little time to enjoy the pleasure of the leaves turning colors.

That was a shame, I thought. I was not taking the time to stop and smell the roses anymore...or the leaves. I was, however, eating more. Before entering into the mother superior's house, I finished my second Clark Bar. With all of the candy I had been eating lately, I was sure that Clark Candies stock had gone up. I crumpled up the bright red wrapper and stuffed it into my pocket.

Sister Mary Francis was waiting for me in the foyer, looking pleasant and professional. She greeted me with a deep, hearty hello. While the older sisters at Divine Providence still wore the traditional garb of a long black dress, white stiff bib, and black and white veil, there was very little about Sister Mary Francis' appearance that gave any clues that she was a nun. Her dress was conservative and classic: a dark blue jacket, below-the-knee skirt, and a white cotton blouse with a modest ruffled front. She wore a silver band on the ring finger of her left hand and a small silver cross around her neck. I guessed from the few lines around her eyes and her salt and pepper hair that she was in her early forties.

I followed her past the chapel where I could hear matins being chanted. "Normally we have them at five in the morning," she whispered, leaning closer to me. "But most of the sisters are getting too old to get up that early. Getting old is one of God's less funny jokes that He plays on us."

I agreed. Lately I had been feeling every bit of my age…plus a hundred years. It was probably the weight I was carrying around. It was a burden, and I was unaccustomed to lugging around those extra pounds.

"In here," the sister said, opening a handsome carved oak door. I felt as if I were entering sacred ground that belonged to women only. The room was richly paneled in mahogany. A statue of the Virgin Mother was inset into the wall and a candle burned at her feet. Behind the wooden desk a picture of the Sacred Heart of Jesus hung on the wall and a pair of rosaries dangled from the frame.

The large wooden chair was surprisingly comfortable.

"A cup of tea?" Sister asked, pouring me a cup from the porcelain tea service.

I took the tea and sipped it. It was sweet and tasted vaguely like flowers.

"Do you like it?" She smiled. Her anxious expression told me that there was something very special about the tea.

"It's very good. Unusual," I commented, taking another sip. "But very good."

"It's my own mixture of roses, herbs and roots that I grow in my garden." Her face glowed with modest pride.

"I'll have to get that recipe out of you," I joked, waving my finger at her playfully.

"It's a secret," she joked back. "You could have me suffer the same pains as Joan of Arc and I still wouldn't tell." Suddenly she turned very serious. "Mike, I have been put in a very awkward and frankly disturbing position."

"Oh?"

"Yes. I have been warned by a caseworker at CYS that it would be in my best interest as well as Adam's if I had no further association with you or Karen. I was told to stay away from you or I would jeopardize the convent's mission of providing temporary safe haven for children. And we both know how important it is to give these poor babies our care."

I nodded reluctantly. This was not the first time temporary caregivers were told to stay away from us. It seemed that CYS used coercive tactics to prevent Karen and me from learning how far the corruption and dirty tricks actually went.

"Guess I'll be going then." I got up to leave. I was not a particularly religious man, but I felt that it was somehow sacrilegious to question the sister. I wanted desperately to learn the name of the social worker who intimidated Sister Mary Francis, but I was sure she wouldn't tell me.

"Don't be silly," Sister said with a smile, getting up and pouring more tea into my cup. "We've got lots to talk about."

I felt like I was ten pounds lighter. As I drank the fragrant tea, we spent the next hour discussing Adam. It was true that an adoptive home had been found, but as CYS was getting ready to move Adam, his natural mother turned up. I couldn't help but think that it was CYS itself that had sought the mother out and hauled her back into the picture.

"For many months after that, Adam remained with us until the mother was finally stripped of her parental rights," said the sister. In my mind, I guessed what had happened: CYS had stretched the process to the limits to get its extra pound of flesh before releasing little Adam from the system.

I learned the name of the social worker involved, Linda Boblin. I didn't know who was responsible for her, but I felt certain that at the bottom of all of this was Jane Worley.

"I know what you're going through," Sister said, offering me a fifth cup of tea. I shook my head, no. My kidneys were beginning to float. "I'd be happy to testify that what I have told you is true. So if you ever need me or if I learn anything that may aid you in your struggle, I will contact you."

As the sister was walking me to the main door, I stopped her in front of the chapel. "Cameron once told me I should tell God about the horrible things CYS has done and that He will take care of it. He says that you do what you do and no one hurts you. Is that true?"

The sister's laugh echoed through the hallway. "I have one piece of advice for you," she said, grinning. "When it comes to CYS, leave the praying to us. You, however, are God's soldier, like Joshua. You go out and kick some ass."

I liked this woman. She had guts.

After a God-bless-you or two, I left the convent. On the way home I stopped at the McDonald's on McKnight Road to use the bathroom. While I was there I bought a Big Mac and a large fries, but instead of my usual Coke, I ordered a glass of water. It was my crazy way of starting to put myself on a diet.

When I got home I dashed off a letter to Jane Worley regarding my visit with Sister Mary Francis. While I was in the letter-writing mood, I wrote to Senator Melissa Hart with an update on Byron's situation and sent her additional information that would help get the new law protecting abandoned babies into place. I also wrote a long letter to Governor Casey, pleading with him to help us fight for Byron. Personally, I did not have much respect for Governor Casey or his politics. Still, he was our governor, and even though I knew he probably had little interest in our situation or in taking a close look at Allegheny County child welfare services, I had to try.

At least Governor Casey did not disappoint me. I received a brief letter from his office within a few days.

...As you must surely know, your case has become a very controversial and highly publicized one. While I clearly can understand the depths of your feeling for Byron and can appreciate your views on the policy and law as they pertain to your situation, I am sure that you can understand while it is neither advisable nor appropriate for any representative of the executive branch of government to become involved in a case in which Allegheny County Court of Common Pleas has clear jurisdiction and currently has under consideration...Thank you for your obvious commitment to our troubled children.

I WASN'T ANGRY OR disappointed at the response. I just wished that Governor Casey was as committed to our "troubled children" as I was. I was relieved to think that his term in office would soon end.

He was right, though: The media was following our fight very closely. It seemed as if every day an article appeared on us, or our case was being compared to others across the country. The editor's editorial section in the newspaper contained commentaries that were sometimes pro, sometimes con. Letters from the public responding to the editors were mostly for us, a few were against. Karen and I were invited on local talk shows, and *American Journal* interviewed us. I was surprised that Judge Lerner also allowed himself to be interviewed by *American Journal*, especially after asking all parties not to speak with the press. Lucy's lawyer and supporters, including the Reverend Johns, took every opportunity to speak with the press, and what they had to say about us was getting less and less flattering. At one point we were accused of trying to bring slavery back into fashion.

As the Reverend Johns became more vocal, the local reporting took more of a racial slant. In the papers we were now beginning to be referred to as the "white couple." I thought this was pretty typical of a media feeding frenzy, but Byron's situation was such an emotionally charged issue that there was no way to contain it.

Every day Karen and I received letters from strangers who felt they'd come to know Byron and loved him. To the public he came to be known as "Baby Byron." To us, he was still little Birdie.

School kids, nurses, doctors, housewives and construction workers took the time to write and call. Their warm encouragement and best wishes did much to help Karen and me, and we responded to everyone who gave us an address.

It was at the end of September that Karen and I decided to take the family to the Cayman Islands. Actually, it was

Karen's suggestion that the family get away over the Thanksgiving holiday. To me the islands were the next thing to heaven. I found an inner peace while diving in the blue ocean and beachcombing the white sands. All the kids, except for Byron, knew the island and loved it as much as I did.

I was glad that Karen wanted to go back. It felt right that Byron would know the islands, too. I wanted our memories of the special place to include him.

Early in November Katie filed a motion with the court asking that we be allowed to take Byron out of the country. Lucy's attorneys were none too happy and filed a motion in opposition to our motion. CYS was not jumping up and down in glee about our request either, but the judge granted us permission anyway.

CYS did its best to hinder our plans, though. We were told that a Ms. Vopel from CYS checked with Customs and found out that, to take Byron out of the country, a court order and a birth certificate weren't enough; she said we needed to have Lucy's signature as well. Bullshit, I thought. By now I questioned everything that came out of CYS's mouth.

I contacted both Customs and U.S. Immigration. Neither had any knowledge of Ms. Vopel or anyone else from CYS. Both entities were curious as to how such false information was alleged to come have come from their organizations.

Immigration in Pittsburgh confirmed that we did not need Lucy's signature. Once again, I dashed off a letter to Jane Worley. This lady had major problems within her organization. The dirty laundry was getting even more rancid. Deciding I had to fight fire with fire, I contacted a private investigator I knew of and asked him to get as much information as he could about Byron's biological family. I also instructed him to get the names and addresses of everyone who could possibly be a part of his life if he were returned to Lucy.

We moved through the Thanksgiving holiday with remarkable speed. I was still reeling from all the activity.

The kids had a school recital, a few relatives dropped in unannounced, and the Christmas shopping season was in full swing.

Karen and I decided to continue our annual ritual of getting new photographs of the children and displaying them on the fireplace mantel, decorated with holly and pine boughs. Up until that year, all the photos had also included the Santa at the local mall, but this year Chris did not want to have his picture taken with the jolly old elf; Chris was twelve now, and just too grown-up for such childhood fantasies. Of course, Connie and Cameron were not.

One morning, Karen dressed Byron in his "Santa outfit"—a red jumpsuit with black "boots" and white cuffs—and we headed to the mall. It was like *déjà vu* as we sat having lunch at the Food Court. A year had passed and nothing had changed: We were still in the middle of a war.

As Karen and the kids ate their burgers and chatted about Christmas gifts and their visit with Santa, I was lost in my own dark thoughts. I had just gotten a report from the PI, and what I had learned was most disturbing. I knew about the aunt; I knew a little about the paternal grandmother, but now I knew exactly where they lived and a little more about their activities. The grandmother, as our anonymous caller had indicated, was a hardcore criminal who lived with a man who supposedly ran numbers. The police pretty much knew what was going on but left them to their own devices.

Even more interesting was the fact that the grandmother's trial for selling heroin and cocaine to an undercover cop was soon to be heard. Amazingly enough, the grandmother was still caring for Georgia, Byron's older sister. It was the same old story: Criminal history didn't matter when it came to taking care of these lost children.

The great-aunt had been living on welfare since sometime in the seventies and had a group of people staying at her place in the projects. As near as the detective could tell, there were Lucy's three oldest sons; a granddaughter and her pregnant fifteen-year-old daughter; and the great-aunt's son, a man around twenty-five who would come and go as he pleased.

That made seven people (soon to be eight) living in a cramped four-bedroom townhouse. I shuddered at the thought that Byron could have ended up with the aunt. What was Lucy thinking? I was sure that Lucy cared deeply for her aunt, but was Byron really better off with her? I couldn't believe this family could do better than Karen and me. Of course, if poverty, welfare and drugs were a way of life to Lucy, then maybe she did not see the inherent problems of that lifestyle.

I knew that if the press ever found out that I hired a detective, they would have a field day with that information. But I was a desperate family man trying to keep his family intact. What else was I to do? The PI's investigation was not anything that I was going to openly broadcast, but if the media did find out and questioned me, I would answer them the way I always did—with the truth. After all, that was why I had hired the detective in the first place, to reveal the truth. I secretly hoped that my undercover man would uncover something horrible that would destroy Lucy's chances of getting Byron. Although I did not hire him for that reason, as much as I hated to admit it, the thought did enter my mind on more than one occasion.

"He does look silly in that stupid outfit," I said to Karen, looking at Byron happily munching on a French fry.

"Listen," Karen said, putting down her tuna sandwich. Her voice was gearing up like a teapot full of steam. "As long as Byron is a part of our family, he'll share in this family's traditions, silly or not. I'll never isolate him. He is no different from the rest of us."

Okay, where was that tough-guy comment coming from? I thought. I was half-afraid to ask, so I didn't.

"Do you know what some black lady said to me in the toy store?" Karen was turning red. She lowered her voice, but the tension was there. "She said Byron was ugly. She said, 'Girl, that's an ugly child you've got there.'"

"That's terrible," I said, tickling Byron under the chin. "Birdie is beautiful."

"And as if that weren't bad enough, she also said I had no right making an African-American a part of our white Christmas tradition. Then she had the nerve to ask me if I knew what the African tradition was and if I didn't know I better find out before I helped commit further genocide on her people. Where does this lady get off?"

If anyone was prepared to handle such a situation, it was Karen. She was well versed in the celebration of Christmas around the world, especially Spain and Africa. Along with the commercial aspect of the Western world, our Christmas at home reflected basic Christian values, along with bits and pieces of rituals from a host of different nations. We had a *piñata*, for instance, as well as tree decorations from the Caribbean and an Italian nativity set and straw goats from Sweden. When Byron was a little older, we intended to celebrate Kwanzi with him, too. Of course, I also knew there were plenty of Christian African-Americans who got just as much involved in Christmas as any white family. "Well, did you dump a bookload of African history on her?"

"No." Karen placed a paper cup up to Byron's mouth. He happily slurped the milk, spilling half of what he drank on his bib. "Why should I have to explain myself? I'm the mother of four kids and I do a mighty fine job with them."

"That's right, Mom," Chris said, leaning over to give her a peck on the cheek.

"That's right," Cameron parroted, placing another kiss on her cheek. "Can I have a frog for Christmas?" Karen laughed and rubbed the spots where her boys had placed their affections. It was her way of making sure the kiss would not be washed off.

"I was thinking, Mom," Connie said, realizing it was her turn to speak. "Don't you think that Santa down there looks like Dad?" We all turned to look over the balcony to Santa's North Pole display. A man faintly resembling me held two children on his knees as they whispered their Christmas dreams to him.

"Why do you say he looks like Daddy?" Karen asked. I already knew Connie's answer.

"Because of his stomach, of course!"

Everyone had a good laugh at my expense.

WE WENT TO JUVENILE Court for the hearing on December 15th, but as in previous hearings we were not allowed into the courtroom. After the hearing, Katie was very upset and I felt that she was beginning to lose the faith.

"The judge put off making a decision," was all that she said, before walking away.

Karen and I looked at each other, not knowing whether to run after her and question her about the proceedings or just leave her alone.

"Let her go," Karen said, bundling Byron up in his new yellow snowsuit. "We'll call her later."

The press was waiting for us as we left Juvenile Court.

"What's the judge's decision?" The anxious reporters asked, following us across the street.

"We feel like we are no further along than we were before the hearing. We know nothing at this point," I opened the side door to the car, then helped Karen strap Byron into his car seat. "The judge," I said, turning to the reporters, "did not make a decision yet." I walked to the driver's side, ignoring the barrage of questions. I was tired and frustrated.

"Mike."

I recognized Vernon Washington's voice. I opened the door and handed Karen the keys. "Warm up the car, hon, I'll only be a minute."

"Did you hear that the great-aunt is claiming she had been trying to get custody of Byron since he was three days old but was turned down because she had lead paint in her house?" I was not sure if Vernon was asking me a question or passing along information.

"I had heard something to that effect from Lucy," I answered, "but I've not seen any documentation. CYS told me that no family members ever inquired about Byron, including Lucy, until, of course, we made the move to adopt."

"Do you believe CYS?" he asked, raising his right eyebrow. What kind of question was that. I thought he already knew the answer.

I took a deep breath. Vernon's questions felt more like a trap than anything else. If I said I didn't believe CYS, would I be interpreted as believing the great-aunt?

"I don't know who is telling the truth in this instance," I answered diplomatically.

"Neither do I," he whispered, diplomatically.

We did not hear from Katie, but we did learn from the six o'clock news that an attorney for Byron, Sarah Biggins, a lawyer in the child advocacy unit of the Legal Aid Society, suggested that instead of abruptly moving Byron to Sojourner House with Lucy or leaving him with us, a gradual move out of our home into Lucy's would be more in Byron's interest.

Biggins believed that Byron's visits with his natural mother should slowly be increased until he was spending some nights and weekends before ultimately living with Lucy.

This made sense to Karen and me. After all was said and done, if Lucy proved herself clean, we would have no compunctions about handing Byron over to her permanently. We would be terribly saddened, but not worried for his safety.

Meanwhile, I began getting conflicting reports of Lucy's progress. The media was reporting that friends of Lucy's testified that she had been off drugs for nine months and was successfully undergoing treatment. However, reports from the detective and people associated with Lucy at Sojourner House, as well as other sources in Lucy's community, were telling us that she was still using cocaine and leaving Byron in the care of strangers when she was out on her own from Sojourner. This last report sounded downright dangerous to us. If only that information would make its way to the judge. But how?

I thought of calling him myself, but that would probably infuriate him. Besides, he couldn't talk to me. He was only allowed to talk at me.

I had a brief conversation with Katie about the events that transpired in the courtroom. Although she did not say anything that aroused my suspicions, I got the distinct impression that something had changed, that the judge was no longer impartial, that his mind was already made up.

"The judge would not let me cross-examine Lucy," Katie said, wearily. "Unfortunately, that cross-examination was crucial to our case."

"What are we to do next?" I asked. I always looked for the bright spot, but they were getting harder and harder to find.

"We wait."

The next five days seemed like an lifetime. As we were sitting down to our evening meal we got a call from Vernon. He was only one of the many reporters that had been camping outside in the cold, waiting for the judge to hand down his decision.

"The judge has reached a decision," he told us, "but it will not be released until everyone involved in the case has been notified."

In a flash, Karen was on the phone with Katie.

"Yes…Yes…Oh, my God!" I heard Karen say. I didn't hear any more. I felt empty inside, as if I had just died. To have come so far and to have finally lost…it was almost more than I could bear. Regardless of common sense, good judgment and compassionate parenting, we were not able to control the decision nor the life of our little boy. I never felt so helpless in my life.

Karen hung up the phone and turned toward me. "The judge decided to return Byron to Lucy," she said through a cascade of tears. "We've got to give him up by ten o'clock the morning of the 28th."

I grabbed the phone and called Katie.

"What can we do?" I was crying as I waited for her answer.

"Nothing, as far as I can see." She was crying, too. She had become so emotionally involved in this case that I knew she was devastated, but I was too torn apart myself to give any support to her.

"I can't accept that," I screamed into the phone. "There's always something that can be done."

"Mike, this whole thing has been a farce since day one. I thought I could lick CYS, but when the NAACP joined forces, we didn't stand a chance. No judge can withstand that kind of pressure. And you know something else? This might go all the way up to the commissioners. I just heard from a reliable source that they regret not 'strong-arming' you at the beginning of all of this."

"Is there no hope?" I was having difficulty catching my breath. I felt myself suffocating.

"There's only one way," she answered. "If Lucy screws up, you could get Byron back."

"She'll screw up," I said, clinging on to the one bright spot in the dark decree set forth by the judge. "I believe she already has."

"We need proof."

"I'll get it," I promised. "I'll get it somehow."

We called the kids together and told them the bad news.

"Birdie's leaving us after Christmas," I explained to the sad, teary-eyed faces. I had let them down. I had failed them. What kind of father was I?

Cameron did not fully understand what was going on, but he cried because he sensed whatever had happened was bad. Connie fell onto the floor and bawled her eyes out. No words from either Karen or myself brought her any comfort.

Chris quietly cried, then through his tears he offered his words of hope. "We'll get him back, Dad, I know we will. We won't let anything happen to our little brother."

I couldn't help but admire his courage, even though I could only pray to God that he was right.

"You promised," Connie screamed at me as I lifted her up from the floor. "You promised to keep us together. Who's next? Me or Chris?"

I couldn't bear any more. I longed to be a hero from one of John LeCarre's novels, if only in the eyes of my children. But I was nothing more than a dawdling old fool who believed that right was right and that was all that mattered. I should have played the game everyone else was playing. But no, I thought, taking Connie into my arms. I couldn't. Then I would have been an even worse parent than I was at that moment.

As if a vacuum had drawn in Karen, Chris and Cameron, they all swooped upon me and Connie. Together we fell in tears to the floor, locked in one big group hug.

I knew then that my battle had only begun.

CHRISTMAS WAS ONLY FIVE days away. Karen was going through the motions of baking cookies, wrapping gifts, decorating the house and doing some last-minute shopping. When Karen took all the kids out to the mall to hear an area school choir sing Christmas carols, I sat alone in the house. There had to be a way to wake up from this nightmare and I was determined to find it.

I stared at our beautiful tree for a while as I thought, then was stuck by something odd. Looking out the window, I noticed how our neighborhood was strangely devoid of colored lights and other decorations. Here and there I'd glimpse a tasteful wreath on a front door or a candle in the window. It wasn't that our neighbors did not celebrate Christmas. These folks just did not celebrate Christmas the way we did back where I'd grown up. Both Karen and I remembered whole houses strung with Christmas lights, plastic reindeer and sleighs on the lawn and luminaria— candles in paper bags lining countless walkways in the old neighborhood. I wanted that kind of Christmas this year.

The lack of decorations made me feel homesick and sad, as if I didn't belong in my own neighborhood. I somehow felt that more decorations would make Christmas feel like Christmas, even though I knew none of us could feel merry if Byron were leaving us.

Ten

HE NEXT DAY KAREN took the kids shopping, leaving Byron with me. I held him on my lap and together we watched the lights on the Christmas tree. He seemed in awe of the red, green and silver lights and could not take his eyes off them. I thought about what that woman had said at the mall, about Byron being ugly, and cringed inside. I turned him to face me and tickled his nose. "'He walks in beauty like the night of distant climes and starry skies,'" I told him, trying to remember Lord Byron's wonderful poem. I meant every word of it, too. Byron was a little dark, but to me he was an exquisitely handsome child.

Byron just laughed and turned his attention back to the tree. We stared at it until Byron fell asleep.

I had been floating helplessly in an endless nightmare since the judge's decision. Why, after all this time, did the judge see fit to take Byron from us? Why at Christmas? This was the single most important time for our family and always had a deep meaning for us. For the past fourteen years of our marriage, we had made it a tradition to visit Karen's family in North Carolina. Because of this heavy cloud of sadness hanging over us, we needed our families more than ever this Christmas. I felt as if I had a child dying of a terminal illness, and this would be his last...our last...Christmas together.

I had literally begged the court to allow us to travel to North Carolina, where the family was celebrating the holidays. Karen's parents were far up in years and for the past several Christmases Karen had been fearful that each one was their last.

I really was not surprised when the courts refused my request. Perhaps they feared that, if we left, we would not return. They did not understand me. I would never do anything that contemptuous. I had stated from the beginning that I would pursue every "legal" means to keep Byron with us. But the court's decision got Karen and I to thinking: It takes a devious mind to imagine devious thoughts.

The doorbell rang, but I didn't answer it. I did not want to entertain anyone this evening. After the persistent caller went away, I got up from my easy chair, put Byron into his crib and slipped a CD into the player. As Elvis Presley was singing "Blue Christmas," I stared out the window. It was only ten minutes to five but already it was dark. A light snow was falling, silvered in the soft glow of my neighbor's security light. A single electric candle burned in his window. These sophisticated people and their subtle decorations! I snorted. What I wouldn't have given for a huge wooden cut-out of Santa and his sleigh or a group of plastic carolers on someone's lawn. At least they would have looked cheerful. And I needed cheerfulness pretty badly.

"Come on, Mike," I said out loud. I had to shake myself out of this doldrum. I had to make this the best Christmas we'd ever have for the sake of the children. I did not want Byron leaving his home in the midst of sorrow, feeling that something was wrong.

When Byron woke up, I plopped him into his snowsuit, pulled my hat, coat, boots and gloves from the hall closet and hurriedly dressed. I wanted to be with my family. The snow had started to fall a little more heavily as I neared the mall, and the roads were becoming slippery. This was not unusual for Pennsylvania in December, but I grew concerned about the amount of snow that was falling so quickly. I turned on the radio just in time to hear that snow warnings were being issued.

By the time I reached the mall, hordes of people were leaving because of the storm. I searched the center court and found Karen bundling up the kids. A sense of relief rushed through me.

"Hey, Dad," Connie waved as I approached. "Are you lost or something?"

"Or something," I answered her.

I helped hurry the kids along. The parking lot and few remaining cars were covered with snow, so I decided to leave Karen's car. "We'll come back for it tomorrow," I said, dusting the snow off the Land Cruiser.

As we drove home we sang every Christmas song we could think of. We did not know all the words to any of them, but we sang at the top of our lungs, as if to scare away the evils that lurked behind the wreaths, the trees and the bright Christmas lights.

I turned onto our street and was shocked to see our lawn and driveway full of reporters, cameramen and vehicles I hadn't noticed before.

"What are they doing out in this storm?" said Karen. "They must want our reaction to the court order," Karen answered her own question, shaking her head in exasperation. "What can we tell them? We hadn't even seen the order yet. Mike, I don't want to talk to them. Not tonight."

I agreed. Besides, I did not want Byron and the other

kids to be apart of a media blitzkrieg. Instead of pulling up to our driveway, I drove to a nearby neighbor's house. While the rest of the family sat in the car, I rang the doorbell. Steve answered the door.

"Hey, Mike," he said, motioning for me to step inside. "Nice Christmas decorations. He pointed to the reporters on my lawn.

"They're the 'in' thing this holiday season," I replied. "I can tell you how to get a few if you want."

"No, thanks," Steve answered, wildly shaking his head. "You can keep them."

I explained our situation to him and he kindly allowed me to park my car in his driveway.

"All right, everybody," I whispered, "here's the plan."

Between Connie's stifled giggles I explained the game plan. We would sneak down to the end of Steve's yard across the field over to our house, where we would quietly make our way to the back door, staying close to the tree line that separated our property from the next door neighbor's. "No laughing," I warned.

We trudged through the snow and without too much of a struggle made it to our back door. Byron gazed up at the falling snow, his eyes round with amazement.

"Wow, this is just like the movies," said Cameron, impressed with our act of espionage.

It was very dark as we entered the family room. The only light was coming from a wall clock in the kitchen. Chris reached out to switch on the lights, but I stopped him just in time. "We're not supposed to be here, remember?"

"But I'm hungry!" he cried out. "I want to make a pizza."

"Me, too!" said Connie.

"But then they'd know we're here," insisted Karen, nodding toward the front windows, aglow with the lights from the media corps.

Karen suggested some crackers and cheese but none of the kids found that very appealing. When Byron started whimpering, I decided it was time for action and I mobilized the troops. We worked our espionage act in reverse, sneaking out the house and back to the car.

"Now what?" Karen asked, staring at me as I swept the snow off the car and began chipping away at the ice that had formed on the windshield.

"We go for pizza."

The tires spun a little as I backed out of our neighbor's driveway, but the Land Cruiser was not to be stopped by a mere snowstorm. Without difficulty we made it to Cranberry where we found a pizza shop still open.

We gobbled up the pizza in short order. I decided to take the family to a hotel for the evening, but there were only two inns in the area and, appropriately enough, there was no room at either one. We had no other choice but to return home. The storm was growing worse.

I returned, just as carefully as we left, but it wasn't necessary. The reporters were gone.

Karen and I looked at each other with a sigh of relief. We spent a pleasant evening together watching *Christmas Vacation* with Chevy Chase. After the movie Karen and I tucked the kids into bed, then went downstairs with plans to snuggle up before the fireplace.

As I was placing a few logs on the fire, the doorbell rang. I did not want to be rude, so I answered the door. It was as I feared—the press. Four reporters and three photographers stood out in the snowy evening, looking like lost travelers. "I wonder if we might have a few minutes of your time, Mr. Derzack," said one woman reporter with a smile.

"I thought we'd finally gotten rid of you," I said, also smiling.

She shook her head. "No, we were just taking a break. We never give up, you know."

I invited all seven of them into the living room, where Karen joined us with a big pitcher of eggnog and a tray of colorful sugar cookies in the shapes of Santas, reindeer, bells and candy canes.

I had already anticipated the questions they asked me:

How do you feel? What are you going to do now? What do have to say about the judge's decision?

"Right now it feels like a terrible tragedy to me and Karen," I said, swallowing hard. I felt like crying. This was the first time I had to talk about this ugly nightmare, and I found it to be some of the hardest work I'd ever done. "I'm still in shock. As much as I would like to blast the judge, I haven't read the order yet so I don't know what his reasons are for taking Byron from us. But right now I'm so angry it's better if I just don't say anything at all."

"Mike, I know this is a difficult time, to say the least, but I did talk with Byron's great-aunt. She of course is elated that Byron is returning to his biological mother. Do you think Lucy is ready to have full-time responsibility for both Byron and his sister?"

I knew the answer to that but decided to give the safe answer. "I have no comment on that."

"We talked to the judge and he said that the reason he was giving Byron back to his biological mother was…" (She began reading from her notes.) "The judge says the mother is clean and that she seems to be doing very well in rehab. She has made plans to get a safe home and a job. He also said that Byron himself helped make the decision. He laughs when he is with her."

He laughs? Of course he laughs! I thought. He laughed with most people because he was a secure and happy little boy. That happiness did not come from Lucy's wonderful, nurturing care…it came from Karen and me. How dare the judge use that against us! The bastard.

"He also stated that the existing laws favor reunification of a foster child with his family in a safe environment. Lucy will provide those things." If the judge saw the insecure and hostile environment of the drug culture as "safe," then I was crazy.

"Is there anything else that you can tell me about what's happening in my life?" I asked the reporter. I thought it strange that I would be the last to know. After all, I was Byron's father.

"Lucy will be holding a press conference with her aunt, a couple of supporters and Reverend Johns."

"When?" Karen jumped into the conversation. Her eyes were wide with anticipation. We had no direct communication with Lucy since the NAACP got involved, and both of us were anxious to hear anything that came out of her mouth.

"Tomorrow."

I listened as Karen answered the reporters' questions about the care Byron received during his stay with us. Her voice and face were filled with pain and a few times she struggled not to cry. Suddenly I made the decision to tell the reporters my worst suspicions about Lucy and her relatives. How could I in good conscience *not* tell them that I was worried that my little boy would be in danger?

"May I make a statement?" I said, after Karen's voice broke off in tears. The reporters nodded. "I don't want to sound as if I'm badmouthing anyone, but I've got to let you know a few things that I know worry me." I told them how, according to my sources, Lucy had not given up drugs, how her mother-in-law was involved in drug trafficking, and how badly Lucy's other children had been abused and neglected. They scribbled busily in their notepads as I spoke.

"So, you see why we feel hesitant about returning Byron to an environment which we do not believe is safe," I concluded.

I was thankful that the reporters listened so intently, recording my every word. I took no pains to hide my anger and despair, and I knew that the reporters believed every word I was saying. I just hoped that they would do their own investigations and report the truth so that the judge would have a way of knowing exactly how bad things were. Then for sure he would allow Byron to stay with his family.

The reporters finished up the last of the cookies and eggnog, thanked us for our cooperation, and went out into the winter storm. I watched from the front window as they scraped the snow and ice from their cars.

It's not easy to do, to scrape things clean, I thought.

🐾   🐾   🐾

THE NEXT MORNING KAREN and I arrived at Katie's office for a strategy meeting. Though we talked for hours, we could not agree on the next step. We wanted Katie to file a motion to let Byron stay with us until Lucy's supposed rehabilitation was looked into deeper, but Katie was hesitant to do so.

I did not believe that I could sink any lower into this pit of horrors I had been cast into, but during our conversation with Katie I found that it was possible to go deeper. Now I understood the term "bottomless pit," because I was in it.

"We've lost. It's time you realize that." Katie's words cut through Karen and me like a cold sharp knife. "I can file an appeal, but eventually the judge is going to take Byron away from you. You've pissed the judge off and there is no way he's going to reward you. Why not just get it over with?"

Her words stung. Neither of us were prepared for our own attorney to give up hope.

"What are you taking about?" Karen snarled. She rose from her seat and walked toward Katie. "How dare you say that we've lost?" Karen was screaming now as she moved closer to Katie. "Don't you ever say that again. If there's an appeal to file, you better file it."

Katie screamed back at Karen and for a moment I thought I was going to see my wife get involved in a fist fight. Then Karen regained her composure. "I know this has been very emotional for you, Katie. I think maybe you have become too involved. The pain you are feeling for Byron and us is too overwhelming, and I believe it is clouding your judgment. Therefore, after you file this final motion, I'll release you from the case and find another attorney."

Katie was relieved. She was prepared to leave us to our own devices, without an argument, explanation or advice.

I felt as if I were losing not just an attorney but also a friend. I was both understanding and angry. My mind told me that Karen's assessment of Katie's emotional condition was correct, but my heart was not agreeing. I was fighting the feeling that I had been betrayed.

I gave Katie a hug before we left her office. "I really do

understand," I whispered to her. Sorting out my feelings toward her would have to wait until later. I only had enough room in my head and heart for Byron.

We stopped off at the grocery store on the way home. What was normally a joyous time for us, shopping for Christmas dinner, now was reduced to just another chore we had to perform to get through the holidays. Halfheartedly, Karen and I chose a ham and tenderloin for the main meal. We haphazardly inspected the yams, the tangerines, apples and nuts before tossing them into the cart. We picked up some essentials—bread, milk, butter—then waited in line, looking and feeling like two Scrooges who couldn't wait for the Christmas season to end.

We had to pull ourselves together in front of the kids, but when we were alone we made no attempt to hide our dark feelings and deep disappointment from each other.

We'll make it through this, I thought. Somehow.

It began snowing lightly on the drive to our home. We picked Byron and the rest of the kids up from the various neighbors who had agreed to watch after them. Then, in an effort to make this the happy holiday season it should have been, we went home, changed into our oldest and warmest winter clothes and went sled riding in North Park.

For a time we laughed and joked as if nothing were wrong. We threw snowballs at each other, lay in the snow, flapping our arms, making snow angels and sucked on icicles that had formed on the tree branches. Outwardly we were a happy, content family. Inside my guts were twisting themselves into knots.

We arrived home in time for the six o'clock news, and we sipped on hot chocolate as we waited for Lucy's press conference to air. She was the headline story. Patiently we waited through a couple of commercials, then Lucy appeared on the screen.

She looked awfully nice. Her black hair was pulled tightly into a braid and held in place by a festive red and white stripped bow that complemented her red turtle-neck sweater. Silver looped earrings dangled from her ears as she read a brief, prepared statement.

"I owe a debt of gratitude to Mr. and Mrs. Derzack for their care and concern regarding Byron. But I do not need their help any longer.

"I did not abandon my children. Byron was never abandoned by me or by my family. I did not just pop up eleven months later and say I want my kid," said Lucy, biting her bottom lip. "A few hours after Byron's birth, when I had left the hospital to eat lunch, CYS took Byron. They took him without my consent and they refused to tell me where they had placed him. The next day, members of my family asked CYS to place Byron with a relative, but CYS refused."

Bullshit! I thought. Who would walk away from their newborn baby hours after giving birth, just to have lunch? It wasn't as if the hospital didn't serve lunch. Did she leave the hospital to get drugs?

I dug my fingers into my chair, straining to keep calm.

"Ever since December of last year, I have been fighting to get my son. I did not learn where he was until the Derzacks appeared on television, complaining about the efforts by CYS to take Byron from them and place him with a black family.

"I feel very bad that Byron was born addicted to drugs, and I want you all to know that I have been off drugs since January 19th. I'd also like everyone to know that addicts are people who suffer from a disease. We're not bad people. We don't get cured, but we do recover. Today I am recovering."

But what about tomorrow? I thought. Lucy freely admitted that she was recovering, not that she had recovered. I was worried and frightened. Her words did not comfort me or convince me that anything she said was true. I prayed to God that I was wrong, but I knew I wasn't.

Lucy did not answer any questions from the reporters but got up and walked back into Sojourner House, escorted by women whom I assumed were aides from the rehab center. Next, Lane Manny, the director of Sojourner House, spoke a few words, saying only that they were pleased with Lucy's progress and looked forward to uniting the entire family. "Lucy's situation is not unique," she said. "Scores of women battle drug abuse every day in Pittsburgh."

But was she clean? I wanted to hear from the director that Lucy was clean. A reporter asked her that question, but she ignored it.

Lucy's attorney declined to answer any questions, stating that he had heard that we had threatened to appeal. However, Reverend Johns of the NAACP did not miss his chance to take a shot at us.

"Lucy has made remarkable progress in the months she has been at Sojourner House. It is regrettable that the Derzacks would resort to character assassination." He went on to talk about the comments we had made to the press and to condemn CYS for placing Byron with us in the first place.

"That's a laugh," said Karen grimly. She aimed the remote control at the television. "I wonder who wrote Lucy's speech—Jane Worley?" The television screen went blank.

"Turn the TV back on and see if we can catch the interview on another station," I said, reaching out for the remote.

"Why put us through more of this insanity?" Karen growled as she held the remote away from me.

"Maybe they'll report something different."

After a few moments, Karen flicked the television back on and turned to Channel Four. Byron's great-aunt was standing beside Reverend Johns and speaking into the camera. We only caught the tail end of her interview.

"...The Derzacks should never be allowed to see Byron again," the aunt said, controlling her emotions. "They are not his family."

Tears crept down Karen's face as she lifted Byron out of his playpen. She sat on the sofa and cuddled Byron on her lap. "How dare she say that? How could she say such a thing?"

I put my arm around her shoulder and stroked her hand.

"She probably didn't," I pointed out. "Probably the reverend told her what to say, or maybe even CYS."

"I wouldn't put it past them," said Karen, holding Byron closer. Chris, Connie and Cameron gathered around Karen.

"Are you going to give him back to that awful woman?" Connie asked, running her fingers through Byron's curly hair.

"Now, young lady," I corrected her, "Lucy is Byron's biological mother. She's not awful, but she is sick and she's trying to get better."

"No, she isn't," Connie flatly stated. "I know a liar when I see one. And I don't care if she is Byron's real mother or not...she's lying."

"Enough," Karen warned her.

"It's true," said Connie, always having to get in the last word. "I can feel it."

"Well, are you going to give Byron back to her?" asked Chris.

"We will do whatever we can do within the law," I answered. "However, the law can force us to do what we don't want to do." The law. What good was a law that did not protect children? And why should I obey it? I was getting tired of doing the right thing.

Somehow, we made it through the following days without too much distraction from the media. Then, two days before Christmas, disaster struck, and it came in the guise of assistance.

Karen and I were so desperate we contacted a representative from an organization that we had heard about, A Place for Us. They had contacted us earlier and expressed an interest in our case. A Place for Us was a group of people founded by a married interracial couple who supported interracial families.

Karen and I spoke to Harriet Young, a representative for the organization, who said she had been following the newspaper reports and believed that she had just the strategy that would ensure Byron's return to us in a matter of a few days after we surrendered him.

"I'll write a press release and send it to every newspaper, radio and TV station in the country," Harriet said, sounding very confident. "You'll get to keep that little boy, I guarantee you."

"Won't you tell us what you plan to do?" I asked.

"No, I'm sorry," she said. "I don't have it all worked out yet anyway. But you'll see the results, I promise you that."

Karen and I talked about it. We did not understand how a press release would be able to perform any kind of magic, but we were at our wits' ends and willing to give it a chance.

"You understand, Harriet," I said, clearly stating my position, "I don't want anything going out about us until I have okayed the release. You can just fax it to my office."

"Understood," she answered.

I hung up the phone with mixed feelings. Should I be trusting a woman I hardly knew, a woman who had her own organization with her own agenda to serve? I convinced myself that she might be a very sharp, savvy lady who could come up with something that would work. Even if she didn't, what harm would there be in letting her write a release? At least it beat sitting around waiting for the ax to fall.

But early the next morning the ax did fall. I awoke before Karen and went downstairs to put on a pot of coffee. It was still dark. As I sipped a cup of coffee and watched the falling snow, I had a sense of peacefulness. It was short-lived.

A loud sound at the window made me jump. The newspaper boy, firing the early edition of the newspaper from a car, had missed the porch and hit the window. Although the window did not break, the sudden noise startled me from my mind's wanderings.

I slipped on my boots and, still in my pajamas, braved the knee-high snow to recover the paper. My feet were freezing when I got back into the house, so I started a fire in the fireplace and made myself comfortable in front of it. I was relaxing with my second cup of coffee when I opened the folded newspaper. I nearly choked when I saw the headlines: IS A WHITE FAMILY KEEPING A BLACK CHILD CAPTIVE UNTIL THEY HEAR FROM PRESIDENT CLINTON?

Please, please, please, don't let this headline be about us, I silently prayed. I closed my eyes and hoped that when I opened them again I would be back in bed and that this whole thing would have been only a bad dream. But it was true. What in the hell did that lady write? I asked myself over and over in disbelief.

I read the article through three times. Although it did not actually say we would not surrender Byron, it boldly inferred that we would defy the court order to return him. We were in deep trouble. This was one morning I hoped that the judge did not read his newspaper.

I wanted to run upstairs and shake Karen from her sleep. Maybe she would have some words of comfort that would ease the blow of the morning's headlines. Instead, I let her sleep. I stared at the flames in the fireplace and breathed in the comforting scent of woodsmoke. In my mind's eye I saw myself walking though the fire. Maybe I'll be like the phoenix, I thought. The flames would consume me and I would rise from the ashes transformed. Or maybe I'd just burn to a crisp.

I heard Karen in the kitchen, pouring herself some coffee. "Paper here yet?" she called.

"Yeah," I answered, fighting the urge to toss it into the fireplace.

"Where is it?"

"In here." I handed Karen the paper and waited.

"Oh, my God! Oh, my God!" Karen was wide awake without the help of the coffee. "This is sheer craziness. No one will ever believe this of us. Will they?"

"No," I lied. Only everyone would believe us capable of this great insult to the law and to Byron because that's what the paper said. And people seemed to always believe what they read or heard in the news.

The reporters gathered in front of house as the sun

began to rise, casting long blue shadows on the snow. Karen and I refused to answer the door and the reporters refused to go away. We couldn't remain hostage in our own home, so we decided to get dressed and take the kids out for breakfast and a visit to the Carnegie Museum in town.

While we pushed our way through the snow and I cleaned off the car, I tried to answer a few questions for the reporters.

"Are you really refusing to give Byron to his mother?" was the first question out of the mouths of the reporters.

As I had answered a million times in the past, I told them that I would do everything within legal means to keep Byron with us. Then I got into the Land Cruiser and drove off, though the reporters were still shouting questions at us.

"Maybe you should adopt them," Connie joked, looking back at the group of reporters standing on the snow-covered lawn. "I'm beginning to feel like they belong to us."

So was I.

I stopped off at the shop to check for the faxed copy of the press release I had requested. It was there as promised. The newspapers reported the news release almost verbatim. I called Harriet Young and demanded that she write a correction and make it clear to the newspapers that we never agreed to the contents of the press release. She said she would, but I knew that the damage of her over-zealousness had already been done. Nothing was going our way. Our world was falling apart faster than I could pick up the pieces.

CHRISTMAS CREPT UP ON us. Things seemed quiet enough. Santa came, bringing lots of toys and surprises to the Derzack household. The kids awoke before dawn and dragged us out of bed so they could open gifts. Byron must have felt the excitement because he was calling to us to be let out of his crib.

"Good morning, little buddy," I cooed, opening the door to his bedroom. Byron was standing, holding onto the rail of his bed. His little body bobbed up and down as he waited for me to rescue him.

"Santa Claus was here," I whispered, lifting him out of bed and placing him on the changing table. "He brought you a whole lot of new toys." I changed his soiled diaper, then took him downstairs where the others were waiting anxiously to open their gifts.

Byron sat in the middle of all the activity, playing with an assortment of brightly-colored ribbons and bows. Connie placed a few bows in his hair and he giggled with delight at the attention he was receiving. Cameron alternately opened a gift for himself, then one for Byron. The bows were getting much more attention from Birdie than the stack of presents before him. Then Cameron showed Byron a riding toy that Santa had brought him—a plastic replica of Byron's favorite TV dinosaur.

"Bar-nee," Byron said, giving it a hug. Chris helped Byron on the toy and he spent most of the morning zooming back and forth across the family room, laughing in delight as he chased the other children.

Karen made us her version of McDonald's egg muffins and allowed us to eat in the family room. This was a special day, indeed. Karen and I watched the kids dig into their breakfast while they played with their toys.

Connie modeled her new Lee jeans and black knit sweater that she had been begging Karen for. I thought the jeans were too tight and the sweater looked too sophisticated for her, but I kept my opinions to myself. In my mind, Connie was trying to grow up too fast, but Karen assured me that was the way girls were. I didn't care for it. I wanted to keep her my little girl for as long as possible.

Chris was tuned into the music playing on his portable disc player. He was wearing earphones, nodding his head to the beat of the music and occasionally bursting out in song. His voice, which was changing, fluctuated between a deep baritone and a high, squeaky soprano. Connie made a face every time he missed a high note.

Cameron was thrilled with all of his toys. He was especially happy that Santa had brought him replacements for his "favorite" toys that were either run over by me or the postman. "I'm going to put them away," Cameron promised, "so they don't get smashed."

"You better," I warned him, "because Santa is all out of those models."

I turned to Karen. "They're a great bunch, aren't they?"

"They sure are," she answered. The smile she was sporting turned sour for a moment. "What sort of system would break up such a wonderful family?"

"A sick one," I answered, swallowing the last bite of my sandwich. "But this is Christmas, Karen."

She nodded. We agreed that for the rest of the day, neither one of us would mention Byron's leaving, the evils of CYS, Lucy's addiction, Reverend Johns' words of criticism or the great-aunt's wish that we never see Byron again.

"Time for church," Karen announced, shooing the bigger kids upstairs to get dressed. While the troops were getting dressed, Karen and I exchanged our gifts.

"I know you're going to say that I spent too much money," I said, handling her a tiny box that the store had wrapped for me. "But please don't. Just enjoy it."

Karen gave me one of those what-have-you-gone-and-done looks, but I ignored it. "Just open your gift."

Karen slowly untied the red ribbon and removed the silver foil paper, then opened the lid of the tiny box.

She gasped as she held the gold and emerald necklace up to her chest. "It's beautiful, Mike," she whispered. "You shouldn't…"

"Hey," I warned her again. "It's Christmas and I love you."

I helped her on with the necklace, then opened my gifts, the traditional gifts I received every year—a tie, a bottle of my favorite aftershave, some socks, some underwear, a couple of undershirts, a new coffee mug and a picture of the X-Men, which Cameron had painted.

"Thanks, honey," I said, gathering up my gifts and placing them under the tree.

"You forgot to open this one," Karen said, slipping a small wrapped box into my hand.

I quickly tore into the package and removed a simple gold and silver ring. "A wedding ring," I said.

"I wanted you to know that I would marry you all over again," Karen explained, giving me a hug.

"I'd marry you a million times over," I whispered. I removed my old ring and replaced it with the silver and gold band. "I guess this means we're doubly married."

"You guessed it," Karen said, heading upstairs to get ready for church.

We all looked so spiffy in our new Christmas outfits that it was hard to believe we had been opening gifts less than an hour earlier. I hated to admit it, but when I saw Connie in her green velvet dress I knew that she was developing into a young lady, and a beautiful one at that. I was going to have a lot to worry about when she discovered boys and they discovered her.

Chris was smartly dressed in his black pants, green plaid vest, white shirt and red tie. Already he was thinking about asking a girl named Jeannie out to the movies. I pitied the girl's parents.

Cameron fussed about his new outfit. The shirt was too itchy, the tie was too tight and he thought he looked like a geek. Karen assured him that he was just as handsome as his brother, but he didn't care. He wanted to get the church thing over with so he could get comfortable in his jogging suit.

Byron wore an all-white outfit with blue snowflakes on the vest. He looked like an angel.

As we entered the church, friends and supporters greeted us with words of encouragement and sympathy. Karen and I were grateful for their consideration.

We filed into a pew close to the alter. I helped the kids out of their coats, and after we were all settled in I knelt down to pray before the mass began.

The church was silent except for an occasional cough. It

always amazed me how quiet we Catholics were in church. I somehow thought it was a sin to talk out loud. Karen, being very strict, would not tolerate, from me or the kids, even the slightest unnecessary movement while the priest was saying mass.

I looked all around the cathedral, taking in the stained-glass windows depicting the birth and death of Jesus Christ and the Ascension of Mary, the statues of the saints looking down upon us and the crucifix hanging above the altar. They were all familiar and comforting to me. I wished that the arms of God could wrap themselves around me so that for one brief moment I would be protected and safe.

I felt Karen tap me on the shoulder. "Excuse me, Mike." She squeezed her way past me and went to the front of the church to light a candle before the Virgin Mary. She knelt before the Virgin, her head bent in prayer. I knew every word she was thinking: They were the same as mine. *Please, Holy Mother, don't let them take my son.*

Eleven

HE DAY AFTER CHRISTMAS was quiet, but not a happy, restful quiet. It was like the stillness that sometimes happens before dawn or the dead nothingness before a hurricane.

The kids were restless; even their new toys couldn't keep them amused. Karen, who was always a mass of nerves and energy, seemed to be at least three places at the same time: making beds, calming the kids, playing with Byron, cooking food, calling neighbors and vacuuming the floors—not once but twice.

I, on the other hand, felt as if all of my energy had quietly seeped from my body. I wasn't calm, but I was still. I had a terrible feeling that something awful was sitting outside the house, ready to pounce on me.

Connie wanted to visit her girlfriend a few houses up the street. At first I didn't want her to leave. I sensed my family was in danger and I needed everyone to remain close.

"Oh, come on, Dad," Connie said, pouting. "I told Melanie I would come over. We're not going to do anything. We're just going to hang at her house."

"Mike," Karen said, "let her go visit her friend's. There's nothing for her to do around here."

"Can't Melanie come over to our house?" I suggested, over cries of protest from Connie. I finally gave in, but I insisted on walking her over to Melanie's house and made her promise to call when she was ready to leave.

"What's his problem?" Connie asked Karen.

"He's just being a father," Karen answered, shaking her head at me.

When I returned from seeing Connie to her friend's house, I found that Karen had allowed Chris to go to the mall with one of his buddies. I was furious. Instead of sharing my fears with Karen so she would understand why I was so upset, I hid out in the library. I had to get a grip on myself.

As the day passed, I grew more and more troubled. I wasn't anywhere near as intuitive as Karen, yet I couldn't shake the glum, oppressive feeling that had been following me around the house all morning. I did not know when the catastrophe would occur or what form it would take, but I knew as surely as I knew Cameron would strew his toys around the house that a catastrophe would happen.

Chris and Connie returned from their outings within a few minutes of each other. As they hung their coats in the hall closet, they argued about whether or not Michael Jackson and his sister, LaToya, were really one person.

"Where do they get such ideas?" I asked Karen. Karen laughed and shrugged her shoulders. I found myself thinking that in my day we didn't have such concerns. Then I realized that my father used to say, "In my day..." and caught myself before actually saying what had been going through my head.

I was relieved when it came time to go to bed. I tucked Byron into his crib and sat with him until he fell asleep. I watched him for what must have been hours. He no longer clutched his fists in pain. There were no more night terrors. No more hurt. He looked happy, peaceful and content. I wanted to soak up as much of him as I could. I wanted to remember him like that.

I thought back to the first day he came to stay with us. He unlocked a whole new world for me, and I was a better person with him in my life. At that moment I hated Lucy for still being addicted to drugs.

There was no doubt in my mind that my sources were correct. They had seen Lucy out on the street, as high as a kite and barely able to walk or talk. They had documented times and dates they had seen Byron being cared for by strangers, with Lucy nowhere in sight. Did CYS know this? Did Sojourner House know? Did the judge? If they knew, did they care?

Even if they did, I knew that the Baby Byron case had become too political and too high-profile for anyone to knowingly rock the boat. I realized then that Katie was right. Even though tomorrow at nine o'clock she would file for an appeal, sooner or later the powers that be would cave into the mounting pressure of the NAACP. Jane Worley would enforce CYS's policy on trans-racial placement and all would be well in the world of family reunification. The only loser would be Byron.

Karen quietly opened the door and tiptoed into the room. "I couldn't sleep," she whispered, sitting down beside me. Together we kept vigil over our little Birdie.

He had grown feathers, but he was not yet ready to fly. He was still weak and dependent and very much in need of all the love we could pile on him. I wondered how long it would take Lucy to push him out of the nest again. A week? Maybe two? Could she possibly hold on for a few months or maybe a year? At least the judge had promised that, if Lucy failed Byron, Karen and I would be allowed to bring him back home. But what exactly did they mean by "failing" him? Hadn't Lucy already failed as a mother?

It wasn't until well after midnight that Karen and I went to bed. I lay awake, listening to the winter wind beating against the windows. Another storm was moving in.

KAREN WAS UP EARLY baking a cake for Byron's farewell party. Strangely enough, Karen and I decided to put up a cheerful facade and pretend that this was a happy day—Byron was going to be with his "real" mother. We invited friends and family over to say good-bye to Byron because we all so desperately wanted Byron not to feel as though we were abandoning him. We wanted his last day with us to be enjoyable, filled with good memories. We all promised, for Byron's sake, not to cry.

I joined Karen in the kitchen and drank my morning cup of coffee while I watched her decorate the cake. Then it occurred to me that we never received a copy of CYS's trans-racial placement policy, which Jane Worley had promised to send us. I wondered now if they even had one, or was Jane Worley lying about that, too?

I picked up the phone and began pushing buttons. "Who are you calling?" Karen asked, licking some of the chocolate icing from her fingers.

"CYS," I answered, impatiently tapping my fingers against the wall.

"What for?"

I put my forefinger to my lips, then motioned for Karen to pick up the other line. A woman I was not familiar with had answered the phone. I asked for Jane Worley, but I was told she was on Christmas vacation.

I asked for a copy of the trans-racial placement policy.

"What is your name?" she asked.

"Mike Derzack."

There was a long pause. Then she asked me to hold. My

name seemed to cause a bit of a stir down at CYS. If anything ever happened to Byron, they really would have something to fear.

"Mr. Derzack," said the woman. I could hear the quiver in her voice as she tried to sound as if she were in charge of the situation. "You will have to call back when Ms. Worley is in. She will not be back until next week."

I hung up the phone. I should have known I'd get the runaround.

"She's lying," Karen said, pouring herself a cup of coffee. "You can hear it in her voice. I'll bet you any money that Jane Worley was sitting right there."

I thought she was, too. There was something that was not right about this policy. Did it exist or didn't it? If it did, what was the big secret?

While Karen finished preparing the food for the after-noon celebration, I straightened up the family room and vacuumed the carpeting. Cameron pitched in and straight-ened up his room, while Connie and Chris tackled the bathrooms.

Finally the first guest arrived: It was Bill, swathed in two mufflers and a goosedown coat. As he entered the house, a flurry of snow came in with him, sparkling in the faint sunlight. "Goddamn CYS," he muttered, extending his hand.

"Goddamn CYS," I echoed, shaking hands with him, as if cursing CYS were a perfectly normal way to greet some-one.

"It ain't going to be easy laughing and smiling our way through this thing," he sighed.

I helped him off with his coat, but when he bent to unbuckle his big black boots, he wavered and gasped, and I was afraid he was about to fall. Grabbing his elbow, I hauled him up straight and helped him into a chair. His face was as white as the snowy landscape outside our door and his breathing was labored. "You okay?" I asked, frightened. I had never seen Bill so weak before.

"Yeah," he huffed, "touch of the flu. I bent down too fast."

"You're working too hard at the shop," I scolded him, genuinely concerned for my old friend. "You should lighten up. Take a vacation."

"A vacation," Bill repeated, taking off his boots. "I'll think about that. Say, here's something for Byron." He handed me a small box clumsily wrapped in the Sunday comics page. As meticulous as he was around the shop, Bill had never learned to wrap a present properly. Bits of tape glistened on the paper, which was crumpled at the corners of the box. Still, it looked beautiful to me.

"Thanks."

"Haven't ya got any cake like ya promised?" grumbled Bill.

"Sure, and coffee, too." I steered him into the living room, where Karen was arranging slices of fresh fruit on a platter. She ran to Bill and hugged him, and he patted her back and spoke softly to her. I hurriedly stuffed Bill's box into the pocket of my sweater; something that small would be just too easy for me to lose.

Soon the rest of the guests filtered in. Even though there was plenty of cake, ice cream, good friends and presents for Byron, the festive mood could not take away the haunting fact that we had less then twenty-four hours left with our little Birdie. I told jokes, even laughed at a few, but I felt as if a death march had begun.

All through the party I still sensed that brooding feeling of a storm about to strike. I constantly checked on the whereabouts of my children: Byron was with Karen, Chris and Connie were playing a complicated board game with some other kids, and Cameron was showing his new plastic dinosaurs to the guests. Although I knew they were safe within the walls of their own home, I was still cautious.

After an hour or so, the party broke up and Karen and I said good-bye to the neighbors. I appreciated the support and love they had shown us, but I was relieved not to have to keep the front up any longer.

Bill kissed and hugged Byron. "You have a good life," I heard him whisper. "I'll watch over you."

"Thanks, Bill," I said, overwhelmed by the tenderness he showed Byron.

"For what?"

"For being such a wonderful friend," I answered, wrapping my arms tightly around him.

"Not that again," he rasped, as grouchy as ever. "Listen." He lowered his voice. "This mother of his is gonna screw up. I've seen it a thousand times. You keep watch. It'll happen. When it does, you scream at the top of your lungs. Announce it to the world if you have to. It's the only way to save Byron."

Karen gave Bill a kiss on the cheek, then rubbed it in. "So it will last forever," she told him. He kissed her hand in return.

He pulled his coat close around him, then opened the door. As he stepped out into a frigid world of high winds, snow and ice, I swore I heard him mumble under his breath, "I love you guys," but I couldn't be sure.

"I love you, too," I called after him, though I was certain my words were lost in the howling of the wind; that was why he didn't respond.

Karen and I cleaned up the remains of the party, then, all too soon, it was time to pack Byron's things. I had been dreading this task. If I could have run away from it, I would have.

Karen and I held hands as we entered Byron's room. We looked around at Byron's crib, his dressing table, his bright-colored toys scattered about the room, the funny poster of a clown on the wall. It's a happy room, I said to myself, but already it was beginning to feel empty, like a shrine.

Karen went right about getting the job done. I envied her strength as I watched her fold Byron's little red sweatshirt with the smiling Santa face and place it in the suitcase. One by one she held each piece of his clothing close to her, as if saying good-bye before surrendering it.

"I can't pack anymore," Karen said, brushing away a few tears. "I'm trying to be brave, but I just can't do this anymore."

"I'll do the rest. Sit down and keep me company." Karen slumped into the rocking chair and sat motionless. I convinced myself to be strong—for Karen.

I took Byron's Barney pajamas from his crib and found myself holding them close just as Karen had done. "Here, smell these," I said, walking across the room to hand them to her. "They smell like Birdie."

Karen pushed them away, then stood up and began to pace around the room. She stopped to pick up a toy, then continued her pacing. "Just put the jammies in the suitcase."

"I'm keeping them," I said, like a child defying his mother.

Suddenly, I remembered that when my grandfather died I had taken his old baseball cap and slept with it until his scent faded away. I somehow felt that if I could smell him he was still around. Now I was doing the same thing with my son's clothing. God, how I wanted to cry! But I would not allow myself. I could not afford to give in to the pain I was feeling. I had to remain strong for my family and true to the belief that those nights Byron and I spent holding on to each other had happened for a reason.

"I keep thinking of you and Byron asleep on the recliner," Karen said, as if reading my thoughts. "What if he can't sleep? Who's going to hold him?"

I couldn't answer her. But I knew that during those long nights as Byron struggled to find some relief from his addiction, it was the sound of my heartbeat that lulled him into sleep. It was my heartbeat that was in his memory. No judge or CYS administrator or attorney or biological mother could ever take that away from him.

I folded Byron's pajamas, walked to our bedroom and stuffed the purple PJs into my sock drawer. When I returned to Byron's room, Karen was opening the window.

"Mike," she said, tugging at her collar. "I can't breathe. It's really hot in here."

"Hope you're not coming down with something," I said placing Byron's red and black striped shirt in the suitcase. Although the four kids had just finished a bout with the flu, I suspected that Karen's reaction was due more to the stress of saying good-bye than some virus. I was feeling the panic myself and the cold air felt good.

"Mike!" Karen whispered, stepping away from the window. "Turn the light off! Come here!"

I didn't think to question. By now I knew to expect the unexpected. I shut off the light and joined her at the window. "What do you see?" I whispered.

"There's someone by the holly bush." We both peeked out the window from behind the curtains.

I didn't see anyone, but if Karen had thought she saw someone, I knew that they were out there. We had both been a touch paranoid since the next-door neighbor in the past two weeks had his front window shot out—twice. Although Karen and I had tried to convince ourselves that it was the result of a careless hunter, we both had our doubts. So did our neighbor. "I think these were meant for you," he had told us.

A gust of wind blew through the room, causing the door to shut with a slam. Both Karen and I jumped. Then, amid nervous laughter, we agreed that it was probably some reporter lurking in the bushes, hoping that we would leave the house so they could fire more questions at us.

"If it is a reporter, Mike," she said, looking sternly into my face, "let's not let him in. This evening is a family evening."

"Aren't they a part of our family?" I asked, only half-joking. I had come to know many of the reporters and was on friendly terms with all of them. It was a scary thought, and even though I knew that they could turn on Karen and me in an instant, they felt like friends. Karen didn't have the same feeling as I did. She was cautious when she spoke to them. She had this thing for being quoted out of context...which was, of course the way of the media.

"Mom! Dad! When are ya coming down?" yelled Connie, in her pre-adolescent whine, from the bottom of the stairway. "You said we could make some popcorn at seven. It's five after! We're wait-ing! When are you com-ing?"

I opened the door and stepped out into the hall. Connie was impatiently tapping her foot on the floor, staring at the ceiling, her arms crossed. What a pistol!

"Ne-ver!" I shouted down the steps, expecting exactly the response I got.

"Oh, Daddy!" she said in a superior tone. Her eyes narrowed as she tossed me the infamous 'Connie look'. "You're real funny." She faked a laugh, then threatened to make the popcorn herself.

"No, you don't," Karen warned, shaking her finger in Connie's direction. The last time Connie put a bag of popcorn in the microwave, she guessed at the time it would take to cook. One flaming bag and a house full of smoke later, she found out that ten minutes was way too long.

I joined the kids in the family room. They were in front of the television watching *Roseanne*. Even though most of the humor was beyond Cameron, he laughed when the others did, as if he were being cued.

Karen made a bowl of popcorn and sat down to join us. Byron was laughing and cooing, soaking up all the attention we were giving him. Chris, Connie and Cameron huddled around him, patting his hands and tickling his chin. Normally, a scene like this would melt my heart and fill me with joy, but this time it hurt to watch, knowing I night never see the children together again.

Connie and I were fighting over the last handful of popcorn when the doorbell rang.

A shot of adrenaline surged through my body, as if I had just missed an up-close-and-personal encounter with a city bus. The kids stopped laughing and the room fell silent. Chris immediately jumped up and turned off all the lights and the TV set; reacting to danger was becoming ingrained in him. "Don't answer it, Daddy," he said quietly. "It's something bad. I can feel it."

I could feel it, too. I knew that whatever it was I had been fearing the last couple of days had arrived. We all sat in a silent circle in the dark. The doorbell rang again, followed by a pounding on the door. A few minutes later the phone rang. The answering machine was on, but no one left a message.

"I'm scared!" Cameron cried.

He had every right to be. That moment, I heard the front door knob jiggling in its socket. Byron began to fuss.

Connie shot up, cocked her hip to one side, waved her finger and tapped her foot. "Stupid reporters! They're frightening Byron! I'm gonna go out there and give them a piece of my mind!"

"You sit down, young lady," I said, grabbing her wrist. "I'll handle this." As I spoke, I wondered how in God's creation I could possibly handle this situation any better than my daughter.

"Well, Daddy?" said Connie, with a smirk. "What are you going to do?"

"Maybe you should just answer the door and tell who-ever it is that we don't want any visitors." Karen picked Byron up in her arms, then placed him back on the floor when he began to whine to be with his brothers and sister. "It could be important, you know."

"It's reporters," I said, "and you told me 'no reporters.' If I answer the door, I'll give in and talk to them."

"Yeah, I know," Karen sighed. "So I'll answer the door."

I told the kids to stay put. Karen and I went together to answer the door, a sort of check-and-balance approach. Karen would tell them to get lost and I would smooth things over by wishing them a Happy New Year.

As we entered into the foyer, a beam of light came through the left doorlight, piercing the darkness and falling in a pool at our feet. "This is no reporter," I whispered.

"Maybe it's a burglar," Karen whispered back. "Call the police."

"Not yet." I motioned for Karen to follow me as I tracked the beam of light, which was now making its way around the side of the house. We all ended up back in the family room, staring at the front door, when we heard the back doorknob jiggle.

Connie let out a frightened yelp.

"Come with me," I whispered, gathering the family close to me. I led my little troop into the laundry room. As I opened the door I warned Connie not to ask if we were going to do the wash. I was closing the door behind me when I heard the garage door fling open and strike against the wall.

"It's the police!" shouted a deep, gruff voice. "We're here to get Byron."

I walked out of the laundry room, closing the door. "Police!" the voice screamed again. "We know you're in here!"

I began to tremble inside. Before me stood four of the biggest cops I had ever seen. One officer was tapping his fingers on his nightstick, while the others stood silently. Their expressionless faces glared at me as I entered the hallway. What had I done to deserve the police breaking into my home?

"Where's Byron?" asked the officer, still tapping his nightstick.

"W-w-where's your court order?" I asked, with as much defiance as I could muster.

All four of the officers walked toward me, forcing me back up against the wall.

"Of course we have a court order," said one of the officers. His face was only inches away from mine. His gray eyes were steady and his thin lips were locked in a firm grimace. I knew that he would not hurt me—police weren't allowed to do that. He's only trying to intimidate me, I thought. "Now where's the baby?"

I paused for a moment. I knew that he knew I was scared. I had never had an adversarial encounter with the police before. How far could I push before they would haul me off in handcuffs or beat me with their nightstick?

"Let me see your court order," I demanded, glaring back at him, feigning courage. Out of the corner of my eye, I saw Jane Worley and another woman whom I recognized as a CYS caseworker enter my home.

The largest and heaviest of the officers came forward and stared down at me. Two against one, I thought. The odds were not looking good. "Look, pal, we don't need a court order. Just get the baby. We don't want to have any trouble now, do we?"

I looked helplessly at Jane Worley. I disliked that woman more than ever. She was cold and heartless, and she was controlling my life. "Do you have a court order?" I asked her. Her refusal to answer spoke volumes. She did not have a court order. If I knew her like I thought I did, she had told the police that she had one, and they had believed her. Why wouldn't they? She probably told them the judge ordered Byron's removal.

At this point, I knew I was being threatened. The police were prepared to remove me from my home and treat me to a stay in the county jail at the taxpayers' expense. Then they would take Byron. I had two choices, as I saw it: Let them take Byron without protesting any further and be free to fight for him, or be locked up and let them take Byron anyway.

Oh my God! I thought. What if they took both me and Karen? Our children would end up in the care of CYS!

Karen, who'd heard the commotion, came out of the laundry room holding Byron, the three older kids lined up behind her. "Dad!" Connie ran to my side crying. "What are they doing to you? Get away from my daddy!" Connie screamed at the officer and attempted to push him away.

"It's okay, baby." I tried to soothe her. "They won't hurt us."

I held Connie as she sobbed. I was pissed. My own local

police were standing in my home, treating me as if I were some criminal. *Jane Worley*, I thought, *one day you will be discovered.* That tiny lifeboat she and the three commissioners were in would begin to sink, and when it did, Jane would be the first one to get tossed overboard. And I was going to make some waves that would cause that little boat to capsize!

I noticed the glare from camera lights shining through the windows of my home as the media tried to capture the terror of the moment for the eleven o'clock news. I inched my way past the officers and opened the front door. "Come in," I called to the reporters. I wanted someone to witness the horror that had been brought into my household.

Jane Worley pushed her way over to Karen and tried to rip Byron out of her arms as Karen held him closer in protest.

"You can't have him," Karen shouted at her. Byron began crying.

Jane Worley stood silent for a moment, her eyes narrowed. She was not used to someone disobeying her. She glanced over at the police. "You can make this easy or hard, Karen," she said. "It's your choice."

"At least let me change him first," pleaded Karen. "He's wet. He'll get cold."

"You have five minutes," she said, casually. "But I want one of the officers to accompany you."

"What do you think she's gonna do," Connie asked, "jump out the second-story window?"

Jane Worley ignored Connie's comment.

"Come on, Jane," I said. "You know us. Why are you doing this?"

"Doing what?" Jane had the nerve to ask.

"Why are you taking Byron away in the middle of the night? The judge said we had until tomorrow and our attorney is going to file a motion at nine. We need the time. Does the judge know about this?"

She turned toward me. "Judges change their orders, Mike." There was no expression in the woman's eyes, and I felt a chill at the back of my neck.

"You old witch," Connie snarled. Under normal circumstances that comment would have cost Connie a week of extra chores, but in this case I agreed with her.

If I had been any less of a man, I would have taken on Jane Worley then and there, but my respect for Byron helped me maintain my own dignity.

Karen went up the steps, clutching Byron close to her. Jane Worley followed, and as the heavyset policeman took his first steps onto my stairs, I said firmly, "Take your shoes off. Take your shoes off first."

He looked at me and grunted, then proceeded to take another step. I walked toward him. "I said, take your shoes off. You're in my home. Take your dirty shoes off. Now."

He took them off, but he wasn't happy about it. I, however, had taken a stand and, as weak as it was, made some sort of statement.

My triumph was short-lived. Connie grabbed me around the waist, breaking down into tears once again. I looked at Chris. He turned away. "I'm coming up to help you, Mom," he called, and ran up the steps.

But where was Cameron? I couldn't see him.

"Cammie! Where are you?" I called. I let go of Connie and began searching for my little boy.

"Hey, where are you going?" demanded one of the officers.

"I'm looking for my son," I answered.

I found Cameron huddled in a corner in the kitchen, three of his fingers stuffed into his mouth. "Come here, darling," I said. "Don't worry. Everything is going to be all right."

He looked at me, his wet, dark eyes full of fear. "It's my fault, Daddy."

I knelt down beside him. "What's your fault, honey?"

He gasped for breath and began to cry. "It's my fault!" he sobbed. "It's my fault they're taking Byron!"

"Oh, no, honey, it's not your fault," I said, lifting him up into my arms. "Why would you say something like that?"

"I...I left...the...the...garage door...I left it open!"

I was so enraged that I could not even speak. How dare Jane Worley, CYS, the judge and the police do this...make my child feel that he was to blame for their sins? My heart ached as I realized that my children had been scarred forever by these people breaking into my home. Was no place safe?

It was sad to think that those who were supposed to protect children had done them so much damage. I feared that now my children, instead of seeing policemen as people they could trust, would fear them. Yes, indeed, this day the good guys had suffered a mighty blow.

I left Cameron with Connie and was almost at the top of the steps when Karen and Jane Worley entered the hallway from Byron's bedroom. Jane Worley turned to Karen and took Byron out of her arms. Karen's expression—the look of a mother losing her child—was forever etched in my memory. That moment I felt for every woman who had suffered the loss of her child.

Then Jane Worley opened her mouth to speak. The words that tumbled from her lips were next to unbelievable. "Your house has such nice carpeting, Karen."

I waited, holding my breath, to see how Karen would react. I knew no lioness or tigress ever protected her cubs with more ferocity than Karen protected her children. It was a good thing that Jane Worley was holding Byron when she uttered those cruel, unforgettable words.

Karen said nothing, but then, Karen is as dignified as she is ferocious. I swallowed hard. I would remain as dignified as Karen, although I wanted to claw that terrible woman to pieces.

Somehow we made it to the bottom of the steps, the cameras still rolling, Connie still crying, Cameron still sucking his fingers, and Chris still trying to be helpful in the midst of disaster.

"Karen, the back door's near the kitchen, right?" said Jane Worley, as Byron began to howl and reach for Karen.

Karen closed in on the CYS director. "Jane Worley, you may have slinked in the back door, but you are leaving through the front. My baby deserves to leave his home through the front door, even though you don't."

We walked en masse. Karen and the children cried while I still held strong, not letting myself break down. We watched as Byron was strapped into an unfamiliar car seat, screaming and fighting. Jane Worley forced a bottle of milk that we had given her into his mouth. Finally, Byron disappeared into the night.

We stood in the cold, long after the taillights of the car vanished.

Oh my God, I said to myself, over and over. They've stolen my child.

I CALLED KATIE AND explained what had happened. She was uncontrollably upset that a court order was not presented and promised to call CYS and the judge. An hour later Katie called back. "We have what I would consider good news," she said. I had my doubts. Too much calamity had arrived at our house lately in the name of good news. "The court order has just been faxed to me. It's handwritten and it was faxed to CYS forty-five minutes after they left your home. They didn't have one when they entered your home."

"How do you know that?" I asked.

"In their haste to calm me down, they faxed their fax to me. They forgot to cover the time that they received it from the judge's chambers."

As she continued, I was silent. In a way I was glad that we had a reason to sue their butts, but I was deeply disturbed that I could no longer trust that the laws that guarded law-abiding citizens would be upheld by our authorities. The world was growing crazier by the minute. Germany's walls had fallen, Russia was now our friend, but we still had enemies: ourselves. We were the ones breaking and entering each other's homes. No, the world just didn't make sense any longer.

"Mike, are you there?" Katie called into the phone.

"I'll talk to you later," I answered. "I don't feel so well."

Actually, I felt awful. My stomach was racked with cramps, and I was dripping with sweat. Finally I went into the bathroom and threw up. My stomach was exploding in pain and I felt I had to purge the ills of the entire world. Afterwards, I stared at myself in the mirror. My red, teary eyes were surrounded by crow's feet, and water ran from my nose. I looked bloated and worn and used up.

"Hurry up, Mike," said Karen, beating on the door. "The news is on."

I washed my face, swished some Scope mixed with water in my mouth and went into the family room. Standing in front of the television, numb and emotionless, I watched the most painful event in my life being repeated. There was me, looking awful; Karen, looking haggard and grief-stricken; and the three kids, as forlorn as new orphans. And there was Byron, screaming, begging us, I imagined, to come to his aid.

Then something happened to jar me out of my numbness. It seemed that the reporters who were at my home had had enough time to cover an African-American ceremony of some sort that was being held on the North Side. They were interviewing Robert Jackson, a local separatist and self-appointed spokesman for the black community. I had seen him many times in association with Reverend Johns.

"There are some concerns about the mental stability of Karen Derzack," Jackson said to reporters. "Her report was the only one not released by the psychologist who tested her. That's because, and I have this from a good source, they are hiding something about her 'condition.'"

I caught a glimpse of Lucy's attorney in the background. Then it dawned on me. He knew that Byron was going to be removed from my home and had set up Jackson to cast a shadow on us. There was a conspiracy going on, I was convinced of it.

Karen did not react to Jackson's remarks. She had been honest with the psychologist and told her the truth about her working conditions with ALCOA and the problems that had ensued. The psychologist assured her that the information would not be made known if she, after review, had determined Karen's history was not a factor in caring for Byron. Dr. Komma obviously was not concerned, for she did not release the information, not even to the judge. But had she leaked Karen's records to the NAACP? Or had she been pressured or duped into releasing the records? I couldn't help but wonder.

Then a picture of Byron flashed on the screen. Inset in the corner were three reasons that the judge had taken Byron away from us. I scanned them: "I'm tired of seeing Mike Derzack's face in the media...Karen Derzack is irrational...Byron is in danger."

"What!" Karen exclaimed. "Those are reasons?"

For our judge, yes. He was punishing us through Byron. We had talked to the media and we were paying the price. Now Byron was "in danger" from the very people who had nursed him through a terrible illness and loved him as their own. It was, as Katie had said, a sad, sad world.

We turned off the television and went upstairs. Chris, Connie and Cameron had decided to camp out together on the floor of the family room. This was their way of comforting each other. I watched the beams of light from their three flashlights, shining into the darkness and eventually disappearing, overcome in shadows.

We got into bed and Karen placed her head on my chest. I stroked her hair as I felt her hot tears falling on my skin. I cried, too. "Birdie," I whispered. "Birdie...Oh, my God! My little Birdie! You're lost, lost, lost!"

Twelve

BYRON HAD BEEN STOLEN away from us. Our home had been broken into, our family violated. We had been treated like criminals. But, according to the law, the judge could do whatever he damn well pleased.

I was in pain. I had failed everyone, including myself. Although I so longed to stay in bed, curled up in a fetal position, licking my wounds and hiding from the world, I had a war to wage. I could not afford the time to mourn Byron. I had to save him—at any cost.

The first point on my agenda was to part ways with Katie. Although it was a sad moment for all of us, we knew that Katie had gone as far as she could. Her personal involvement and negative outlook were hindering our case. Yet I was grateful to her and I knew that, if nothing else, she would remember us in her prayers; we would certainly remember her in ours.

We sought out the services of a new attorney, Peter Fischer. Peter was a kindly, older gentleman with thinning silver-gray hair and soft blue eyes. Because Peter reminded me of a combination of my grandfather and an uncle who I had loved very much, I was comfortable with him as soon as we met.

Karen and I went to Peter's office one bitterly cold December morning and poured out our guts to him. Months of frustration streamed out of our mouths like foul, brown water. I was somewhat embarrassed at exposing my feelings to a virtual stranger and not a little ashamed at hearing my own words as I demanded that a federal lawsuit be filed against the police who broke into our homes, Jane Worley and her assistants, the judge and anyone else who had hurt Byron. I truly despised these people, and it had grown almost impossible for me to find any redeeming qualities in them. My anger was causing great anguish for me, for I needed to believe in people, not disparage them.

Peter remained calm, understanding and sympathetic throughout our tirade. He allowed us to vent our frustrations, and, when it came his turn to speak, he put the events in order, repeated them back to us, then made the decision to take our case. He thought a federal lawsuit was in order. I felt that we were finally moving in the right direction.

Karen had mixed feelings about Peter, but I liked and trusted him. When he asked for a ten thousand dollar retainer, I didn't question the price, even though money was getting tight. I'd been sorely neglecting my duties at the shop. I was the sole source of new commercial accounts, but I had been spending most of my time fighting for Byron, and the shop had started to nosedive. Although I knew I would need to take a deep dip into our savings to cover the ten thousand dollars, I reached inside my coat pocket and without hesitation wrote out a check for Peter.

My hand shook as I placed the check on the desk in front of our new attorney. I would need some time to transfer the funds.

"I've postdated the check..." I began to explain.

"Let me know when it's okay to cash it," Peter interrupted, dismissing my comment with a wave of his hand. "Now let's get down to business. About this federal lawsuit—now is not the time to file it."

"Why?" Karen demanded, tapping her fingers on the mahogany desk. She was feeling out of control and I could sense she was not happy with Peter's advice. Karen liked action.

"I'm personal friends with the judge, and regardless of what you may have heard, he does listen to reason," Peter said, smiling reassuringly. "Just give him time to work his magic and Byron will be back with you in a couple of months. Then we'll talk about the suit. If we file now, it would be like sticking a bee in the judge's bonnet...and we don't want to do that, do we?"

"Who cares about the judge?" Karen said, in disbelief. "Our concern is Byron and the treatment he's received. These people were wrong and deserve to be punished so they'll think twice before they hurt some other little kids. I say sue 'em all. Maybe we should place a few bees down the judge's pants and really give him something to holler about."

"I understand your feelings," Peter said, reaching out and placing his hand on Karen's. "But you'll need to trust me. I can handle the judge."

"Trust him, Karen," I urged.

Karen was silent for a few minutes. She looked at Peter, then at me. "Okay. We'll do it your way. For now."

We talked about the upcoming hearing and it was decided that Peter should file a motion requesting visitation rights for me and Karen. It left a bitter taste in my mouth to know that we would have to pick up our little Birdie up at his new home—a drug rehabilitation center—but anything was better than not knowing how he was doing. We also requested documentation from Sojourner House, stating that Lucy was clean.

"We accomplished a great deal today," Peter said, giving me a pat on the back as we left his office. "I'll fax you a copy of the motion."

Karen didn't have much to say about Peter that was very flattering, but her opinion of him didn't affect mine. I was sure that we had found an attorney that would fight for us. Karen, on the other hand, thought he would do more fighting for the judge than for us. "He's hiding something," Karen said, finishing up her analysis of Peter. "You just wait and see. There's something going on behind those sweet, sad eyes of his, and it's not in our favor."

We pulled into the drive where Sam, our postman, greeted us with a sack of mail. "You're now bona fide celebrities," he said, handing me the bag.

"Is this all for us?" I asked. The mail sack was filled with letters and postcards.

"All for you," he smiled. "I hope it's all good news. I know the letter my little girl wrote you is."

Karen opened the door and I carried the letters into our home and dumped them on the library floor. They covered the carpet and slid under the desk—a mountain of mail. I was overwhelmed by it all.

Karen and I ripped into the letters, devouring the words of encouragement as if they were manna from heaven. There was not a negative letter in the bunch: Everyone was in support of us getting Byron back. From the letters, we could see that people were fed up with CYS, the legal system and the Allegheny County commissioners. I just hoped they voiced their opinion at election time. A few folks sounded like Rush Limbaugh, commenting on the sad state of affairs across the United States. It was "the country's going to hell in a handbasket" routine, and I found myself agreeing with that shadowy forecast.

"Oh, Mike," Karen said, handing me a handwritten letter. "This one is special."

I took the letter and rested my back against the sofa. The letter had the faint smell of apple pie. I held it closer to my nose and sniffed. Definitely apple pie.

Dear Mr. and Mrs. Derzack:

I have followed your much publicized legal case involving your son, Byron, and would like to offer a few words of encouragement and praise.

There are many children in the U.S. in need of a home. Usually, it is easy to obtain a newborn or toddler who is black. Yet there are those who literally travel to the ends of the earth—Romania, Russia—in order to adopt a white child. Happily, you have distinguished yourselves by opening your heart and home to a little boy who needed both. And, in doing so, you have engendered great emotional and financial expense to yourselves.

As a black woman, let me reassure you that the biased and narrow-minded opinions shared by a few loudmouths are not held by all. Sure, the little boy needs his own parents. All children need their own parents. If this were a perfect world, issues of this sort would not even come up and dysfunctional families would be non-existent.

However, the world is not perfect—yet. The social problems we as humans face are too much for us to handle and await the resolution that only God can give.

In the meantime, fight for your little boy. In twenty years he will do more for the black community after being brought up in a stable and loving home, hopefully going to college and becoming a contributing member of society, than he would be wearing a black hood, standing on a street corner, draining my and other taxpayers' resources by living in Shuman Center.

Teach him that there is a whole class of blacks, a secret society as it were, who go to work every day, pay their bills, take nice vacations, own homes, don't use drugs, don't wear droopy drawers, don't like rap music and take care of our kids. Unfortunately, some people don't believe we exist. Guess we'll surprise them some when the secret gets out.

Would that I could offer some financial help for your legal battles, but alas I cannot. However, if you'd like to talk or would like a positive opinion, please feel free to contact me.

In any case, best wishes to you.

Carole Hart.

"Carole Hart," I whispered. "I don't know who you are, but God bless you." I folded the letter and placed it in my wallet. I planned to use it as a reminder that there were people in the black community who put Byron first. My moment of euphoria was short-lived as Karen spread the daily newspaper out on the floor in front of me.

"Read this." She pointed to the headlines: NO VISITS FOR DERZACKS, BYRON'S GREAT-AUNT SAYS. "Who is she to be making decisions about who can see Byron and who can't?"

I read the article and wasn't surprised that the great-aunt was giving her opinion. She had been enthralled by the media attention. I knew from the first time I had seen her in front of the cameras, weeping and gnashing her teeth over the fact that a white family was caring for her great-nephew, that she would not deny the press a comment or two. The more outrageous, the better the likelihood of seeing her name in the paper.

I was, however, very concerned about the judge's remarks. It was obvious to me that the judge was indeed capable of irrational behavior. He had defended his decision to place Byron in a drug rehabilitation center with Lucy because he thought it would be racist if he didn't. According to the article, he was afraid that, had he allowed Byron to remain with "a nice, white suburban couple," people would misconstrue his action to mean that he thought African-American women weren't good mothers.

Hey, I thought, she was the drug addict that almost killed her two youngest children. That was the way he had described her earlier. Black or white, such a person did not make a good mother.

"I can't believe this!" I slammed my fist on the paper.

"Well, the judge does have a point," Karen said sarcastically. "After all, aren't all whites nice and living in the 'burbs?'"

"Yeah, right," I answered, not finding Karen's remark very funny.

"If you want a real treat, read the part describing how Lucy convinced the judge that she was intelligent and competent to care for Byron. That's a real joke. I wonder who pronounced the judge intelligent and competent—Lucy?"

I pondered over the article for a while and wondered why the judge had sugarcoated Lucy's condition. Either he chose to ignore the wisdom that years on the bench should have given him regarding human nature, drug addiction and the shortcomings of the CYS...or he was simply incapable of learning...or he was getting a lot of pressure from some outside source. In any case, I believed the truth would eventually show itself.

I knew from my informants that Lucy was hanging out in bars and reportedly still doing drugs. I knew the grandmother was nothing but trouble with a criminal record that stretched a mile long and included attempted murder. Her trial for selling cocaine and heroin was on the docket. If she were found guilty, then maybe, just maybe, Byron's sister would be moved to a better home.

The great-aunt had me baffled. On the surface she seemed clean, but I knew that a threat to the kids under her care was lurking in the shadows. In a family that dysfunctional, there wasn't likely to be much positive influence.

The truth, I said to myself. How would I find it? I remembered the saying that Karen had used on many occasions—be careful for what you wish, you just may get it. What would I do with the truth if I found out that my sources were wrong? What if Lucy had recovered? What if the judge was right? What if Byron were better off with Lucy?

No matter. The truth was paramount. There could be no other way to live. I promised myself that, no matter the cost, I was willing to suffer any adversity to get to the truth...even if it meant that Byron was lost to me forever.

I picked up the phone and dialed the number of a woman who had previously identified herself to me (through the detective I had hired) as "a friend." She was well connected with the police and the elite of Pittsburgh, as well as the dark side of the law. She wasn't normally a woman I would want to know, but this was war.

"This is Mike Derzack," I said into the phone. "I need help."

We talked briefly. She called herself "Regina." I was enchanted by the lyrical sound of her voice, which had a slightly British sound to it. Although she was careful with her words, every once in a while her pronunciation betrayed her Pittsburgh upbringing.

I told her I needed her help to verify Lucy's current condition and how Byron was being cared for. Although she said she could help, I still had my doubts. "How can I be sure that you are telling me the truth?" I asked her.

"I'm not doing this for you," she said. "I'm doing it for me. Just call it payback time. As far as I'm concerned, I've got to tell you the truth. If you don't believe me, well, you'll just have to check my information for yourself."

She went on to give me explicit instructions to call her, in the future, only on Wednesdays, and then only from a payphone.

I hung up the phone feeling that I had been sucked into a world of foreign intrigue. Code names, dubious characters, high-placed people. It was scary and exhilarating.

I relayed the conversation to Karen, who felt that we would get more help from Regina than we would from the whole legal system and our other informants put together. And if we didn't, what did we have to lose?

NEW YEAR'S DAY CAME and went. We celebrated with the traditional Polish dish of pork and sauerkraut—for health and wealth. Karen and I went alone to church. Not many people were there. There was nothing particularly special about the passage of one year into the next. Neither Karen nor I felt like celebrating, so we stayed home, drinking wine in front of the fireplace. When the clock struck twelve, it reminded me of the day that I had etched Byron's name into the inside panel of the grandfather clock. Byron and I had built that clock. I sawed, polished and glued the pieces together while Byron laughed his support, occasionally pointing out my tools as I named them aloud—hammer, nails, file. I planned to give the clock to him when he got married, a memento of his old man and how much I loved him.

What was my Birdie doing this evening? God, I prayed, don't let him forget me.

The days that followed passed at a snail's pace. Business at the shop had slowed even more and I had to lay off the receptionist. This put a panic into the rest of the employees and Bill was worried that they would begin to jump ship, leaving us in even greater disarray.

My mind wasn't on work, though; it was consumed with Byron. I was spending most of my time hanging around Pinegrove Terrace and down at the Mission of Light on East Street. I needed to understand all that I could about this wayward, depressing lifestyle. I stood outside of the Mission, shoulder to shoulder with men down on their luck, as they waited for a bed or a meal. I listened to their stories. Some of them had families in other states they hadn't seen in years; some had never married but had drifted from job to job and finally to nothing; others had been well off at one time, but had put all their money into the bottle or needle. I began to understand how poverty, homelessness and drugs could happen to the best of people.

The New Year was well under way, and I could feel a change occurring within my own heart. I had changed since that night the CYS had taken my Birdie away from his family. I was wiser, calmer, maybe a bit jaded regarding the law and the court system. I wanted to trust the values that my father had given me about the police and the American system of justice, but I knew that I couldn't.

But those weren't the only differences in me. Down at the Mission, I'd been kicked in the stomach by racists and slapped in the face by the homeless. I'd tasted the helplessness of a drug addict who had cried in my arms, fearful of the drug that had become his master. As a result, I was becoming more like Bill—less judgmental, much more accepting and willing to lend a hand to a stranger. I felt like I was a part of humanity. Wherever I went now, I went on bended knees, yet I had never stood as tall as I did at the Mission house.

In the smallest of events, I saw a greater picture. I often worked on the soup line, and whenever anyone smiled at me, I felt as if that person had handed me a twenty-dollar bill. When they frowned, I understood their fear and anger.

I no longer felt so secure about myself, my job, my place in the universe, but it was a good feeling. Sometimes it seemed to me as if I had closed my eyes and stepped off a mountain top, trusting that I would land safely. I had learned to yield to the unknown. But the unknown was a difficult master. In all my wanderings downtown and at Pinegrove and from all my conversations with Regina, I learned much about myself but nothing about Byron. It was as if Birdie had been swallowed up by a black hole.

The word on the street was that Lucy was in her third phase of Sojourner's program and was allowed weekend passes with Byron. Although my sources had seen Lucy now and then standing in front of Jake's Bar and Grill and on the corner of East Street and Federal, no one had seen Byron. Who was taking care of him, if he weren't with Lucy? I was going crazy with worry.

Finally the day of the January hearing arrived, the coldest day on record in Pittsburgh. As we expected, based on prior experience, Karen and I were refused entry into the courtroom. We sat in the hallway waiting for our attorney to tell us what had transpired.

The hearing did not take long, maybe twenty minutes. At last we saw Larrence Franklin, Byron's attorneys, a couple of CYS staffers, Alice LaPort and Peter filing out of the courtroom. From Peter's smiling face, I assumed that the hearing had been a good one for us.

"Well?" Karen asked. "How did it go?"

"Not bad," Peter said, still smiling. "I don't believe Sojourner's going to release Lucy's records, but the federal lawsuit will take care of that. The judge has agreed to four visits with Byron, one every other month. They're still fighting about the times and who will transport Byron."

"Every other month." Karen sounded as if her hope had flown out the window. "That's not enough."

"I'm sorry, Karen," Peter said, touching her shoulder in sympathy. "I know how you feel, but please be patient and allow the system to work. The judge has agreed to keep you and Mike a party in this. If Lucy is not able to care for Byron for any reason or for any amount of time, Byron will be returned to you. And it will happen. Have patience. Okay?"

"Okay. Patience. I'll try," Karen conceded. I heard her words but I knew she was not convinced.

"It's already happening," I said excitedly.

"What is?" Peter asked.

"Lucy has been seen without Byron. That means we should be able to at least babysit while she goes out." Karen nodded in agreement.

"Yes. That does sound reasonable, but you will first have to prove that Lucy is without Byron for longer than just a few hours or so. I don't think Judge Lerner or CYS is going to agree to give you Byron if Lucy has to run to the corner supermarket for shampoo." Peter sighed and smiled his slow, sad smile.

"Well, I suppose you're right," I said, raising my eyebrows. "But I don't think Lucy's making trips to the corner store."

"Get me proof and I'll place it before the judge." Peter lost his smile. His brow wrinkled slightly, as if what he was about to tell us caused him a great deal of pain. "One other thing. I know you're not going to like this, but I think it's for the best. The judge has placed a gag order on both of you, so whatever you do, don't talk to anyone in the media about this case."

Karen lost her cool. Her face seemed to crack and come apart, then coalesce into a fierce mask. "You allowed him to gag us! For months we've been fighting that order. The first time you go into court for us you get us gagged!"

"Calm down, Karen," I pleaded. I noticed a few people looking at us, then quickly losing attention as they concentrated on their own problems.

Peter motioned for us to step out into the stairwell. We continued our conversation, our words echoing up the stairs and rolling back to us. Karen tried to keep her voice below a roar, but she wasn't having much success at it. The unheated stairwell was icy cold, and my nose was beginning to drip. Without missing a beat, Karen pulled a tissue out of her purse and handed it to me. Peter waited quietly for Karen to finish her harangue, then lunged into a speech when she paused for breath.

"The judge doesn't think family reunification works," he began. "He knows Lucy's going to go back to her drugs, and he wants you to have the child. But by being so verbal, you have brought attention to the case, and in doing that, everyone in God's creation got involved and applied pressure on Judge Lerner. The NAACP is the most glaring example. Had you just kept quiet, this thing would have already been settled in your favor. Give the judge a chance to work things out. Play it by his rules this time. Trust me."

Maybe I had screwed up. I had been warned of the judge's vindictive behavior inside of his courtroom. I should have kept my mouth shut. Maybe I did contribute to Byron being taken from us.

"All right, Peter," I said, looking at Karen. "We'll play it by the judge's rules. I'll do anything to get Byron back home."

Karen remained quiet. I could see her mind at work. "Peter," she said, glaring at him, "I don't like anyone taking

away my right to freedom of speech, even a judge. I believe
what Lerner did was against the law and he did it to protect
his own butt. However, I'm willing to listen to your advice.
But, and I mean this, if the judge screws us over, I'll scream
holy hell from a mountain top and he won't get a night's
sleep for the rest of his life. Understood?"

"Understood." Peter was smiling again. "And here's a
copy of a motion that I think you'll find very interesting.
Byron's attorney, Merinda Blake, intends to file this with
the judge next week. Read it when you get home, then call
me."

Karen shoved the pages into her purse.

As we left the courthouse, a barrage of questions flew
our way from the reporters anxious for a story. We ignored
them without explanation. We were gagged. That's the way
the judge wanted it, so that's how we would remain. Not
because I respected or agreed with his decision, but because
I wanted to appease him. I'd kiss his feet and shine his shoes
for the rest of his life if I thought it would bring Byron back
home.

As I approached the car, I spied Vernon Washington
sitting on the bumper of the Land Cruiser. "Hey, buddy," I
said, holding out my hand. "How are you? Long time no
see."

"What's wrong?" he whispered looking around at the
horde of other reporters running toward us. "You kill
somebody or something?"

"Can't talk, now," I said, unlocking the door. "I'd like to,
but I can't."

"That son-of-a-bitch! He gagged you, didn't he?" Vern
said. He slapped his hand against the back window with a
reverberating thump. "Are you gonna comply?"

"No comment."

"Hey, Mike, don't do this, man," Vern said, grabbing
my arm. "The judge has already barred us from the courthouse. He's makin' us freeze our asses off out here. Next
thing you know, he'll be gagging us."

"Come on, Vern," I pleaded. "I've gotta think of Byron. I'm sorry, but screw freedom of speech. I gotta do this for my kid."

"Some great country, huh? We got freedom of the press, we got freedom of expression, and what have we got? Nothing! Well, good luck, man. Let me know if you need my help."

Vernon turned away from us and waved to the reporters. "He ain't talkin'. He's been gagged."

"I never said that!" I yelled. "I want to go on the record as saying nothing more than NO COMMENT!"

Vern's face fell. He looked as if I had hit him, and I felt like a heel. Freedom of speech was what made America great. Everybody learned that in their fourth grade history lessons. What a sorry fool I had become!

Karen was all charged up over the judge's gag order. I would have rather faced a thousand reporters with sharpened pencils and hot spotlights than listened to Karen all the way home screaming about the judge and Peter. But I hadn't that option.

"I don't believe Peter and I don't trust him. How can it make sense that Katie never allowed us to be gagged and Peter does? How close a friend is he with the judge, anyway?"

"Karen, just stop it," I said. I remained calm because that was my way, just as it was Karen's way to speak her mind— loudly when need be. "Katie didn't prevent Byron from being taken away. Give Peter a chance to get him back."

"I don't like it, Mike, not at all. But, if you feel strongly that Peter is doing right by us, then I'll trust your decision."

"But you will keep quiet, right?" I asked.

There was a long pause. Finally I heard Karen whisper, "Yeah, right."

As we were pulling into the drive, our kids were being dropped off by a neighbor who had driven them home from school. I watched them laugh and horse around as they plowed their way through the snow. Connie threw her bookbag onto the ground, then made a snowball and pitched it at Chris. It hit him in the back and splattered snow into his collar. Chris chased her, pushing her into the snowdrift and washing her face with a handful of snow. Cameron, coming to Connie's defense, tugged on Chris' coat to pull him away from her.

My children, I thought. Then suddenly I remembered that I had to pick Byron up from the babysitter's. I began to back out of the driveway.

"Where are you going?" Karen asked, one foot already out of the door.

"To get Byron," I answered.

"Mike! Honey, stop!" Karen's voice caught on a sob and she almost fell out of the car.

Then I realized it: Birdie wasn't my child any longer. He wasn't mine to hold, to teach, to tuck into bed. I stopped the car and lay my head on the steering wheel. When would these thoughts go away? Would I always feel that one of my children was missing, that I had to help him, get him, free him, rescue him?

"I miss him, too," Karen said softly. "God knows, I sometimes wake up to check on him. I still change his sheet, and just the other day I put some Barney vitamins in the shopping cart for him before...before I remembered."

I reached out for Karen, and for a moment we lost our worries in each other's arms.

"Are you two necking?" Connie asked, tapping on the window. "If you are, then stop it. The neighbors will talk. You're too old for that sort of stuff." Connie, I thought with a smile, was one in a million, and I was lucky enough to be her dad.

I pulled myself together and joined my three kids for a brief snowball battle while Karen went into the house to start supper. As we played, I kept thinking of the fun Byron was missing. Would I ever throw a snowball at him? Take him sledding? Be a father to him again?

Karen called us to dinner. It took a few minutes for us to change into dry clothes, but at last we sat down to what smelled like spaghetti. I was right. Meatballs, garlic bread, the works. My mouth was watering as I waited for my serving.

"None for you," said Karen. She handed me my "lite" dinner of boiled chicken breast, a boiled potato, no butter or salt, a serving of unbuttered green beans and, for dessert, half of an apple. I did not protest my meager meal. I even left a bite of potato on my plate. For effect.

Perhaps, I thought, I had gone just a little too far with the dramatics. Karen was eyeing me suspiciously as she cleared the plates from the table. I should have complained just a bit, or at least eaten all the potato.

I was gaining weight despite Karen efforts at getting me to slim down, and there were plenty of good reasons—all of them fattening. I had gotten pretty skillful at hiding Snickers bars and sneaking out of the house to down a hamburger or two. But, I had blown my cover. Karen suspected something.

I was stacking the dishes in the washing machine when Karen remembered the motion Peter wanted us to read. "Let's take a look at this thing," she said, waving the slim sheaf of papers at me. I wiped my hands on the dish towel, then joined Karen at the table.

"It looks as though CYS is having some internal problems," I said, reading the motion. This was good. Hopefully they would split their forces and start to make mistakes serious enough to stir the judge into action.

On the surface it appeared that Byron's attorney, Merinda Blake, was acting in the best interests of Byron and requested that Byron's case be removed from Alice LaPort's region and moved to another CYS office. She accused LaPort of interfering with the orders of the court and using her position with CYS to exert undue pressure on the outcome of the case.

"It says here that Byron's counsel caught LaPort giving legal advice to the great-aunt after a special meeting they held regarding our visitation," said Karen.

I shook my head in disgust. Why was the great-aunt, who was not a party in the case, invited and not us? More underhanded maneuvering from CYS, no doubt.

"Looks like LaPort told the auntie how to resist the judge's orders," I said. "Whoa, pretty serious charges."

"The judge won't do anything," Karen said. "She's black and that scares him."

"Look, it gets better." I read aloud a section that accused LaPort of meeting privately with Lucy's attorney, while refusing to even accept a phone call from the child advocates. However, she did hold a public meeting for the African-American community in which she proposed a separate agency within CYS to be run by blacks for blacks, on the assumption that only members of the same race were equipped to deal with children of that race. I supposed that education, caring and training had nothing to do with taking care of a child if the color was wrong.

"Oh, no," I laughed. "Listen to this! LaPort accused a black attorney who is supportive of us of 'not being a woman of true color.'" I guessed that LaPort meant blacks were not really black if they disagreed with her.

"The woman's pathetic." Karen took the newspaper and began cutting out the article. "You know, Mike, if you or I or any 'nice, white, suburban couple' would have publicly said these things in the course of our job, we would definitely have been fired, and justly so. Am I right or what?"

Karen was right, but the rules of behavior that applied to us did not seem to apply to LaPort. A few days later, Peter attended a hearing on Blake's motion. LaPort was present with her attorney. After hearing testimony that contradicted itself, the judge ruled to deny the petition, just as we expected he would. Peter explained it away by saying that the judge did not want to tie up the courtroom with CYS internal problems. "If counsel feels strongly enough about her complaint against LaPort, she can always appeal." Byron's counsel obviously did not care enough: No appeal was filed within the allotted time.

But there was good news! We were scheduled to have a meeting with Byron on February 12th, our first meeting with him in a month. February 12th was the day I was living for, just two days before Valentine's Day, the whole nation's official day of loving. I would get to hold my little Birdie again and try make up for our time away from each other. February 12th—an eternity away.

A WEEK LATER, JANUARY still held the city in a deep freeze. During one of my sorties to the Mission House, I met a ragged man who told me to follow him: He knew some friends who had information on Byron, he said. Wary of a trap, I followed the man underneath a bridge near Three Rivers Stadium, where a group of street people had set up housekeeping. It was a regular rat's nest, full of old sofas, torn mattresses and other discards, but it was home to the ragged man, two women, three old geezers and a little girl about three years old. My heart went out to them. They huddled close together over a pathetic campfire, shivering in the cold.

One of the women told me that a party was being held for Byron and Lucy at the Hill House in Herron Hill in honor of their return to the black community.

"I wasn't invited," said a toothless old man, who wore layer after layer of clothing.

"You ain't black," said the ragged man.

"That's true," the old man answered, "but I still wanna go."

"Well, you can't," said another old fellow.

I was surprised how news traveled in the circles of the homeless. While their information sometimes proved incorrect, most of it was either right on or contained at least a sliver of truth. I thanked them for their help and gave the ragged man a twenty dollar bill, telling him to buy some food. I hope he did.

The following Saturday, I found that the street people were right. The local paper reported the party and hailed it as a success, even though Lucy and Byron had not made an appearance.

"Something bad is going on," Karen said, holding the newspaper in hand as we sat at the kitchen table, eating breakfast. "Lucy's attorney is quoted as saying that legal problems prevented Lucy from attending. Call Peter. Maybe he knows what's going on."

I was a little disturbed to find out that Peter had already spoken to the judge about the news report but did not think it was important enough to call us. I could hear Karen taking deep breaths to calm herself as she listened on the other phone.

"Mike, Mike," Peter said calmly. "Everything's under control. The judge called Lucy's attorney this morning. The judge was satisfied that the legal problems did not directly concern Lucy, but had something to do with the NAACP and Mr. Franklin, Lucy's attorney."

"An ex-parte communication?" I asked, growing angry. The judge never thought of calling my attorney when he read the denigrating article on us. He just had the police break into my home. The judge had his head on backwards.

"Yes, you might say that," Peter explained, "but I wouldn't make a big deal out of it. It happens all the time. It makes the legal process a little more friendly."

"I suppose," I conceded.

"You suppose?" Karen interrupted, her voice just short of a roar. "Where in the hell was *our* sprinkling of friendliness from the judge? Or don't we get any because we're nice white people? Peter, Lucy is in trouble. They're covering for her."

"Proof, Karen. Without it, there's nothing we or the judge can do."

"File an emergency motion," Karen said. I could tell she was fighting to remain calm.

"On what grounds?" Peter asked.

"Think of something!" she yelled. "You're the lawyer." Karen hung up the phone with a crash and stomped into the kitchen.

"I gotta go," I told Peter, and hung up. Karen paced back and forth, fanning herself with an empty envelope.

"They're lying, Mike. Lucy's screwed up already, and they're covering for her. It's just...not...FAIR!"

I believed Karen was correct. Why would Lucy's attorney's legal problems with the NAACP affect Lucy's party? They wouldn't, of course. Something else, something damaging to Lucy, was at the bottom of her absence. But the bigger question was, why was the judge buying this bunch of crap?

Thirteen

ESPITE THE FRIGID TEMPERATURE and the doom and gloom forecast of more snow and cold weather, I was in a great mood. The day for our court-allotted five hours with our son had arrived. Karen and the kids had been preparing for days, stockpiling Byron's favorite foods, buying duplicates of his old toys and adding a few new ones to the pile, and cleaning his room. It had been nearly a month and a half since they took him away, and I dearly longed to hold him and hear his tiny laughter.

Not one of the kids had to be told twice to take their showers and get dressed for the reunion. This was a special day—like Christmas.

"Gee," I said to Connie as she made a grand entrance

into the family room, wearing her Sunday best, a pink floral dress with a rounded white collar. Her sandy-colored hair was decorated with bright pink ribbons. "I don't know if Byron is going to recognize you."

"Oh, Daddy. Really!" Connie rolled her eyes.

It was exactly noon when we all piled into the car. We chattered nervously about little nonsense things—the weather, Chris' upcoming basketball game, Cameron's favorite *X-Men* episode. We kept our conversation light because we did not want any heavy, unhappy news to spoil our day. After stopping to pick up a celebration cake— Byron's favorite kind, chocolate with buttercream icing— we made our way through city traffic to Sojourner House.

Because we were five minutes early for our designated one-thirty pickup, we were not permitted to enter the building. We stood outside in the frigid air, waiting for someone to notice us. Karen and the kids huddled in the doorway, trying to keep warm as blasts of cold wind pounded against us. I stood on the sidewalk, staring at the large window covered with small red hearts made out of construction paper. A metallic red "Happy Valentine's Day's" greeting was strung haphazardly across the top of the window. The display looked festive enough, but all the cheeriness in the world could not hide the fact that my little Birdie was in a place he did not belong.

I cleaned a small peek hole by wiping the dirt and road salt from the window with my gloves and peered in. I could see a receptionist busy answering phones and jotting down notes. A woman walked into the lobby but I couldn't make out if she were the staffworker designated to do the exchange or not. My breath froze on the window, obstructing my view.

I made myself another peek hole. This time I could see a little boy. I took my scarf and cleaned a bigger space. Yes, it was my Birdie. "Hi, honey!" I called, tapping the glass.

I watched as a woman carried Byron past my window on the way to the foyer. Byron spied me and began to reach out and call to me, but the staffperson did not stop. Byron began to scream as we lost sight of each other. I ran to an adjoining window, trying to keep up with them. "Dad's here!" I shouted to him, my heart galloping in my chest, but the staffperson moved Byron to her other arm and he lost sight of me.

I joined Karen and the kids in the doorway and waited for the staffperson to bring Byron to us. After five minutes or so, the door opened halfway. Two long arms poked out, holding Byron, dressed in a thick, blue snowsuit. I could not see the woman's face and she ignored my "thank you" as I took Byron into my arms.

It felt so good to have him with me, to feel his warm, wriggling body in my arms. I didn't care if it were for five seconds or five hours. My boy was mine again. He clung to me like a squirrel on a tree and buried his face in my chest.

"Hi, darlin'," said Karen, pulling his hood back a little so she could see his face. "It's Mom...Aunt Karen."

I knew how difficult it was for Karen to be reduced to an aunt. She had hoped that Lucy would agree to allow Karen to be known as Mommy Two, but Lucy requested that if Karen insisted on referring to herself as someone important in Byron's life, it should be as an aunt.

Chris, Connie and Cameron smothered Byron with hugs and kisses. Byron laughed, a hearty, happy laugh, and eagerly returned their affections. We were complete again, if only for a few hours.

We hurried back to the car and once everyone was settled in a seat, I headed home for Wexford. Karen slid a tape of music into the cassette player and we all sung along. Byron bobbed his head up and down, singing "love you, love you" with gusto. Karen and I noticed immediately that Byron's vocabulary and annunciation had deteriorated.

"We're home, Birdie," I said, as we neared the house. Byron squealed with delight as we pulled into the garage. Everything was familiar to him and it seemed like he had never left us. Byron rushed to the kitchen, opened up the "goodie" drawer and rooted around until he found a package of graham crackers. "One," he said to Karen, holding a cracker in each hand.

"Two," Karen laughed. "You have two crackers. One in each hand. You can have two."

Byron ate the crackers while Connie poured him a cup of milk. Byron was king for a day and we were his willing subjects, seeing to his every need. He loved the attention.

It did not take any time at all for Byron to settle into his normal routine, chasing Cameron all over the family room and playing with his toys. But, as Chris was setting up a beanbag game, Byron stopped playing with his red fire truck and ran to the corner of the room, his head bowed as if he were ashamed.

"Hey, buddy," I said, lifting him into my arms, puzzled. I had never seen Byron react in such a manner. I did not know what in particular had triggered this behavior, but I fully understood who was to blame for it.

I was warned by Dr. Lipinsky to expect some strange reactions from Byron. I thought I was prepared, but I wasn't. Watching my son acting timid and ashamed in his own home stirred emotions in me that I could not readily identify. "Who's the best boy in the whole world?" I cried, tickling his neck with my fingers. "Birdie's the best!"

He didn't respond to me at first, but, after I repeated myself a few times, he pointed to himself and said "best."

We played a few games of beanbag toss and, funny thing! Byron won each game, with a little help from Cameron. As I was on my knees about to play horsy, Karen asked me to go to the basement and get a fresh carton of ice cream out of the freezer.

"Be right back, Birdie-boy," I said, giving him a quick kiss on the forehead.

As I was about to open the door to the basement, I heard Byron screaming. I ran back to the family room, afraid that he had hurt himself. He stood in the middle of the room, head bowed, sobbing uncontrollably. "Daddy's back," I said, holding him. "What's the matter? You want to help Daddy get the ice cream?"

Byron nodded. We walked down the steps, with Byron counting each one aloud. "One, two, four..."

"Three," I corrected. I would miss teaching my son.

We ate our pre-dinner snack, then bundled up in our winter coats, scarfs, gloves and boots for our drive to the Strip District of the city to have dinner at the Spaghetti Warehouse. Spaghetti was Byron's favorite meal.

When we entered the restaurant, Byron giggled with delight at the life-size Indian statue in the foyer, then ran to the counter and grabbed an all-day sucker from the display.

I shook my head. "Dinner first."

"Dinner first," he repeated, handing the sucker over to me.

The hostess seated us at a table in an old wooden trolley that took center stage in the large dining area. Byron stuck his head out the window and stared at the folks eating their meals. A woman, her mouth filled with food, pointed to Byron. "You're Baby Byron, aren't you?" she called, giving us a thumbs-up.

Byron was becoming recognizable and that concerned me. We had always been careful to hide his identity, but reporters, being the bloodhounds that they are, were always more concerned about the scoop than Byron's safety. I frequently found myself wishing that there was just one reporter that would probe deeper into this mess. CYS was as rotten as a three-month-old cabbage in the back of the fridge—if only someone would take the time to look.

We ordered our meal and ate with delight. It was evident from Byron's sauce-covered face that he really got into Italian food, literally and figuratively. None of the kids wanted dessert, so we sat and talked while Karen and I had a cup of coffee. We kept up a brave front even though all of us, except Byron, were well aware that our time was running out.

Time is our enemy, I thought, as I glanced at my watch. It was six o'clock. We had thirty minutes left before Byron's check in at the drug rehab center.

"We better go," I said, wiping Byron's face with my napkin.

"All ready?" Connie moaned, reaching out and hugging Byron.

I nodded.

"Dad," Chris asked, "what would happen if we didn't take Byron back?" Chris was dead serious.

"We would be guilty of kidnapping," I answered. Byron began to fuss as Karen zippered up his snowsuit. I took Byron into my arms and he began to entertain himself by playing with my glasses. "Besides, they would throw us in jail, feed us only bread and water, and make us watch re-runs of *That Girl* until we died of sugar diabetes."

"Mike, stop it." Karen gave me a slight punch to my right arm. "Your father's joking about the bread and water."

It was a short drive to Sojourner House and we arrived on time. Once again a pair of arms greeted us through a half-opened doorway. Before surrendering Byron, we all took turns saying good-bye. Connie began to cry, Cameron sucked his fingers, and Chris gripped his mother's hand. The scene was all too reminiscent of the night CYS stole Byron away from us.

"I love you, Birdie," I whispered, handing Birdie to the staffworker. "Daddy will be back for you. Be brave, sweet-heart."

Byron screamed and kicked, reaching out for me. Then the staffworker closed the door. Byron was gone, but I could still hear his screams.

Although I would never have traded spending the day with Byron, as we drove home I wondered if our visits hurt him more than they helped him. I feared that he would feel we deserted him because he had done something wrong. Children always seem to blame themselves for the hurt around them.

I remembered the time when my father was ill and in the hospital with a particularly nasty virus. Connie confessed that she had given her grandpa a kiss on the lips when she had a cold and she was very worried that she was the one who had made him sick. I has assured her she was innocent, but she only half-believed me.

Byron was far too young to understand that all of us

were being held hostage to a dirty game of politics and political correctness. We were as helpless as he was. I was learning the rules and knew I would eventually beat them at their own game. But would I win in time to save Birdie?

As was the routine, when I arrived home, I immediately checked for messages. A few reporters wanting to know the details of our visit with Byron...my mother...Karen's mom...Regina. I called Regina first.

"What's up?" I asked.

"Good news for you, bad for Lucy," Regina answered in a soft whisper. "Lucy missed her check-in time at Sojourner House a couple of weeks ago."

"Do you know the date?" I asked. My heart was pounding. "January 9th."

"Tell me all you know." We were on to something.

"Well, Lucy didn't show up for a party. No one knew where she was. The grandmother was embarrassed, so she sent her live-in to look for her. Old Mort found Lucy and her boyfriend holed up at her sister's apartment. They were both flying high."

"Is your source willing to come forth?"

"No, I don't imagine so. It was Mort that told me." Regina was remarkable. She had ties to everyone in town.

"Where was Byron?"

Regina paused for a moment. "I'm afraid I don't know. Mort certainly didn't have a clue."

"Does Sojourner suspect anything?" That was a dumb question. They were the professed experts: Of course they would know.

"Probably, but don't count on the records to show anything unusual. They're out to make Lucy and their program look good."

I agreed.

Regina abruptly ended our conversation. I erased the messages, then called my mother. I didn't have anything to say to her; I just wanted to hear her wonderful, comforting voice.

≈ᔕ   ≈ᔕ   ≈ᔕ

IN THE WEEKS THAT followed, and after many discussions, Karen and I came to the conclusion that our visits were probably more disturbing than helpful to Byron. Though he was always happy to see us, he screamed like a banshee whenever we parted. We decided to have one more visit, then ask the judge to help us work out some sort of visitation that was less unreasonable and emotionally traumatic.

It was our feeling that Lucy should be present for our meeting with Byron and that the visits should be on a more regular basis. This would give us the opportunity to form a relationship with Lucy. Byron could have two families to love and to give him love. Just because the court ordered that Byron should grow up in Lucy's home, it didn't mean that we could not be a part of the "extended" family unit.

Both Karen and I believed that if Lucy had the opportunity to know us better, she would find she actually liked us. We could help her, see her through her rough times, take Byron to baseball games, give them both love and guidance. These things were not beyond us. We had loads of love to give.

But would the judge serve the child or his own agenda? This question nagged at me. The judge had recently issued a statement that he had been "as impressed as hell" with Lucy's testimony at the January hearing. This deeply concerned me.

It was becoming obvious to me that Peter's assessment of the judge's attitude of "waiting for Lucy to fail" was wrong. I was convinced that the judge wanted to believe that Lucy was straight, although he had no proof, other than the word of CYS. He had no blood tests, no records, nothing. Why didn't he ask for proof? After all his years in family court, I found it incomprehensible that the judge could be fooled by a drug addict. A witness that looked good or sounded good didn't necessarily have to be credible. He should have known that. If I could find out that Lucy missed her party and checked in a day late at Sojourner, and then put two and two together, certainly The Honorable Judge Lerner had enough wherewithal to do the same.

The judge was beginning to remind me of those monkeys depicting tolerance: hear no evil, see no evil, speak no evil. Good advice for the common folk, maybe, but not a very wise position for a judge to take. The judge was wearing blinders, and he himself had placed them over his eyes.

I went to the shop early one morning and sat at my desk, toying with the idea of calling the newspaper. The judge had in essence bought my silence with promises of sending Byron back to us when—not if—Lucy fell from grace. I knew she had fallen, and so did everyone else at Lucy's party that night. But the NAACP involvement was too intense; CYS was too strong, and my attorney was not aggressive enough. I was losing Byron.

Everything kept leading me back to the media: They were the key. The heat needed to be turned up, and no one knew how to do that better than the press. The judge needed to know that I would not roll over and play dead. But I was under a gag order. I couldn't talk. Could I?

"Whaddya thinking, boy?" Bill asked, poking his head through the doorway. "I can smell that brain cooking all the way down in the storage room."

Bill was beginning to worry me. The color of his skin didn't look right. His ruddy complexion had, in the past few weeks, taken on a sort of grayish-white color. Every once in a while I'd catch him rubbing his arms, as if he were in pain. Both Karen and I urged him to see a doctor, but Bill didn't believe in doctors. "Damn sawbones," he'd say. "They can't help me."

I had long ago learned not to argue with Bill. I knew I would only lose.

"I'm thinking about breaking the court order," I said.

Bill smiled.

"Well, what do you think?"

"I'm pure amazed that the cork in your mouth has not popped by now," Bill said, raising one eyebrow. "I was getting concerned that one day you'd just explode."

"Who's right? The judge or me?" I asked. I knew the answer, but receiving Bill's blessings was like receiving dispensation from the Pope.

"This country will go to shit if people like you don't speak the truth." Bill took a deep breath and rested back in his chair. He looked tired. I was worried for him.

"Why don't you go home and get some rest?" I suggested. "You look beat. I'll cover for you."

Bill scratched his stubbly chin, as if he were thinking very hard. "That's a good idea. I believe I will."

I gasped aloud, but I was pretty sure he hadn't heard me. Bill almost never went home, even when he was sick. It scared me to think how horrible he must have been feeling. "Please, let me take you to see my doctor," I begged him.

He shook his shaggy head. "Naw, I'm not that sick. Just awfully tired. I don't want to make any mistakes, see? If I go home and get a good rest, I'll be back tomorrow morning, fresh as a daisy."

I doubted that, but I knew it was hopeless to argue. "At least let me drive you home," I offered, grabbing my keys from the desk drawer.

"What do you think I am, an invalid or something?" He stood up and puffed out his chest. For a minute he looked like the old Bill, full of piss and vinegar. "Before I go, I'm going to finish stacking up the paper in the storeroom."

He's going to be all right, I persuaded myself. Maybe he just didn't sleep well the night before. He was probably just very tired.

After Bill left, I picked up the phone and called Karen. "I've decided."

"And?"

"We talk."

"Good."

I left the shop shortly after Bill. I took a drive past some of the local bars, checking out the urban scenery, looking for my "moles" who had been feeding me information about Lucy and her family. The streets were quiet for the most part, but it was only six o'clock, much too early for any serious activity.

The McDonald's on Forbes Avenue glared into view. Although I knew I shouldn't stop, I did anyway and went inside. There was no drive-in window, which was just as well since I couldn't risk bringing any food into the car, especially hamburgers and fries. Karen would have smelled them out like a bloodhound.

I stood in line, trying to decide between a Big Mac or a double cheeseburger, when I heard a familiar cry. I spun around. Byron was sitting in a booth with four people—one man and three women, none of whom I recognized.

"Shut up, you little fucker," the woman sitting closest to Byron said, loud enough for everyone in the restaurant to hear. She raised her hand as if she were going to strike him. I made a move to intervene, but she lowered her hand when Byron cowered down in his seat and began sucking his thumb.

The woman saw me, but she did not recognize me. I was wearing work clothes, dirty and sweaty from the grime and heat of the shop. I gave her a hard stare, then left the McDonald's without buying anything. I had no appetite. I cursed at myself for not taking Byron with me, but I couldn't. That damn judge wouldn't let me.

I called the police anonymously from the car phone and reported the incident. Byron was with strangers, and that was against the court order. I felt it best to leave and allow the police to do their job. The press was already having a field day with the fact that I hired a private detective to keep an eye on things, and I couldn't risk being accused of spying.

I rushed home and told Karen about the incident. She was boiling mad. Since Lucy had entered her fourth and final stage at Sojourner, reports from all of our sources confirmed that she was back on drugs, seen drunk in the local bars, and leaving Byron and his sister with their paternal grandmother for days at a time. One source had told us that it was the grandmother who returned the kids to Sojourner House, not Lucy.

When we questioned this, we were told that grandchildren where allowed to visit with their grandparents. CYS saw no problem with this.

I called Peter and urged him to file an emergency petition to remove Byron from Lucy. He agreed to do so. Lucy was not caring for Byron, and by the looks of things no one really was. I had witnessed for myself the abuse that my Birdie was being subjected to. No more, I thought to myself. This shit ends here.

"One more thing, Peter," I added. "I'm going to talk to the press. I just can't keep quiet about this."

Peter was silent for a moment, then he began to strongly advise against any contact with the press. Inexplicably, he suddenly changed his mind. "Maybe you should," he said. "I think the judge has lied to me."

"About what?"

"About our chances." Peter was quiet for a minute. I could tell that something important was bothering him, so I waited for him to gather his thoughts.

"I'm going to tell you something about the night Byron was taken away from you," he began. "I hoped I wouldn't have to because it sounds so cruel, and I really don't think the judge is a bad guy, just a man who has managed to get himself situated between a rock and a hard place. I was with the judge the night they took Byron."

"What!" I screamed into the phone. "You were with the judge?"

"In a way," he explained. "I was sitting behind him at a Pitt basketball game. While your son was being taken from you, he was bouncing his little girl on his knee, looking quite the family man."

"That bas..." I began to interrupt.

"There's more. After awhile he was paged, then left the game, looking a bit distressed. He never returned."

"Are you thinking what I'm thinking?" I asked. Was it

possible that Jane Worley acted on her own, then covered her tracks by forcing the judge to write and fax the court order forty-five minutes after my house was broken into? Or had she talked to one of the commissioners who gave her the okay? It was either one or the other.

"Something's terribly wrong here," Peter said, treading very carefully. "I'm not advising you to break the gag order, but I do believe that the judge has violated your civil rights. Understand, however, that the judge may take strong action against you when he learns that you've basically told him to go to hell."

"I've been to hell," I said. "It's not very comfortable. Maybe a trip there will do him good."

"Then send him."

Karen, who had been on the other line, hung up the phone and stared at me. I knew what I had to do, but that didn't stop me from feeling nervous and frightened. I sat down for a few minutes to compose my thoughts, then called a reporter from the newspaper. After introducing myself, I told him that Karen and I would give him an exclusive interview.

"You're breaking the gag order?" The reporter sounded quite amazed.

"I prefer the word 'challenging'," I answered. My voice was shaky. "I'm challenging the validity of the judge's ruling."

"Mike," she murmured, "I agree with what you're doing. I just want you to know there's a good chance the judge will have you locked up."

"If that's what it takes," I said, "then so be it."

Karen and I agreed to meet with the reporter after our next visit with Byron. The judge would be angered and as a result he would take our visit away. The judge was getting pretty easy to predict. I was well on my way to locating all of his "hot" buttons and in time I would be able to push any one of them at will. This judge was not the type to think first, then act; he reacted, then thought.

"There's one condition," I explained to the reporter,

"Karen cannot be quoted. I'm the one challenging the judge, not Karen." The last thing we wanted was for both of us to be thrown into prison so that our biggest nightmare would come true: CYS would take our children. It was a scary thought, but to us it was a real possibility.

That evening, for the first time in months, I slept easy. That confirmed for me that I had made the right decision. I wondered if the judge slept as soundly as I did.

Around noon the next day, as if to add insult to injury, we received a call from one of our sources. A beer distributor, stopping off an order at a downtown tavern, saw Byron that morning, playing in the barroom. Byron was behind the bar, holding an empty beer bottle. The brave distributor said he was willing to come forth as a witness if need be.

"Call the judge," I said to our informant. "Tell him everything you know."

"I already did, Mike," she said. "But it ain't gonna do no good. To him, Byron is just another black kid."

"What? What did he say?"

"I didn't talk directly to him, but I told the lady that answered the phone. She said the judge would look into it."

"When?"

"Didn't say. I didn't ask. But don't hold your breath."

I hung up the phone feeling as if my chest were being squeezed by a pair of giant hands. I became short of breath. The sound of my heart pounding in my ears made me feel nauseated, and I began to grow weak. I'm having a heart attack, I thought.

"Oh my God," Karen cried, rushing over to me and helping me to the kitchen table. She pulled out a chair and I sat down, dizzy and disoriented.

"I'll call 911," Karen screeched, grabbing for the phone.

"No," I choked, "call Dr. Hale."

As Karen spoke to the doctor, I began to calm down. I took the phone from Karen.

"Doctor," I assured him. "I'm just suffering from a slight anxiety attack. Nothing serious." I explained my symptoms to the doctor, who punctuated my ramblings with an occasional "I see."

"Put Karen on the phone," he said. I handed the phone back to Karen.

"I see, Doctor. Yes, of course. Okay." Karen turned to me. "You're to see the doctor at one o'clock today."

I was right. It was stress. But it was also my weight and high blood pressure. Much to the delight of Karen, the doctor placed me on a diet.

It was difficult getting through the week with no extra goodies to give me solace, but I was determined to gain control over my body.

We had another visit with Byron. Everything that we had noticed a month ago during our previous time together was exaggerated. He spoke less and cringed more often. Every time I left his side, he wailed like a siren. My Birdie was heading downhill.

The judge denied our motion to revamp the visiting procedures, as we knew he would, but at least we tried. A few days later, we (and the judge) awoke to the headlines, DERZACKS CHALLENGE JUDGE.

"Oh, boy," Karen said, reading the newspaper and calmly sipping her coffee. "The judge is not going to like this very much. If I were you I'd go hide under the bed. The police should be here any minute."

"Thanks, Karen," I said. "You'll probably point out my hiding place."

"Don't need to do that," she said, a little nervous smile appearing on her face. "I already told the coppers where you'd be."

Actually, I did feel like hiding. Breaking the law, whether it was a good law or bad one, did not sit easy with me. It was not the way I had been brought up. But I had no time to think about the finer ethical points of my actions: I had made my decision and I would accept the consequences. If I were to suffer imprisonment or fines, I was first going to make it worth my while and talk to everyone who would listen.

I began with Ann Devlin, the host of a local radio show. Ann had graciously allowed us on to air our story a couple of times. She was sharp, witty and tough in her questions, but she was fair and knew her audience well.

The program director scheduled us for the afternoon show that same day and began to announce during commercial breaks that we were going to be live with Ann at four.

I was worried that people would begin to view me as a press prima donna, although I wasn't that sort of person. Dealing with the press, even though I felt I was handling it okay, was not an easy thing for me to do. It was, however, something that I had to do. I couldn't worry about my public image. There was no chance I was going to walk away and trust the system to do the right thing.

Karen and I hurriedly adjusted our schedules, putting off calls from the rest of the media. We asked a friend to schedule a formal press conference for the next day.

Rush hour traffic was just beginning as we drove across town to the radio station. I glanced over at Karen a couple of times, but her expression was always the same. Her jaw was clenched and she stared straight ahead as she picked at a label on a folder she had across her lap. Her family was her world. She was worried for us.

"I see the new prison is coming along just fine." I pointed to the red brick multi-story structure that was being built on the riverfront. "I wonder if they'd give me a room with a view of the Allegheny?"

Karen looked out the side window. "You know, Mike," she said, thoughtfully, "I was reading that eighty-five percent of children in foster care don't finish high school. Seventy-two percent eventually end up in prison. That's sad, isn't it?"

"Yes, sweetheart, it is."

"If we don't get Byron back, that will be his home someday." Karen nodded at the prison, then grew silent.

I believed that. It seemed odd to me that instead of correcting the problem with a foster care system, we built new prisons. It was all economics. Humanity had nothing to do with it. I couldn't think of anything redeeming about Allegheny County's CYS. Restructuring wouldn't help; it would be like reshuffling a marked deck of cards. The system would have to be totally disbanded and turned over to a private agency, which would have to answer to the government. As it stood, CYS was the government and answered to no one.

I found a parking space in the lower lot. The walk to the station felt good. Spring was once again in the air and I was getting itchy to work in my garden. We signed in at the front desk, then a guard ushered us back to the studio where Ann greeted us with open arms. She was a young woman just over thirty, with short blonde hair and a strikingly beautiful smile.

"I have to tell you," she said, as we took our seats. "Reverend Johns called and demanded to be allowed to be a part of today's show."

"I don't want this to be a battle with the NAACP," Karen stated. "We don't have anything to say to them or to Reverend Johns."

"I agree," said Ann, "so I told him we could have him on at a later date. He was none too happy to hear that. Just be aware that he may call in during the show."

"Hey, that's fine," I said, talking into the microphone so the technician could get a voice check. "I'm willing to listen to his opinion. If he has a question, I'll be glad to answer. But I will not do battle with him on the airwaves."

"I understand." Suddenly her voice took on a brisk, professional quality as she spoke into her mike. "Welcome to the Ann Devlin show. Today we have Mike Derzack..."

Ann laid the ground rules for the show, repeating the number for the listeners who wished to call in. Then Ann began firing questions at me.

I answered every question without hesitation. I told her about my sources, about my reason for challenging the judge, Lucy's suspected activities, her dubious family background, and my suspicions about a cover-up designed to keep Lucy looking good.

"I feel sorrow for Lucy," I said. "She's as much a victim in this whole mess as Byron is. The NAACP is using her in the name of racial matching. They don't care about her. They don't care about Byron. They care about pushing their own separatist beliefs at the risk of losing some of their own. They are the ones who turned this thing into a race issue, not me. Not Karen."

I paused for a few seconds to catch my breath when Ann asked, "Why should we believe you, Mike?"

"That's a good question," I said, taken aback. Although I admired her directness, it sometimes shocked me. But that's what made Ann the best at what she did.

"I've told my story many times," I answered. "Every time it's been the same. I have no need to lie. If I thought Byron was adequately cared for, believe me, I'd back out and leave well enough alone. But in the end, people will have to judge for themselves whether or not to believe me."

We went to a commercial and were talking about Byron when the program director interrupted us on Ann's private line. "No, absolutely not," she said, looking at me. She covered the receiver with her hand as she whispered, "The judge is on the other line. He's demanding air time."

Karen jumped out of her seat. "We can't talk directly to him, can we?"

I shrugged. I didn't know what to do. I never expected the judge to call into a radio talk show to discuss a case that the right to privacy act was supposed to protect.

"Tell him," Annie said, "that I wouldn't allow Reverend Johns to talk, so I can't allow him to be a guest. However, he can call the private line and we'll take his call live."

Ann hung up the phone. She had just told a judge "no way" and did not seem the least bit perturbed about it. I wish I had her courage and savvy.

A few seconds later the phone rang again. "I'll handle it," she said, then picked up the phone. I looked out the window to the control room and saw the techs busily rushing around. Something was happening.

"The judge hung up on us," Ann said. "They think he was calling from his car phone and lost the signal...Back with Mike Derzack."

Then Ann did the unbelievable. She spoke directly to the judge over the air, giving him the private number to call. She explained the situation as we all waited on pins and needles for the judge to call in.

"Wherever you are, Judge Lerner, please call in now," Annie sang into the microphone. "He must not be listening or he's changed his mind. Let's open our lines to our other listeners."

I wasn't as focused during the first call as I would have liked, but I was still thinking about the judge. His actions had to be a first. I wasn't surprised, though; it was just another example of how he reacted to a situation before thinking about it. He was getting more and more predictable.

The comments from the listeners were mixed. As I had feared, many people were growing tired of hearing about the case. I had three particularly bad calls in a row. One listener, an older woman who identified herself as a mother and a grandmother, gave me some motherly advice. "It's time to recognize things for what they are," she said. "This isn't about a child's welfare. This is about one race hating another. You are not going to get Byron back. I think it's time you faced that and got on with your life."

I thanked her for her opinion, then listened to the next caller.

"Hi, Ann," a husky voice said, identifying himself as a first-time caller. "I'm calling from my car phone while I'm sitting in traffic trying to get through the Liberty Tubes. You know, I don't agree with the judge's decision. I think he was really off base sticking that kid in a rehab center. But I get tired of hearing about this problem. Every time I listen to your show, I hear something about the Derzacks. I agree with the last caller. Move on already, Mike."

I was beginning to feel a little uncomfortable, but reminded myself that everyone was entitled to express an opinion, so I thanked him.

The third caller identified herself as a friend of Lucy's family. "Instead of disrespectin' Lucy, you should help her. I hear you're rich. Why don't you give her some money so she can take care of her children? That boy's great-aunt is a good woman lookin' after Lucy's kids. If Lucy can't take care of Byron and Georgia, Auntie should take 'em."

"Thanks for your calls, listeners," Ann interrupted, disconnecting the caller. "We have sixty seconds left for one last call."

"Hi, I'm Sandy, a first-time caller. I have three quick points. To that mother and grandmother out there—just the fact that you have children is reason enough to fight for the safety of all children. It's not a racial thing; it's a loving thing. If you're too old, too tired or too cynical to do something good, then instead of throwing stones at Mr. Derzack as he's climbing the mountain, you could at least cheer him on, for you granddaughter's sake.

"The man calling from the car phone—hey, wake up. If you think the judge's decision was wrong, call him, not Ann. Speak your mind to him. After all, he's shaping the world you live in. You may find you don't like the results.

"And to the friend of Lucy—the great-aunt is living in government housing, receiving welfare and I'll bet donuts to dollars she's getting a check every month courtesy of the taxpayers to care for Lucy's three children. Take away the money and let's see how fast she gets rid of the kids. A real family opens it doors as well as its heart, no conditions. They help because they're family, not because there's a price tag. And if you give money to Lucy before she's licked her habit, where do you think that money's going to go? To the kids? Get real!

"Don't let those people get you down, Mr. Derzack. For every hundred of them, there's one of us. Those aren't bad odds, because we are willing to take the beating, and they're not."

"Well, thank you, Sandy. Your comments were well thought-out for a first time caller. That's it, folks…"

What a way to end a show! My only regret was that I didn't get a chance to thank my champion. In any case, it was good to know that she and people like her were out there, supporting us.

Fourteen

A MOTION WAS FILED with Judge Lerner by Byron's child advocate attorney, Ms. Biggins, that Karen and I be held in contempt of court for violating the court order. Biggins did not waste any time—I spoke to the press, the motion was filed, the hearing was scheduled, I was scared.

Oh, I joked with friends about metal files being baked in chocolate cakes, but inside I did not find my predicament funny in the least. However, I knew that I would make the same decision, even if the judge held me for trial. In a way, I felt that I was going one on one with the judge. I couldn't call him out in some back alley and pound the spit out of him, so this was my only way to do battle.

I doubted whether the judge had the guts to do anything

to me. The press would have a field day if I was led off to the county prison in handcuffs. I would be the noble father, a hero of sorts, and the judge would look like a heartless fool.

I had long lost my patience with the judge, CYS, the NAACP, the whole kit-and-caboodle. My generosity toward Lucy was all but gone, since I had witnessed for myself her lack of care for my Birdie. I knew the truth—she was a full-blown drug addict, and the only "child" she truly cared about was her crack habit. Once she had to fend for herself, she would go back to work, all right—as a prostitute.

While Lucy was receiving special care and treatment, I was on my way to court because I had opened my mouth and spoke out against the system. Rocking the boat, I discovered, was not a thing to do in Allegheny County. I wasn't going to be happy until the whole boat capsized. A father's fury, I was finding out, was just as strong as a mother's.

The day before the judge was to hear the motion, I learned from Peter that Judge Lerner had had another ex parte communication regarding the gag order. The judge, it seemed, had no idea how the gag order was put into effect. He accused Peter of agreeing to one.

"Of course, you know, Mike," Peter said, defending himself, "I never agreed to anything of the kind. I told the judge he was confused. It was Lucy's attorney who demanded that you stop talking to the press. I fought against the gag order with all my might."

I believed Peter, but Karen was absolutely convinced that Peter was lying. She picked up the phone and dialed Peter's office, though he did not accept her call.

"Listen, Darlene, you tell Peter I want to see a copy of the court transcript when the judge gagged us," Karen barked into the phone at Peter's secretary. "Not that I think he'll get us one, but give him the message anyway."

That evening Karen and I had a major fight over Peter.

"What is it with you?" Karen demanded, pointing her finger in my face. "Why do you blindly trust this guy?" I did not say anything. I didn't know why I did. I just did. If I gave Karen that answer, she would accuse me of being no older and wiser than Cameron.

Our argument continued for some time, and when I finally had had enough, I opened the French doors to the deck and walked outside to cool off. Karen followed me, still yelling about Peter.

Inside I was seething. I had never known such rage before. Although I loved Karen more than anything on earth, I was enraged I could not find a way to get her from badgering me.

Then I caught sight of four elegant terra cotta planters I had commissioned from a local artisan. Karen loved them, and hardly ever noticed them without commenting on their beauty. "Do you like these planters?" I said.

"What?" Karen questioned, adjusting her glasses on her nose.

"Just answer the question," I said calmly. "Do you like these planters?"

"Yes," Karen answered cautiously. "You know I do."

"Good." I lifted a planter above my head like a superman and threw it down with all my might to the cement patio below, where it smashed to smithereens. Two others followed suit, but the fourth was spared destruction when it landed safely in the grass.

Karen stared at the broken pieces for some time, too stunned to speak. "I'm subtracting the cost of those from Peter's bill," Karen said at last, still taking in the devastation. "Wouldn't you like to see some more things I like? Maybe you can break them too."

I followed her into the family room where she pointed out a crystal vase filled with red tulips. "I really like that," she said, handing me the vase. She didn't think I would do it, but I walked back out on to the deck and tossed the vase over the railing. After I heard it hit the patio with a satisfying crash, I turned and smiled at Karen.

"You're worse than a child." Karen was furious but I didn't care. I felt like trashing the whole house. The year and a half of playing the nice guy, calm and cool, had come to an end. While I couldn't throw CYS off the balcony, I could take my anger out on helpless crockery. I searched the deck for something else to throw.

Karen grabbed a plastic cup one of the kids had left on the end table and put it behind her back. "That's enough, Mike."

No, it wasn't. I was still like a raging bull. I lifted the oak table, gave it a heave-ho, and it too went plummeting to the ground. I stared down at my handiwork, a sort of collage in splintered wood, shattered terra cotta and disintegrated crystal. Now I was finished.

Karen didn't talk to me for the rest of the day. I cleaned up the debris and stuffed it in the trash. The kids noticed the missing items but had enough sense not to ask what had happened. Well, two of them did.

"Dad, did you accidentally drop the planters and table off the deck?" asked Connie when she got home from school. I detected a slight sneer on her lips.

"Yeah. You wanna be next?" I asked, stepping toward her. She squealed and bolted, giggling as I chased her through the house. Finally I grabbed her about the waist and began hauling her toward the door.

"Help, Mom!" she pleaded, reaching out for Karen. "Dad's gonna obliterate me!"

"You're on your own, sweetheart," Karen said, stirring the spaghetti sauce that was simmering on the stove.

I dragged Connie out onto the deck and eventually subdued her giggles. "Go down on the patio and lie there. When I give you the high sign, scream," I instructed. "I want to play a joke on your mother."

When Connie was in place, I gave her the signal. She screamed wonderfully well, a real blood-chiller. I waited for Karen to come running from the kitchen. I waited a bit longer.

"Scream again, but louder," I whispered down to Connie. "I don't think she heard."

"I heard," Karen said, sneaking up on me. I jumped out of my socks. "Get up here, Connie, and set the table."

"Spoil sport," I said, sticking my tongue out at Karen. She didn't find me funny.

"Five-year-old," she retaliated.

That evening she went to bed still very angry with me. We didn't dance that night.

WE ARRIVED IN COURT the day the motion was being heard and were informed that we were not allowed in the courtroom. I found this odd, since I was in the hot seat, but that was the judge's decision.

I entertained myself in my usual fashion while Peter went to my defense. I observed the other people, made up stories in my mind about their lives and argued with Karen about Peter's ability to keep me out of trouble. She still didn't trust him, and for the life of me, I still couldn't figure out why.

After twenty minutes or so, Peter motioned for us to meet him in his "annex office"—the second floor stairwell.

"So far so good," he said, wiping a few beads of sweat of his forehead. "The judge has given us a short recess so that I may discuss your options with you. First, he's holding both you and Karen in contempt…"

"But I never said anything to the press," Karen cried. "Did I, Mike?"

"That's right," I answered. "Not a word." That, I thought, showed remarkable restraint on Karen's part.

"That doesn't matter," Peter explained. "You were there during the interview with the media, so you're a party. The judge sees you two as one, so whatever happens to Mike is going to happen to you."

Karen let out a deep sigh of disgust. "Then I should have screamed my lungs out."

Peter waited for Karen to regain her composure. I was beginning to get the feeling that Peter did not care for Karen, either. This is great, I thought, a battle within a battle.

"Second," Peter said, "the judge says he'll forget this whole thing if you agree to waive your rights in this case."

Karen started laughing, and her laughter shot up the stairwell and echoed back to us. It was like hearing her in stereo.

"You're kidding," she choked. "Tell me you're joking." Suddenly Karen stopped laughing. "The judge wants me to give up my rights?"

Peter nodded.

"No."

"Well, hold on a minute," said Peter, leaning against the wall. "You might want to reconsider your answer. I think the judge is being more than generous here, because if we don't settle this matter today, you truly may find yourself in court and possibly in jail, paying a fine. Biggins is asking that you make monetary compensation to Byron. She included that stipulation in her motion."

"What?" I could not believe my ears. We had said publicly a million times that we would pay for Byron's education and see to it that his needs were taken care of. We were in the process of setting up a trust fund for him. Now they wanted a cash settlement? No way.

What kind of people were these? I guessed this was a situation where someone decided to rob from the rich and give to the poor. Unfortunately, we were not wealthy—just comfortably off, and we were getting less comfortable with each check we wrote to Peter.

"The judge may go for it if you choose to fight," Peter warned. As the sweat poured from his forehead and dripped down his face, he pulled a handkerchief from his coat pocket and mopped his glistening brow. The stairwell was chilly, but Peter was roasting.

"So what if he does?" Karen was defiant. She puffed herself up as much as she could, trying to look bigger and taller than she was. Karen was scared, but brave.

"I don't think you realize the trouble you are in." Peter's voice was beginning to quiver. I could tell he was growing more and more frustrated with Karen. "The judge has three options before him…"

"Listen, Peter," Karen said, stepping closer to Peter. "I know I'm in deep, but I want you to listen carefully: I am not afraid of what the judge can do to me. You tell him we will not, under any circumstances, give up any of our rights. You also tell him we will not roll over and play dead. If he wants to send us to jail, then tell him to do it and get it over with."

Peter looked at me, his eyes begging for help. "I agree with Karen," I murmured.

He was none too happy with our decision, but he finally agreed to present it. When he returned to the courtroom, Karen and I took our seats in the hallway. We believed in our rights to speak our minds.

I could not believe that Peter was even hinting that we should cave in to the judge's demand. He wouldn't suggest that, I told myself. I must have misunderstood what he was saying. He was just explaining our situation, like any good attorney would do.

Another twenty minutes passed. Peter emerged from the courtroom looking tired and disheveled. His silk tie was askew and his silver hair, normally English boarding-school neat, was sticking up like the fur of a frightened cat.

"Should we go home and pack our toothbrushes?" I asked, straining to keep my teeth from chattering as the three of us walked back into the stairwell.

"The judge decided to keep the motion open," Peter said with a smile.

"What does that mean?" Karen demanded.

"The judge is giving you another chance. If you're good, the contempt charge will just go away. However, from now until the judge feels like putting this matter to rest, you are under the threat of being hauled back into court."

"In essence, the judge is trying to blackmail us again." Karen paced back and forth in the tiny stairwell, then turned to Peter. "Why did he really do this?"

"Well, legally speaking, it was a good move. If he would have ruled on the motion, you could have appealed and possible gotten it moved out of his courtroom. I don't think he wants to lose that control."

"You bet he doesn't," said Karen. "He knows what he did was wrong."

"Well, please—stay out of trouble," Peter said, trying to sound as if he were joking. I knew he was serious. I couldn't help but feel that Peter would be beside himself with joy if we never talked to the press again.

A group of reporters were waiting outside the courtroom. Karen and I looked at each other. We knew what we had to do. When they fired their questions at us, we answered every query in detail. I came down harder on the judge than I had in the past, and I hoped, when he read my comments in the morning paper, they would feel like blows to his jaw.

It was one of those long drives home. Karen spent the entire trip pointing out Peter's deficiencies, and I defended him as best I could. Even so, I had some nagging doubts about the events that had taken place in the judge's courtroom.

Lucy was released from Sojourner House a few days after our court ordeal. The director publicly stated that Lucy had "graduated" from the program. When I asked a Sojourner representative if Lucy was off drugs, the woman simply said, "She's graduated."

I went ballistic. Did Lucy "graduate" with an A or D-minus? Was she clean or kinda clean? Why was everyone covering for this woman? All I wanted was a straight answer and documented proof that what I was being told was indeed true.

Peter filed a motion that Lucy's records be open for review by Karen and me. Since we were still a party to the proceedings, we were entitled to know that our Birdie was in safe hands. But, as was expected, the judge denied our request. I doubted that even he had reviewed Lucy's medical records and progress reports. Truth wasn't what the judge was interested in: Keeping in favor with the powers that be was.

A few days later, on April 15th, Karen and I were back at juvenile hall. We wanted to know before the press did if the judge was going to allow Lucy to care for her children outside of the auspices of Sojourner House. As it turned out, he allowed Byron and Georgia to live with Lucy in her new home, but he did not release either child from the "protective" care of CYS. A caseworker was to monitor Lucy's progress and Byron's care.

I shook my head when I heard the results. If CYS looked after things the way they did when they first dumped Byron on us, then Lucy was free and clear. CYS might make a few feeble attempts at keeping tabs on my son, but even if Lucy were standing in front of Jane Worley, snorting cocaine, I was convinced the judge would never know about it. It would make CYS look bad if Lucy failed.

As if they could look any worse. Jane Worley had in the past week attempted to justify CYS's decision to return three children to a father who was charged with killing his wife. "There isn't any law against it," she was quoted as saying, in the newspaper. Fortunately, a judge in Juvenile Court reversed CYS's decision, claiming that CYS had not informed him of the man's criminal record.

Hey, judge, I thought to myself when I read the story in the newspaper, criminal records don't count, remember? If they did, Byron's sister would not be with her drug-pushing grandmother.

One last hope remained for Karen and me. The judge had not yet removed Byron from the state's protection and would not be making a final ruling to remove him from the courts until June 15. That gave me two months to prove to the judge that Lucy indeed was incapable of caring for her children.

I called Regina as soon as I got home from court. She already knew about the ruling. (News traveled fast in Pittsburgh, proof that our small-town mentality still existed.)

"You gotta help me," I begged. "I have to find out where Lucy's living. I've gotta know that Byron is okay."

"I've already put my feelers out, but so far, everyone is real hush-hush," Regina said. "Someone is going to great lengths to keep that lady hidden. I'll keep in touch."

Our conversations were always short, but they were normally very sweet. I trusted that Regina would learn Lucy's whereabouts in the next few hours.

I was wrong.

Weeks passed and nothing transpired. I was out of my mind with worry. Lucy had dropped completely out of sight; however, Byron and his sister were seen from time to time in the care of their grandmother.

This put me into heart failure. The grandmother had recently pleaded guilty to selling coke and heroin to an undercover policeman. She did not receive a jail term, but was paroled without probation. What was wrong with this picture? The woman was a habitual criminal. I guess crime did pay...or else someone was paid off. I was growing more and more cynical with every passing second.

When the news broke about the grandmother's guilt, CYS scrambled to revoke the granny's visitation privileges, and she was not allowed to see Byron or his sister. Of course, the law had required CYS to do a check on all placements, but somehow the grandmother had been overlooked. CYS had another embarrassment to add to the list. But it didn't matter how many oversights, mistakes or murders took place—CYS, like the judge, was beyond the law.

I called a good friend who was outraged over the gross misbehavior of CYS. She organized a postcard campaign aimed at bringing attention to CYS's inadequacies and our concern over Byron's safety. Thousands of postcards, all pre-addressed to Judge Lerner, were distributed to area churches and businesses, but by the time he received the first postcard, the press was already onto the story. A local reporter accused me of orchestrating the whole thing, then condemned my friend in an article in the next morning's newspaper.

The tide was turning against us in the media. As far as they were concerned, Lucy was clean, happy and a great mother; after all, Judge Lerner had said so. What was the Derzacks' problem? Articles began to appear in the newspaper praising CYS and their efforts to help children. When an article came out about a group called CASA, a volunteer program overseeing CYS's placements, I questioned what was going on.

I met with one of our sources, code name "Margo," to question her about the new CASA program. Margo, who was in her late seventies, had succeeded in forcing the county into having public hearings on CYS's questionable practices. The hearings resulted in a ton of suggestions, but the county commissioners never implemented any of them, including a CASA program. The judges and CYS were adamantly opposed to having independent volunteers overseeing the judge's decisions and CYS's placements. Why all of a sudden did CASA now seem like a good idea to CYS?

"Well, what do you think?" I asked Margo, as we sat down on her living room sofa.

"I think it's more or less an attempt to get good P.R.," she answered, handing me a glass of lemonade, which I downed in one gulp.

"Whoa," I choked. "A little on the tart side."

"Good, ain't it?" she chuckled. "Here," she said, handing me an envelope, "I just received this information."

I opened the envelopment. It was the budget for the CASA program. Damn! I said to myself. CYS was funding it.

"Are they allowed to do this?" I asked. It didn't seem kosher that independent volunteers were funded by the organization they were supposed to oversee. What if CYS did not like the recommendation of a volunteer regarding a particular placement? Those that had the money had the control.

"Weird, huh?" Margo said, taking a swallow of lemonade. "I haven't been able to find out where CASA's offices are yet, but my source tells me that the University of

Pittsburgh is tied into this somehow. I know the second in command is from CYS's ranks."

"Who trains the volunteers?" I asked.

"CYS." Margo's answer did not surprise me.

"Are they allowed to do this?"

"I'm looking into it," she answered. "Right now, it appears that if a CASA program can't get funding, CYS is permitted to get it started. At some point CYS should step completely out."

"Did they try getting funding anywhere?" I was filled with questions.

"Don't know yet. I do know that a judge in the central part of the state is as mad as hell over Pittsburgh's CASA. He said he's willing to make a public statement that CYS should not be funding this sort of program."

"Great," I said, refilling my glass. The tart taste was beginning to grow on me.

"Well, maybe not," she observed. "Who from the media is willing to investigate? I'd say, from the recent wonderful articles on CYS, that no one is."

"Maybe you're wrong on that one," I said. "I have a close contact and I think she'll look into it."

"Mike, sometimes I think you're plain stupid." Margo shook her head. "Things just aren't that cut and dried. How do you think these articles came to be? I bet you any money Jane Worley or someone with even bigger connections had a meeting with the newspaper and convinced them to do a few favorable articles. After all, CYS has been getting beat-up pretty bad lately. "

So a little politicking was going on. It made sense and it was okay by me, because CYS was going to screw up again. It was only a matter of time.

On my way home from Margo's, Regina called me on my car phone.

"Mike, I've got some news for you," she said in her usual low whisper.

"Is Byron all right?" My pulse began to race.

"As far as I know, but I'm not calling about Byron, I'm calling about Lucy. She's in the PennFree program. I'm relatively certain that they have supplied her with housing. If Lucy screws up, they'll get rid of her in a heartbeat. They're not into playing games."

"Where is she living?" I asked.

"Somewhere on the North Side. However, Byron and Georgia are with grammy dearest most of the time. I've already had someone call the judge about it."

"Thanks." I hung up the phone and turned into my neighborhood. It was obvious that CYS didn't give a hoot what the judge's orders were. They were supposed to prevent the grandmother from seeing the children unsupervised, but I didn't trust them any further than I could throw Jane Worley. In fact, it seemed to me that CYS was using the situation with Byron's grandmother as just another ploy to get more money. I could just hear their reasoning: "We're understaffed and underpaid and overburdened...give us more money." The only thing that caused CYS problems, it seemed to me, was that they simply did not care what was best for the kids, law or no law.

It was not until the second week of May that I heard from Regina again, this time with bad news. Byron had been in and out of Children's Hospital since Lucy left Sojourner House, and he was there now.

What was the matter with my baby? What had those people done to him now?

I grabbed Karen and rushed out of the house. I was going to see my boy come hell or high water. Karen was on the car phone to every newspaper, radio and television station in a fifty mile radius. If this tip proved to be truth, I wanted the world to know my boy was sick enough to be hospitalized three times in one month. What had Lucy done to my Birdie?

I ran into the lobby of the hospital and went directly to admissions. "What room is Baby Byron in?" I panted.

The receptionist looked up at me, then asked me to wait while she checked.

I was in a cold sweat, shivering with fear. My poor boy. He never had so much as a scratch when he was with us. My poor boy. I paced back and forth like a coyote in a cage.

Two security guards entered the lobby. "Are you the one asking about Baby Byron?"

"Yes," I answered.

"Please come with us." Oh my God, I thought, this was worse than I imagined. What if he were dead?

The guards escorted me to the door, then told me to leave or the police would be notified and they would remove me.

"What the hell is going on?" I begged. "I just want to see my child. Please."

"I'm sorry, Mr. Derzack," one of the guards said. "I can't allow that. Please, just go home."

I considered making a run for the elevators. At least, that was what my heart was telling me to do, but my head ordered me to leave the hospital. Maybe, I reasoned, the press will have better luck than me.

Karen was waiting on the sidewalk in front of the hospital, crying into a tissue. "Is he all right?"

I explained the situation to her as we walked to the car. I called a few of our contacts at the newspapers, but they couldn't give me any information either. In fact, they too had been warned to stay away from the hospital.

Peter placed a call into Judge Lerner and was advised by the jurist's secretary that the judge was aware of the situation, and had already looked into the matter. Byron was suffering from a cold.

Right, I thought to myself. A cold, and he's in the hospital. Worse yet, the judge believes this bullshit. Or maybe he was the one making it up.

It took some doing, but finally a few of our contacts persuaded a hospital insider to give us information. It wasn't much to go on, but we learned that Byron was probably having a nervous reaction to being moved around so much. Byron's records were removed from the computer and his file was supposedly locked safely away in the administrator's office. Lucy did not have the power to make these things happen, but CYS did. I was beginning to believe that the judge was a mere figurehead; it was Jane Worley who was the real power source.

A few days later Byron was released from the hospital and was seen back in the care of his grandmother. Lucy had been spotted with a new boyfriend, a known drug dealer.

In desperation I called PennFree to ask how Lucy was doing. Although they were friendly and seemed truly compassionate toward me and my family, they would not confirm that Lucy was a part of their program. I understood their reasoning but I was not about to accept their wishy-washy answers. Still, there was nothing I could do.

I was hitting an all-time low when I returned to the shop late one evening to catch up on the bookkeeping and heard a message on the answering machine for me to call Bill's sister, Sally. I wrote down her number on a scratch pad, then got distracted in the back room as I checked up on the workload. Nothing had gotten done that day. I noticed that Bill's initials were missing from the daily employee checklist.

A wave of fear spread over me. Bill was sick.

I called Sally right away.

"Mike, I'm glad you called," Sally said, clearing her throat. "I'm sorry to say this, but I have some bad news for you."

"Is Bill sick?" I interrupted. Please say he was only sick.

"Bill died this afternoon. His heart gave out on him."

I began to cry. I thought my heart could not possibly shatter any more than it already had. I was wrong.

"Mike," Sally said, "Mike, it's okay. Bill knew his time had come. He went peaceful, in my arms. It's okay."

No, it wasn't. Bill—my friend, my mentor, my advisor—was gone. No, it wasn't okay. He left me when I needed him most. And what about Charles? He had left Charles alone, too.

I calmed myself down long enough to learn that Bill had

already been cremated. He didn't want anybody staring at him, saying how much he looked like himself. That sounded like Bill. No funeral either.

"He just wants me to sprinkle his ashes," Sally said.

"Where?"

"He said something about his battlefield, but I don't know where that is."

"I do," I said, wiping the tears from my eyes. "Please, if it's okay with you, let me take care of it, okay?"

"Sure," she answered. "Bill would like that."

"Sally, if you ever need anything, you call me." Taking care of Sally was the least I could do for Bill.

She said that she would be fine and thanked me for my offer. After a little more conversation, we hung up.

Now I felt truly alone. I walked around the shop, thinking it would never be the same again. Who would curse at and cajole the presses, calling them by name (Huey, Dewey and Louie)? Who would remember everyone's birthday and bring in soda pop and cupcakes? Who would be there to pick me up when I faltered?

No, nothing would be the same without Bill.

I studied the plasterboard wall that by now had received seventeen blows. I turned to leave the room, then thought, *What the hell* and delivered one final punch. For Bill.

Karen already knew about Bill, and although she loved him dearly, she was relieved that he went out on his own terms. No doctors, no "life-saving" machines, no one having to take care of him, no ceremony. Karen was right, of course, and maybe someday I could see Bill's passing with the same stoic attitude. But for now, I wanted to be left alone to mourn.

Fifteen

THE JUDGE TOOK AWAY our final visitations with Byron because I had challenged the gag order. It did not come as any surprise to Karen or me. In fact, instead of punishing us, the judge had made an important decision for us: We now no longer had to decide whether we should continue to put Byron through the emotional torment of returning him to Lucy after a day with us.

Bill was now fertilizer for the two sickly-looking pine trees in Pinegrove Terrace. I had carried out his last request and hummed taps as I did it. I quickly came to realize that as long as I remembered Bill, he would still be alive. So I vowed to keep him in my heart until we were both up in heaven, swapping war stories and drinking Iron City Beer. I loved that old man and, God help me, I was missing him something fierce.

I searched out Charles and finally found him in a decrepit video game arcade near the Terrace. Charles turned away from me after I told him the sad news. "Don't matter," he said, over the beeping and whirring of the infernal games. He put a quarter to "hold his place" on the machine that another boy was playing. "He was just some crazy old man that was always poking his nose in where it had no business being."

"Yeah," I agreed. "That was Bill. He was a nosy old coot."

Suddenly Charles' face grew dark with fury. "You sayin' his death don't matter?" Charles said, grabbing hold of my collar. I started to push him away, but stopped myself. He was only up to my armpits, but he had quite a grip. He also had quite a lot of grief.

"Come here, boy," I said, wrapping my arms around him and pulling him close to me. "It's okay to feel bad." He began to cry like a baby. I cried with him. Almost none of the other boys in the arcade blinked an eye or even looked in our direction. They were used to bad news happening all around them.

"He was a good man, can't nobody say he wasn't," Charles whimpered, rubbing his eyes. "That's God's honest truth."

It sure was. This poor child had lost his father. I wanted to wipe his pain away and make the world good and right for him.

"I was thinking, Charles," I said, acting as if I were the helpless party. "I need a pal right now, someone who can help me get over losing Bill. You willing to talk with me now and again?"

He sniffled, then straightened up. "Yeah, sure," he said regaining his cockiness. "But if we're to be 'pals,' let's get a few things straight. First, I know who you are. You're Bill's boss. He got a hoot out of you givin' me those batteries. Said it damned near drove him crazy lookin' for those things. He told me, too, if anything ever happened to him, you'd be a wreck, and I'll be damned if you ain't. He asked me to take care of you. I shouldn't even try, 'cause you sure look like a hopeless case, but I promised him I'd look after you. Second, I ain't doin' this to get at your money or nothing. I know easier ways to make bread. I'm doin' it for Bill."

"Understood."

"Good."

His turn came up on the machine, and he offered to let me play. It was a vicious hand-to-hand combat game, full of blood-letting and bone-crushing, and I just didn't have the stomach for it. "Maybe another time," I said lamely.

He smiled. "Okay, another time. You can play something less gory."

I guess, in a way, Charles had inherited me.

After I left the arcade I headed toward Peter's office, picked up a copy of the lawsuit we were filing, leafed through it in the parking garage, then continued on home.

We were suing just about everyone on God's green earth, or so it seemed: the county, CYS, the commissioners, Jane Worley, the NAACP, and Reverend Johns, among many others for racism, and the police, for breaking and entering into my home without a search warrant. All and all, thirty-six individuals and organizations were named in the suit. I was serious about getting access to records on Lucy, and I'd come to believe this was the only way to do so. I'd hit them where it hurt, in the pocketbook. Peter had been dragging his feet getting the lawsuit drafted, and it took more than one phone call from Karen to put his butt in gear. I didn't understand why Peter had not filed earlier. I thought the suit should have been filed before the April 15th hearing. That might have given us some bargaining power, and I did not want this suit to appear as if it were being filed as a matter of sour grapes.

It was being filed to prevent this from ever happening to anyone else ever again. I wanted it to cost CYS dearly, to force them to think twice before playing with another child's life.

As the tall buildings of the Pittsburgh skyline receded in the rearview mirror, I let my mind wander. Karen, Peter and myself had a major go-round about naming Judge Lerner in the suit just a few days earlier. Karen and I wanted to do it, but Peter had advised against it. I shuddered when I thought back on the conversation Peter and my wife had had, because I knew I was about to walk into one of the same magnitude in just a few minutes.

"You're just afraid of getting the judge angry with you," Karen accused Peter. "Who are you working for, anyway?"

Peter had sat quietly and taken the abuse. Sometimes I couldn't help but wonder if there were not some truth in what Karen was saying: Whose side was Peter on?

"Mike, you have one more shot at getting Byron, so don't get the judge any more upset than he already is," Peter had pleaded. "Let's wait until after the June 15th hearing. If he releases Lucy from the court and the kids from the system, then we can always add his name in later."

"Now!" Karen screamed. "Why is it that when I speak to you, you don't hear me? Who in the hell do you think is paying your bills? It's not the judge, it's me. Now, you will do as I say?"

Peter had nodded, seemingly acknowledging Karen's request.

But now I knew I was in trouble. I had looked at the suit, and the judge's name wasn't in it. The closer I got to home, the more I dreaded Karen's reaction. She would notice in an instant that Judge Lerner had been left out.

Karen greeted me at the door, anxious to read over the suit. We had spent a month fine-tuning it and, except for the missing judge, I thought it was ready to be filed.

"I knew it," Karen said, picking up the phone. She dialed Peter's number, got his answering service, and left a message for him to call her, no matter how late it was.

When he did not return her call, Karen left two more messages, both with his secretary. By the time Karen spoke to Peter it was too late to add the judge's name. The papers had to be filed that afternoon.

"Convenient, ain't it?" Karen shouted, actually throwing the receiver into its cradle.

"Peter's only doing what he thinks is right," I said, defending him.

"Peter is doing what's right for the judge," Karen countered. "What is your problem, anyway? Why can't you see Peter for what he is and get us a new lawyer?"

"If that's what you want..." I shrugged my shoulders and locked myself in the library to read the newspaper. Peter was becoming a sore spot between Karen and me. It seemed all of our fights were because of him. But if Karen wanted a new attorney, let her find one.

I sat down at my desk and scanned the paper. An article on CYS's trans-racial placement policy immediately caught my interest. The report made reference to the written policy that was adopted December 15, 1992. So it did exist after all.

Karen and I had been trying for almost two years to get a copy of that policy; now it was public. I called CYS and for the millionth time asked them to send me the policy. I referred to the article and this time I felt that CYS had no option but to comply. But I had been wrong before. After I hung up with CYS, I decided to call the reporter who wrote the story, and she agreed to fax the policy to me. This was getting exciting. I finally was going to be given a document that explained to me why Byron had been taken away.

I shared the news with Karen. She was so relieved that she momentarily forgot about Peter. "They really put into writing a policy that is discriminating?" Karen asked, pouring me a glass of grapefruit juice. It was supposed to help me lose weight. "That was stupid, don't you think?"

It sure was.

The next morning I arrived at the shop a couple of hours earlier than usual. Instead of arriving at seven o'clock, I was sitting at my desk, drinking coffee and reading the fax before five A.M.

I was no attorney, judge, or lawmaker, but I knew that CYS's trans-racial placement policy was wrong. It basically forbid people of one color to take care of a child of another color. Strangely enough, it droned on at length about providing a black child with proper ethnic hair care, but it failed to go into such detail when it came to providing that child with a safe home.

That afternoon, I received another copy of the policy, this time from CYS. But there was a major difference: Some of the pages were missing, and other pages had sections that had been blacked out with a black magic marker. Poor CYS, they weren't smart enough to change the table of contents to match the document they had sent me. I knew from the complete document what they were trying to hide: They had tried to make the policy less "colored-oriented."

I dialed Margo's number and much to my delight I caught her at home. I needed her advice on how to handle the discrepancies in the two policies.

"Have a few minutes?" I asked.

"For you, always." Margo sounded out of breath. "What's up?" I explained the problem.

"That's real interesting, Mikey," she said, pausing for a moment. "I just read about the written policy myself in yesterday's paper. I'd say that up until now CYS was pretty good at keeping this thing under wraps. I've been working all morning to track down what is going on, and I think there are three versions in existence—the one you have, the one the newspaper has and the one CYS is enforcing. Whatever's going on, you can bet it stinks."

"You think this kind of policy is even legal?" I questioned, staring at the date it was implemented. December 15, 1992. Damn it! That was around the time CYS attempted to steal Byron the first time.

"Let's put it this way. In all of my years as an advocate, I've never heard or seen any other organization putting this kind of thing in writing. I think you should feel honored."

"Why?"

"Looks like CYS did this just for you." She chuckled a little, then took a deep breath, as if she were taking a puff from a cigarette. "Write a letter to the U.S. Department of Health and Human Services, Office of Civil Rights in Philadelphia. Have the address?"

I had never even heard of them, so I grabbed a card from the rolodex and began to write as Margo spouted out the address. "They should have a field day with this one," she said, her chuckle turning into a full-fledged laugh. After all the time Margo had put in working to expose CYS, she deserved the first laugh.

"One more thing. Did CYS ever have a trans-racial placement policy before December '92?" I asked.

"Not a written one." She was still laughing when she hung up the phone.

This twisted attempted by CYS to cover the truth was not only sloppy but also, as Karen would say, "plain stupid." It also warranted a call to Jane Worley. A sympathetic CYS board member had given me Worley's private work number. I loved it. The only way she'd be able to avoid me now was to change her number. If Jane were in, she would have to speak to me. She had no other choice. I dialed the magic number.

"Yes?" Jane Worley breathed slowly into the phone. I felt that she was expecting a more intimate caller than me.

"Good afternoon," I cheerfully greeted her. "How are you this fine day, Ms. Jane Worley?"

"Who is this?" she asked, sounding a little confused.

"Your favorite ex-foster parent, Mike Derzack," I chirped.

"What do you want?" she demanded, her voice as cold as January.

I paused for a moment and took a sip from my steaming coffee. I leaned back in my chair and put my feet up on the desk. I liked having the upper hand for once. "I got the trans-racial placement policy your people sent me. Thanks for getting it to me so quickly. What's it been? Two years? Are you using messengers on horseback?"

"I have no time for your sarcasm," she hissed. "Get to the point of your call."

"Well, Jane," I said, feeling a little like a cat that had caught a mouse, a rat, a pigeon *and* a canary all at once. "There seems to be a little tiny problem. You forgot to send the whole thing. A few pages seem to be missing. Oh, I know you're very busy, but..."

"Did you check the envelope?"

"Wait, let's see." I paused, pretending to check the envelope. "I checked the envelope."

"Well, there were some changes recently made to the policy. Maybe that's the copy you received," she said, covering her tail.

"I wished you would have sent me the December 15, 1992 version, not last night's version," I replied. "But, never mind, I secured a copy on my own."

For the first time since I had met her, Jane Worley seemed at a loss for words. I could just imagine her running through a mental list of people who had access to the original policy. She would never believe that her own source at the newspaper had turned on her.

"Well, it seems that you have what you need, so if you haven't any other..."

"No, there's nothing else...for now," I said as pleasant as pie. Jane Worley—what a pill.

I hung up the phone, then dashed off a letter to the Civil Rights Office and enclosed a copy of both policies. While I was at it, I wrote an extensive letter to the Judicial Conduct Board in Harrisburg regarding Judge Lerner. I enclosed all the articles to date where the judge's bias showed and a copy of the all the motions and court documents that I was able to secure. I heard that the Judicial Conduct Board was just as hard on judges as the AMA was on doctors, which is to say, not hard at all. But, what the hell, I thought, it was at least worth a shot. Now and again they made an example out of someone, just so they could show a reason for their existence. Maybe I'd be lucky. Maybe they would find Judge Lerner to be a little unfit.

⚜   ⚜   ⚜

THE BIG DAY ARRIVED. It was June 15th, hot and sunny. Karen and I made yet another trip to juvenile hall. This was the day the judge was expected to declare Lucy freed from the courts and Byron and his sister no longer wards of the state. We had received reports from our sources that Lucy was planning to move out of state with the two children as soon as she was financially able. We were told that Lucy thought living in Pittsburgh was too "hot" for her, that she needed to get away where no one knew her.

Lucy did not have a job, but that didn't seem to matter to the courts or anyone else. She was still provided living quarters courtesy of PennFree, and, to our knowledge she was back to her old tricks, so to speak.

We had filed a motion to prevent the judge from releasing Lucy and the kids, but I knew that it would be denied. Our day in court had not yet arrived, yet I still clung to the hope that one day the truth would win out.

Peter, Karen and I had agreed not to speak with the press right away if the ruling was in favor of Lucy. I needed time to gather my thoughts. I knew I would be in no condition to speak and I did not want to sound bitter toward Lucy. I wasn't, really. I knew Lucy was incapable of taking charge and pulling herself free of the forces that had gathered around her. She was, from the start, as vulnerable as a child.

Karen and I sat in the courtroom, knowing that we would not be permitted to speak. Against all hope I prayed for a miracle. I knew God heard me, but He didn't agree with my timing. Our requests to be heard were denied; a lawyer from the Civil Liberties Union who wanted to present a brief objecting to Karen and me being held in contempt was told to leave; and the judge announced that "both kids are friendly and well adjusted. The bottom line, they are being well cared for by their mother."

I knew we had lost. I tried to prepare myself for the final verdict, but when the judge ruled in favor of Lucy I felt as though I had been flattened by a steamroller. Then as if I had not been crushed enough, the judge ruled us out of Byron's life completely. We were not allowed any visits.

"Has any good come out of today?" I asked, walking out of the courthouse. I held my head high and took a deep breath to steady myself. I had nothing to be ashamed of. I had fought a good fight. Although it appeared I had been knocked out, I would learn to box differently the next time.

Before Peter could answer, we noticed Lucy carrying Byron in her arms and holding on to Georgia's hand. "Let it go, Mike," Peter said, putting his arm around my shoulder. "Another day, another time."

The press gathered around her, shouting questions.

She looked scared as she repeated over and over again, "No comment. I said, no comment."

Her attorney did the same.

I repeated my question. "Has any good come out of today?"

"No, not much," Peter said, looking over at the group of reporters. He smiled and waved to them. "But we do have one thing to be grateful for?"

"That is?"

"He didn't find you in contempt..."

"...At least for today." I finished his sentence for him. "Did he allow any of our information to be entered into the records?"

Peter, still smiling at the reporters, shook his head, no.

"Did he answer any of our concerns about the grandmother caring for Byron?" Again, no. The judge no longer had to wear blinders. He was already blind.

"I'll call you when I get back to the office," Peter promised. "Maybe we should arrange a press conference or something."

"Maybe," I said.

The media was not pressing Karen and me for an interview. We made our way across the street to our car with little problem. I found that unusual. Normally they would rely on us to give them information regarding the proceedings since the hearing was closed to them and they had no other way of getting information.

I glanced back at juvenile hall to say farewell to that old brick building, but something told me I would be inside those walls in a very short time. Lucy was still talking to reporters, her supporters gathered about her, having their say, too. This was their day of victory. For Byron's sake, I wished they had something to celebrate, but I knew they couldn't protect Lucy forever.

A handful of reporters were talking to Peter, who was taking an awful long time to say "no comment."

"What is that guy doing now?" Karen asked, glaring at me. "He better not be speaking for us."

Karen felt as though we were cursed with Peter and had persuaded me to talk with other attorneys. We met with several but could not find one willing to take the case. A few were willing to take pieces, but the scope of the federal suit and our fight for Byron seemed to them to be "too time-consuming."

Eventually, I convinced myself that Peter was fated to be our attorney because he had a role to play out in all of this. It would all make sense in the end, I was certain.

With nothing better to do, Karen and I went to the shop. Bill's absence left a huge hole in the place, and I did not feel very comfortable there anymore.

Peter took his sweet time calling us at the shop. When we finally heard from him, we learned that there would be no reason to hold a press conference. The judge had already held one.

What! I thought. A judge holding a press conference regarding a Juvenile Court decision? I was flabbergasted. His twenty-minute hearing took him two hours to explain to the press. If only he had used the time to search out the truth of his decision, our life—and Byron's—would have been different.

"I guess we'll have to wait to read about it in the morning paper," I said to Peter, more curious than angry that the judge had out-maneuvered me. It was a good move and I respected that. He got to the press before we could. He suckered them into believing that he was welcoming them back to his courtroom. He was using them, but it served the media's purpose as well as his. It wasn't often a judge spoke so openly to the press. I would have ignored my side, too, for a scoop like that.

I knew the moment the newspaper arrived. Karen was standing by my side of the bed staring down at me, slamming the newspaper against her hand. Her face was scarlet and I swear I saw steam coming out of her ears.

"Bad news?" I smiled feebly.

"I guess that depends on which side of the fence you're on." Karen eyes narrowed. "And, since our attorney seems more on the judge's side than ours, I'd say that yes, for us it's bad news."

"No use in dragging it out. Let me have the paper." I sat up as Karen handed me the front page. What had Peter done now?

Suddenly I spied his name. "...Attorney for the Derzacks said that, 'the judge had conducted a fair hearing and addressed a number of our concerns.'" That may have been his opinion, but it wasn't Karen's or mine. I couldn't understand why Peter would say such a thing.

"What are you going to do about it?" Karen demanded.

"I'll ask him not to talk to the press anymore," I answered. What else could I do? What was done was done. I couldn't call the newspaper and tell them that my attorney talked out of turn. It would make our ranks look confused and disorganized. I could not let anyone know that there was any dissention.

"Don't ask, Mike. Tell him. Put it in writing. Gag him if you have to."

I shook my head. "Karen, let's not be too hasty. It's easy to get caught up in the press. You know that. They seem to have a way to drag answers out of people. Peter probably just isn't too skilled in dealing with them." Nevertheless, I knew we would have to reprimand him for the damage he had caused, and I knew that reprimanding Peter would be like yelling at my father.

🌿   🌿   🌿

KAREN AND I TRIED to get our lives back to normal, but without Byron that would just never happen. We all desperately wanted to believe that Byron was safe, but we had no way of knowing for certain. The federal lawsuit would force CYS, Sojourner House, the police and the commissioners to surrender their records on Lucy. But by then, if we didn't do something else to hurry the process along, it could be too late. I lived in sheer terror that Lucy would leave Pittsburgh. It would be easy for her to just disappear to some other state, get on welfare and place Byron and Georgia with some other CYS.

Our letter to the Civil Rights Office caused such a stir that they launched an investigation into our allegation that CYS's trans-racial placement policy was unconstitutional and racially biased. The newspapers picked up on the story because, if CYS was found in noncompliance with federal policy, they would have sixty days to fix the problem or face losing their federal funding.

Jane Worley, in an interview, said that the policy had been changed a few weeks prior to the hearing, but wouldn't say what those changes were or produce a copy of the new policy. She was a slick one all right. The changes that were made were a few deletions in an effect to conceal, not improve. Jane Worley had better be wearing a life jacket, I thought. She was about to be tossed overboard.

"Listen, Mike," Karen said one evening while we were in the kitchen, pouring over the state of our affairs concerning Byron. "Since the court has released Byron, and CYS no longer has any say over us or Byron, maybe we can deal directly with Lucy. No lawyers, just people talking. Like it should be."

"How will we get in touch with her?" I asked, liking the idea. Before Sojourner and CYS conspired to keep Lucy from us, we had been doing just fine. I think Lucy even liked us. Maybe one on one, free from the NAACP, Reverend Johns, and people like LaPort, we could make things work. Of course we could. We would make it work. People left to their own devices often accomplished the impossible.

"I'm going to call Byron's great-aunt and invite them over for a picnic and a swim. Maybe they can come tomorrow. It's supposed to be really hot. It'll be nice for them to get out of the city. I'll ask her to extend the invitation to Lucy."

Surprisingly, the aunt was receptive. She and Karen chatted for a little while. Even though the aunt declined our invitation, she said it was fine by her if Lucy wanted to take the boys, and she promised to deliver the message to Lucy. "She'll call you back," the aunt assured us.

It was as easy as that. Lucy was going to call. We were headed in the right direction.

After waiting a few hours by the phone, Lucy finally did call. Karen and I were in seventh heaven when she accepted. We both spoke to Lucy. I thought she sounded a little shaky and she seemed to ramble a bit, but I figured she was probably nervous. We had been through a lot together. She probably heard that we had grown two heads, a tail and fangs, so no wonder she was nervous.

"I'm real sorry about all this mess," Lucy said. Her voice suddenly grew soft and low, like a child hoping to get back in the good graces of an angry parent.

"We're not blaming you for anything," Karen said. "Whatever happened is water under the bridge. What matters now is that we talk over our problems. Who knows, Lucy? You may just discover that Mike and I aren't such bad people after all."

"Oh, I never, not once thought that you were anything but kind people." Lucy's voice quivered; she was nervous again. "It was everyone talkin' at me that messed up my head. It was hard being watched all the time...but like you said, 'that's water under the bridge.' I have lots to share with you about CYS. They ain't such good people, you know. They lied to me all the time. They said I was nothing but dirt. It's true. I heard them say it. I'll bet you thought they were for me, but they weren't, they..."

"We can talk tomorrow," Karen said. We both could tell from the excited tone of Lucy's voice that she was getting agitated. We would have plenty of time tomorrow and hopefully in the months and years to come to talk about CYS and straighten out our differences.

"Okay, tomorrow," she said. "I think you'll be real happy to see how Byron is doing, but don't be alarmed or nothing because he has a cold. Just some sniffles. But, he's doing fine…real fine. It's just a cold."

"The other kids are welcome, too," Karen repeated for the fourth time.

"Okay, I'll bring 'em all, if I can get someone to bring us," Lucy said with a hint of resignation. Maybe we were doing too much to soon.

"It won't be a bother for us," I said quickly. "But if it's too much for you, then we can have the brood over another time. It will give us a chance to talk without too much interruption. And, if you need a ride, you call us and I'll be right over to pick you up. I'll pick up your whole family, okay?"

"Thanks, but I think my new boyfriend will be able to drive us over. He's been talking about meeting you," Lucy said, then added very quickly, "You don't mind if he comes, do you? He's a really nice guy and I know he'd enjoy meeting both of you."

"That'll be fine," Karen answered. "He's more than welcome."

"If something happens and we can't get there, I'll call you around eleven to pick us up. If you don't hear from me, then I'll see you all around noon."

Lucy began to say something, then her voice started to crack and I heard her sniffle. "I must be coming down with something, too."

"You take care," Karen instructed her before hanging up.

Karen was much more optimistic than I was about the picnic plans. I had some serious doubt whether Lucy would even show up. If she didn't, I was willing to bet it would only be with her boyfriend and Byron. I couldn't help but think that I was going to get shaken down for something by

Lucy's new love. Mike, I said to myself, you're getting way too cynical. Maybe everything would turn out fine.

Naw. I knew better. Karen was going to be in for another heartache when Lucy didn't show. I was getting very close to becoming a complete cynic.

Sixteen

LUCY DIDN'T CALL AT eleven, nor did she show up at noon. By one-thirty I had given up what little hope I had of seeing Byron. Karen still had an ounce of optimism left and began making excuses that getting the five kids ready for a visit had put Lucy behind. Chris, Connie, and Cameron were still hopeful. When two o'clock rolled around, the kids had given up but Karen decided to give the great-aunt a call. I took my station and picked up the phone in the hallway.

"I'll have her call," the aunt promised, not sounding surprised that Lucy had forgotten us. "I think she's over at her grandmother's. I'll get in touch with her as soon as I can. I'll try to get her to call you as soon as possible."

"When do you think that will be?" Karen was hopeful to the end.

"I'm not sure she'll even call. But I'll say shoot for three o'clock today."

Karen was feeling miserable. She believed that open, honest communication would bring us all together and we would become one big "extended" family. It was a nice idea, but to make it work, both sides had to cooperate.

I kept reminding Karen that Lucy had problems that went far beyond keeping appointments, and that mere talking wouldn't straighten her out, but Karen did not want to hear it. On this point she was like I was with Peter— bullheaded and closed-minded.

At three-thirty the phone rang. It was Lucy. She sounded horrible, listless and near tears.

"What's wrong?" Karen asked.

"Oh, nothing," Lucy said, sounding as if she were in pain. "I can't make it today. I'm having dinner at my grandmother's, but I need to talk to you. It's very important. Can we have lunch tomorrow?"

"Sure," Karen said, her face full of strain and weariness. "I'll meet you at Stein's, that kosher deli on Ohio River Boulevard...or would you rather I picked you up?"

"I'll get there on my own, somehow." Lucy's voice sounded muffled, as if she had put her hand over the mouthpiece. "I'm on the phone," I heard her call to someone.

"Sorry," she apologized. "There's lots happening here so I can't talk long. I wanted you to know that I won't be bringing Byron this time. You and me have to talk some first. I'll see you at Stein's around one-thirty."

"That's fine with us," Karen said. "Is everything all right?"

"Why do you ask?" Lucy shot back.

"You sound troubled, that's all," Karen offered, backing off slowly. "I know you're busy, so we'll talk tomorrow. Call if you can't make it."

"I'll be there," Lucy promised. Then the line went dead.

Karen's eyes meet mine. There was still a glimmer of

hope in hers and I fed off it. "She'll come," Karen said. I didn't know who she was trying to convince—me or herself.

The next morning Karen and I went into the shop together. There were a million and one things to do and very little time to get everything done. The business had been hit pretty hard lately, and for the first time I was beginning to worry about the financial end of things. But Byron came first. That was just the way it had to be.

We hurried through our duties, half-heartedly paying attention to what we were doing. Karen was helping me roll the paper cart into the storage area when I gave it a mighty thrust, rolling it accidentally into Karen's ankle.

"What are you trying to do, break my leg?" she said, hopping about on one foot. "That's it. I'm done for the day. I'm tired. I hate this shop."

I was beginning to dislike it, too. It used to be fun, but now it seemed to get in the way of helping Byron.

When the time arrived for us to meet with Lucy, Karen and I were at each other's throats about the littlest of things. Neither one of us had been sleeping or eating on a regular basis for the past couple of weeks, haunted by the thought that no one was looking after Byron's welfare. Even if CYS wasn't doing their job very well, at least someone should have been held responsible if anything happened to Byron. Bad supervision was better than none at all.

We locked up the shop. I never found the time to replace Bobby or Bill, and the part-time receptionist I hired was on vacation, so we were running at half-mast. I never closed my doors during business hours before and felt mighty guilty about doing so now, but I promised myself to run an advertisement for help in the Sunday paper.

The deli, half-filled with the tail end of the lunch crowd, was quiet and private enough for Lucy and the two of us to get reacquainted. I looked around, but Lucy had not yet arrived. I expected her to be late, so Karen and I ordered a salad and coffee.

We slowly munched our way through the lettuce and tomatoes, looking up at the door every five minutes. It was now two o'clock and still no Lucy, so we ordered lunch—baked chicken and rice, with a bagel and matzo ball soup. I was just finishing my fourth cup of coffee when I glanced at my watch. Two forty-five. Still no Lucy.

"She's not coming," Karen finally conceded.

"Maybe she'll come."

At three o'clock, Karen folded her napkin on her plate. "She's not coming."

"Give her another ten minutes."

At three-thirty, the dining room was closing to prepare for the dinner crowd. "She's not coming," I said gently, laying my arm on Karen's shoulder.

"How could she...do this?" Karen sputtered in anger. "We just want to help her. She must know that."

I patted her shoulder. "Don't blame Lucy for this mess," I said softly. "At some point, she stopped being a responsible human being. You might just as well blame a tomato for being rotten than blame Lucy for not being trustworthy. Remember what Dr. Lipinsky said?"

She nodded. "Never trust an addict. It's just so sad, so sad. If only she'd let us help her."

Lunch was over. I paid the bill while Karen called Lucy's aunt. She had no idea where Lucy was, but Lucy had never mentioned our luncheon plans to her.

Lucy, I said to myself, all we want is to help you. Let us help you. But Lucy was young, irresponsible and addicted. Worse yet, my senses told me, she was headed for even bigger trouble.

"I guess it's over." Karen gave me a faint smile of resignation.

"At least for the moment," I said, kissing her on the cheek. "But the tide will turn. Give it time."

We drove back to the shop and finished every job before we left late that evening. We were exhausted, but the workout helped relieve some of our frustrations. By the time we put the lid on the last project, Karen's face was smudged with blue and red ink and I looked like as though I had been swimming in an inkwell.

What a powerhouse, I thought, looking over at Karen. She gave a hundred and ten percent of herself at everything she did. We were buddies. Through everything we stood together, sometimes not very closely together, but close enough to lend support to each other. That was what marriage was all about. Ours was a good marriage.

Karen and I held hands as we walked to the car. We talked of old times: College classes, our first date, the night Cameron was born. The drive home didn't feel so long.

The house was dark and lonely when we arrived, since the kids were staying overnight with friends. "I don't like it to be this quiet," Karen said, turning on the television.

We sat down before the TV, staring at the screen like some old couple on their last legs. It was an old episode of *I Love Lucy*, and though it looked as dated at hell, it was awfully funny.

"Dinner?" Karen said after a while, tilting her head in my direction.

"Yeah," I answered, flicking through the stations with the remote control, looking for something half as amusing as Lucille Ball.

"What are you hungry for?" she asked.

"I don't know. What are you hungry for?" I asked, settling for an episode of *Bewitched*.

"Don't start, Mike," she warned. "Just pick something."

"A sandwich."

"What kind?"

"I don't know."

"For God's sake," Karen snickered. She went to the kitchen, and soon I heard the sound of pots and pans banging and cabinet doors opening and closing. Pretty noisy sandwich-making. I went into the kitchen where Karen was busily preparing a T-bone steak, homemade French fries and a big tossed salad.

"What's the occasion?" I asked, delighted that I was going to finally get a full-course meal after weeks of dieting.

"There is none," Karen answered, slicing the peeled potatoes. "Just felt like cooking." That was good enough for me, because I felt like eating.

I opened a bottle of wine that we were saving for a special occasion, and as I helped Karen prepare the meal, we toasted everything, from ants to zebras.

I set the dining room table with our best china, silver and crystal. I even used our best linen napkins. Then I cut a few fresh roses from the garden. Everything was complete and perfect. It was nice to think that something was going right.

As we sat down to eat, the phone rang. At first I was going to let the answering machine take a message, but with the kids not home, I figured that maybe one of them was calling.

It was Regina. "Mike, tell Karen to pick up the other line," she said excitedly. "I want you both to hear this."

"Hi, Regina. What's the matter?" Karen said.

"Lucy's been thrown out of the PennFree program." Regina's words dropped on us like a bomb. "They caught her doing drugs last night. Her blood test was positive."

"That's why she didn't sound so good," Karen whispered to me.

I wasn't sure what to think. If what Regina said was true, Lucy would lose her housing. But where would she live then? More importantly, where would Byron and his sister live?

"Has it been made public?" I asked.

"Yes. It will be the talk of the town tomorrow. I just want you to be forewarned. You'll probably be getting some early morning phone calls from the media."

"Can you fill us in on the details?" I asked. I was curious. Why, all of a sudden, after all the reports we heard about Lucy using drugs, did the drugs show up in her blood now and not earlier?

"It's rumored that Lucy really upset a few people at PennFree. She wasn't cooperating with scheduled blood tests, and Byron and his sister weren't in daycare like they were supposed to be. PennFree just had enough. A caseworker saw Lucy buying drugs and followed her back to her apartment, then called PennFree. They did a surprise test."

"Where was Byron when all of this was going on?" Karen asked the question that was going to be the next thing out of my mouth.

"CYS suspected Lucy wasn't clean before this and took the kids away from her," Regina answered. "They're staying at their great-aunt's in Pinegrove." So while Lucy was taking our calls and agreeing to meet with us, she was already in trouble, desperate trouble. She never even had custody of Byron. No wonder she couldn't bring him with her.

"No! How can that be?" Karen cried. "Who gave Byron to his aunt? CYS?"

"It appears so." Regina sounded just as upset as Karen. "But it's only temporary. I hate to tell you this part, but CYS didn't supply as much as a bed for the two kids. They just dropped them off, and rumor has it that Byron is sleeping at the foot of his aunt's bed, while Georgia is sleeping at the head. They're squeezed in like sardines, poor things.

"Don't worry. The judge will hear the case soon. He'd have to be some flaming asshole, excuse my French, not to send Byron home with you."

"Well," I said, "the judge is a flaming asshole. But I'll get my boy back one way or another."

"Just one more item to mull over," Regina said. "The auntie's son has been charged with rape and beating up a woman. She'll say he's not living there, and maybe that's so, but I know for a fact that he spends a lot of time there."

"Oh, Christ," I whispered. I wasn't sure if we didn't go from bad to worse. A rapist…or a drug addict? Not much to choose from.

Over the months I'd felt a wide range of emotions, but the one I was experiencing that moment was one I could not readily identify. It was caught somewhere between rage and disbelief, a sort of emotional limbo. I wanted to strike out at someone at the same time as I wanted to run away and hide from the hideousness of the world.

Karen and I did not feel vindicated with Lucy's relapse. In fact, we were saddened that her fall had to be so public. It was bad enough to take a tumble in private, but literally everyone in Pittsburgh was watching this poor woman. We were terribly upset that Byron was moved to yet another house, when all he needed was to be allowed to come home.

I felt bad for the black community in general. Although Karen and I were never certain just how many from that community supported Lucy, those who did were very verbal, making headlines at every opportunity. Just a few weeks before Lucy's regression, a black activist was passing out blue ribbons to show support for Byron being returned to his mother. Although he ignored the facts about Lucy's drug addiction and criminal history, his stand was clear and simple: Black children belonged with a black family, regardless of the drugs that might be pumping through the parents' veins. I refused to believe that he spoke for the black community at large, because he and people like him only served themselves. The black community deserved a better spokesman and I hoped they would find one.

I couldn't wait for the morning paper to be delivered, so Karen and I drove downtown, where the newspaper hit the stands at eleven-thirty P.M. We waited in the car in front of a newsstand until a truck pulled up and a young man filled the stands with papers. Then I threw two quarters into the slot and pulled a warm paper from the rack. BABY BYRON'S MOM BACK ON DRUGS. The headline hit me square in the eyes. It was true. Lucy had been caught red-handed.

Byron would be coming home soon. I knew he would.

I called Peter's home from the car phone but his answering machine was on. "Peter, call me right away," I said, excitedly. "It's urgent."

That night Karen and I didn't sleep a wink. We did however have a late-night, cold dinner of gray steak, dry potatoes and wilted salad. It tasted delicious.

&   &   &

MOTIONS, COURT DATES AND hearings were happening so quickly it was hard to keep track of all the comings and goings. At the July hearing, Connie went with us. She wanted the "experience," she said, of seeing our justice system in action. At first she was a little shy in her new surroundings, but she soon struck up a conversation with a boy around her age. I overheard him tell her that he had been accused of breaking into a neighbor's house. Connie listened intently as he tried to persuade her that it was a case of mistaken identity. From the look on her face, I guessed that she was not convinced of his innocence.

A courthouse employee interrupted my eavesdropping with news that Byron was being held upstairs in a play area while Lucy and the great-aunt were in the courtroom. "Just thought you should know," he said, shaking my hand. "I think what you and your wife are doing is great. There should be more people like you."

"Go on up and see him," Karen urged, giving me a slight tug. "You are his father. You have a right to at least look at him."

It didn't take much for Karen to persuade me. My little Birdie was only two flights up from me.

"I wanna go, too," Connie whined. "He's my brother."

I took Connie by the hand and we both rushed up the stairs. Whew! I was out of shape. It took me a few minutes to catch my breath, then I gently opened the door and searched out the play area.

It wasn't hard to find. Children's voices and laughter echoed down the corridor, coming from a large, glass-enclosed room. I could see Byron playing inside. He looked tired and old, and it frightened me to see him looking so dispirited.

His grandmother was inside with him—alone. This lady never ceased to surprise me. Every time I saw her she was dressed to kill, and today was no exception. Her floral two-piece dress and white wool jacket looked brand new and expensive. Her eyeglasses alone probably cost a mortgage payment. She actually gave the appearance of being a classy lady, and, if it weren't for her vast criminal record, she may just have been able to pull it off.

"I miss him," Connie whispered, blowing a silent kiss in Byron's direction. "I want him to come home."

"Soon, honey," I promised.

"Mr. Derzack," a voice behind me interrupted my precious moment. It was a kind caseworker who had been helpful to me in the past. "Would you like to go in and see him?"

"You think I should?" I said, opening the door and stepping inside. Of course, I knew I shouldn't, but what did I have to lose? "Birdie," I called.

Byron came running over to me and wrapped his arms around my leg.

"How's my little boy?" I said, scooping him up in my arms. Byron hugged me with all his might.

"'Onnie." Byron reached out for Connie. She gave him a big kiss and told him he would be coming home with us very soon.

We played a few games, rolled around on the floor and hugged a lot. Strangely enough, his grandmother watched us the whole time and never said a word. I believe she was surprised to find out just how close we were.

"Daddy," Byron said, pointing to a game piece that resembled a king, so I handed it to him. "Good Daddy," he said, giving me a hug. It was then I realized that he was referring to me, not the game piece.

One of the aides looked at me and we both started to cry. Birdie had not forgotten who I was in his life. I was still, after eight months of separation, his daddy.

I was holding Byron in my arms when a bailiff from Judge Lerner's court came storming into the room. His voice was stern and gruff. "The judge has ordered me to remove you from the playroom, by force if necessary. You are to have no contact with the baby Byron."

"I understand," I said, giving my son a kiss on the forehead.

"I'll go peacefully." I understood, all right. I understood that the judge was a heartless pig and nothing short of an idiot. Or else he was a frightened fool under the thumb of some powerful organization. I couldn't be with my son, but the grandmother could. A woman who probably gave her own son drugs was to be trusted more than me.

"Sorry," the caseworker whispered. "We tried to keep your visit a secret."

"Thanks," I said. "I appreciate your efforts."

By the time I reached Karen, the hearing was being let out. Peter explained that the judge ruled to reinstate Karen and me as parties to the case, but did not give us custody. He ordered that Byron and his sister were to stay with the great-aunt.

Karen and I were very upset about the judge's decision. From everything that we knew about the aunt's living conditions, they were too crowded to force two more children into her home. Why was the judge doing this? Did he know about the cramped living quarters? More importantly, did he know about the aunt's son? It was hard to tell what he knew and what he didn't. It seemed that CYS gave out only the information that suited them. But that did not leave the judge off the hook. It was his court and he was responsible.

The judge announced that he would make a decision in August naming who would go home with "the prize"—his lousy term for a little boy without a stable home. He said that Byron would either go to a family member, another black family or us. The fact that he brought up the possibility of another black family entering the picture did not surprise me. Margo had told us that CYS always used a model black family, "The Johnsons," whenever they got into a bind. In the end this perfect family would back off, as they often had in the past.

I didn't know what family would want Byron and his sister for keeps. The aunt wouldn't get any money if she adopted them, and that, I felt, was a high priority to her.

Judge Lerner also asked, rather nicely, that Karen and I

not grant any interviews or speak with anyone from the media. We agreed. We thought we were so close to getting Byron that anything we had to say about the case could wait for another day.

Karen and I felt as if our lives were totally out of control, without means of expression or getting information. We couldn't talk to the press, and we couldn't file any more motions than we already had. When we asked Peter what to do, he dropped the verbal equivalent of an atomic bomb on our heads.

"I've been made an officer of the court," he explained. "That means the judge has forbidden me to tell you the details of what went on during the hearing."

I was speechless with shock and anger, but not Karen. "Then the judge is paying you," she told him in no uncertain terms, "because we're not. Why should we, if you're not going to do what we pay you to do?"

I had never heard of an attorney taking the side of the judge before, but I supposed since Judge Lerner ordered it and Peter complied, it must be a fairly commonplace legal procedure. Nevertheless, I agreed with Karen: As long as Peter refused to tell us about the proceedings, we were *not* paying him.

The first thing I did after the hearing was to ask the county housing department how many people were permitted in a three-bedroom home in Pinegrove Terrace. They were pretty sly. They didn't give me a straight answer because they knew who I was and why I was asking.

A few days later one of my informants told us that the aunt had been moved to a bigger apartment in the projects. I hoped that it was true. I prayed that Byron was no longer crammed in some bed with his aunt and sister.

Two weeks before the August hearing, we received a copy of a petition for legal custody of Byron and his sister, Georgia, filed on behalf of the grandmother. This was a joke, I thought. She didn't stand a chance getting the kids. No judge in his right mind would...But then again, we weren't dealing with just any judge. Didn't he give custody of Byron to a practicing drug addict? Maybe we did have something to be concerned about.

Peter thought the grandmother was just grandstanding and would not pursue the petition. I thought the family was laying groundwork to sue the county and Karen and me if the judge ruled in our favor.

We also learned from Regina that Georgia had broken her arm, but there were conflicting stories on how this had happened. The aunt contended she saw Georgia hanging over the upstairs railing and the next thing she knew, Georgia fell, breaking her arm. The other story, confirmed by two of our sources, held that one of Georgia's older brothers got angry with her and broke her arm in his hands, like a stick. I didn't want to believe that, even though the psychological reports had detailed the boy's aggressive, often violent behavior.

The month passed slowly. I was feeling pretty confident that the judge would give Byron back to us at the August hearing, but that was only wishful thinking. Instead, he ruled that he would make a final decision on September 16, another month away.

The judge had some other, more interesting decisions as well. Karen and I were, once again, to be evaluated by Doctor Komma and were granted two visits with Byron, five hours each. The judge ordered CYS to find a family who would adopt both Byron and Georgia, to keep them to-gether.

We immediately let it be known to the judge that we would adopt both children. The prospects of having an-other girl in the family delighted Karen to no end. I think the judge was a little surprised at how quickly we made our decision, but when it came to adopting children, our answer was always "yes."

The judge also apparently came to his senses and or-dered that Lucy's parental rights be terminated. All of Lucy's attorneys made an impassioned plea that Lucy be given another chance, but the judge was not very sympathetic.

"Where is Lucy today?" the judge asked, glancing around the courtroom. Lucy was nowhere to be seen. Judge Lerner glared at Mr. Franklin and asked him again, "Where is Lucy?"

"Your Honor, it's like this," the attorney answered. He stood up and tugged at the back of his suitcoat, then straightened his tie. "Lucy just began a new job, and even though she wanted to be here, she was afraid she would lose her job, so I advised her to go to work. She's trying hard to make amends."

"Mr. Franklin, I have seventeen cases to hear this morning. Every one of those parents cared enough to take the time to be here. I find Lucy's excuse and her absence inexcusable."

"Your Honor, it was at my advice that Lucy isn't here today. She begs the court to give her another chance. She loves her children and does not want to lose them. She wishes the court to enroll her in another drug rehabilitation program."

"If you remember, the county has assisted Lucy in this matter at some length to no avail. If she still wants to enter a program after today, CYS can advise her on the programs available to her. This will not affect my decision to terminate her rights as a parent."

Mr. Franklin took his seat, wearing an expression that said, "Well, I'm not surprised to hear this."

The judge acknowledged our cooperation in not talking with the press. It sounded like a dogowner praising his beagles for sitting and staying. Nice boy. Good girl.

WE WAITED PATIENTLY FOR Doctor Komma to call to arrange an appointment with us, but, when after a week's time, she didn't call, I contacted CYS to find out why. Coincidentally, the doctor had just taken her vacation and wasn't expected back for a month. Perfect timing. The judge did not want another psychiatrist to evaluate us, since Doctor Komma was so familiar with the case. I once again requested an evaluation by an independent psychiatrist, but was denied.

CYS was to arrange for a CASA worker to set up a time for our visits with Byron, but it took a call from Peter to prompt them into making a decision. After talking to the CASA volunteer, Peter learned that the adoption of Byron was going to go through an Ohio agency because of the publicity in Pittsburgh surrounding the case. I didn't understand how any amount of publicity would affect an adoption agency's job, and no one seemed to have a good answer. CYS just decided to have it that way. He also learned that there were two black families interested in adopting Byron, an unidentified couple and the Johnsons.

CYS sent over a twenty-six page questionnaire for us to fill out, which Karen and I completed in one evening. I called CYS to find out if this was normal procedure. It was not. They were just trying to keep us distracted. Then a CASA volunteer informed us that they had to "observe" Karen and me in our home with our children.

This notion drove me crazy. A volunteer, who had less than twenty-four hours of training, in a program that was barely four months old, funded by CYS, was evaluating *me*? Who would ensure her appropriateness and impartiality? CYS, the framers of the "trans-racial" placement policy? This whole thing was getting past ridiculous and moving into the blatantly absurd. The "evaluation" was a network of red tape being used to keep Byron in the system while CYS squeezed the last penny from the state and federal agencies for his care. I wouldn't put it past CYS to start kidnapping children and losing them in the foster care system, just for the bucks.

I wasn't far from wrong about the CASA volunteer, a young black woman with the personality of a cement wall, totally devoid of warmth. She spoke in a dull monotone, as if her words had no importance to her and she spoke at all only because others expected her to. People like her scared me. They were too detached from the world and other people.

The CASA worker had learned well from her CYS training; she was three hours late. "Car problems," she said. She made up for it, though: Our meeting went on for three excruciating hours. It was torturous to try to maintain a conversation with the woman, though normally I could talk with little or no effort to anyone. She preferred answering questions in words of one syllable, but when pressed could say as many as five words at a time. I learned that she did not have transportation back to Pittsburgh, so Karen and I drove her home, another forty-five minutes of nonstop entertainment.

The next day Peter called, bright and early, to inform us that the unidentified couple had dropped their "bid" to adopt Byron. Our chances were improving. Also, the CASA volunteer decided that Byron and his sister were not very close after all and did not need to be adopted as a pair to the same family. I found it amazing how much of an authority this woman had become in a few short hours. She didn't even have a degree in child development, and apparently had never even worked very closely with children.

"What about our visits with Byron?" I asked Peter. I was anxious to see my Birdie again.

"There's a problem. CASA wants the visits to take place on Saturday, but CYS says they don't deliver on Saturdays, so now it's a problem of how to transport the boy."

"Oh, for Christ's sake!" I barked. "Not that again. He's not a pizza, after all. Tell them I'll pick him up."

"You'll have to go to Pinegrove Terrace." Through the phone lines, I could actually feel Peter shudder. He was in the country club set. Raising money for charities through golf tournaments was one thing, but laying eyes on the unfortunate up close and personal was something else again. That was certainly his loss, just as it had been mine.

"Why don't you come with me?" I said, very seriously. "After all, you're my attorney. You should be there if anything goes wrong."

He laughed. "I charge double on Saturday. Karen wouldn't like that."

He had a point.

THE ANTICS AT CYS continued and went far beyond organizing their own force of poorly trained volunteers. At last, CYS was caught in a lie.

Karen contacted an acquaintance of ours, who was fighting a battle with CYS over the removal of a child in her care, and asked her to write CYS and request a copy of the revised trans-racial placement policy. Much to her surprise and mine, CYS wrote a letter claiming that there had been no change in its policy since its inception in December of 1992.

This was contrary to a previous news article on the matter, as well as my conversations with Jane Worley. I contacted an official at the Civil Rights Office and asked him what was going on. I was led to believe, I said, that CYS had changed its 1992 trans-racial placement policy to meet federal guidelines. Had this been done or not?

The Civil Rights Office was just as confounded as I was.

Obviously, we were not the only ones concerned. A reporter from one of Pittsburgh's two major newspapers gave me the courtesy of a phone call to inform me that Jane Worley had lied to her about the trans-racial placement policy. Although this particular reporter had at times been at odds with Karen and me, I thought she was pretty good at her job. She managed to get her hands on court documents and persuade Judge Lerner to talk when no one else could. She had also gathered the "inside story" on the private adoption proceedings concerning whites who were adopting blacks, and reported on them, "because the black community had the right to know." She was well connected, as well as a bit arrogant. I gave her scoops now and again because it served both of us for me to do so.

The minute I heard the reporter's angry voice I knew she

was boiling mad. Jane Worley accused the journalist of not reporting the truth in an article on the Civil Rights Office investigation.

"She actually told me that I had 'misunderstood' her and that she never told me that there was any adjustment in the policy," the reporter complained. From the sound of indignation in her voice I could tell that she was surprised that Jane Worley had dared to treat her in such a manner. After all, she was the press. "If she thinks she's going to get away with telling me I don't know my job, read Sunday's paper."

I read Sunday's paper with intense delight. The reporter's article only made front page news in the regional section, but that was good enough for me. Jane Worley had crossed the wrong people. She forgot rule number one: Don't screw with the press. The newspaper that had for so long been singing the praises of CYS were now on the attack.

The article proved that our federal lawsuit against CYS for racism had merit and that our suspicions about Jane Worley were true. She had implemented the trans-racial placement policy against the advice of the county law department. Although CYS claimed that they had the full support of both the law department and the county commissioners, those two groups begged to differ. They never gave their approval, they said in the article. Although the county thought they could defend her, they admitted that it was wrong for Jane to work outside the advice of the law department and to attach the commissioners' names to something without first consulting them.

So-o-o long Jane Worley. The commissioner tossed her overboard and now she was nothing but fishbait. Although I did not believe that the commissioners were totally innocent, I wasn't naive enough to think that they would refuse to sacrifice one of their own to save their skins. That was politics in Allegheny County. Jane Worley was a casualty, and rightfully so.

Karen was elated when she read the article. Just as the judge was my nemesis, Jane Worley was Karen's. In the back of my mind I couldn't help but believe that Jane Worley was too firmly connected to the "right people" in Allegheny County to ever completely fade from the county's payroll, but I knew her days as the coordinator of CYS were numbered.

The next day I was at the shop, mulling over Jane's state of affairs, when Karen gave me a call.

"Mike," she said, "you're not going to believe what the judge was quoted as saying in an article on Baby Byron." Oh, I wasn't so sure about that. The judge could do or say little or nothing that would surprise me.

"Let me have it." I took off my glasses and rubbed my aching eyes.

"Says here that he stays awake in the middle of the night wondering if he did right by Byron," Karen said. "If the judge were standing in front of me, I'd tell him to his face, if you're losing sleep over your decision, then, honey, you didn't make the right one."

"Why don't you call him?" I found more than a little humor in that—Karen and the judge talking to one another. How long would it take for their cozy chat to deteriorate into a screaming match? It was rumored that the judge liked "his wine and his women." If he came head to head with Karen, he would swear off women and drink more wine.

"I love you, sweetheart," I whispered, with a smile in my voice.

Karen returned my affections with a snort. "You sound guilty. You were thinking something unflattering about me."

"Honey! How could you think such a thing?" I protested, perhaps a bit too much. She slammed down the receiver, sending a sudden jolt to my eardrums.

As September 16th grew closer and closer, I became a little worried about the psychological report—there was none yet, because Doctor Komma had not had a chance to meet with us. But we had it from a good source that the missing report would not hold up to the judge's ruling. The very next day I learned that the date of the hearing would be moved to October 5th in order to allow Doctor Komma to complete her testing; the September 16th hearing would be no more than a status report. How much longer could they delay the inevitable? How much longer would they force Byron to suffer?

CYS had been exposed to great embarrassment; the judge, although trying to pose as a tortured man, was losing public credibility along with CYS. The commissioners were on the hot seat because our federal lawsuit was going to cost the county a ton of money. If they gave Byron to some other black couple, simply because they were black, our suit would be as good as won. There was no doubt in my mind— Byron would be coming home.

Karen and I had fought hard for our child, and we had scars to prove just how long and valiantly we did fight. We hoped they would soon become scars of victory.

I came home from the shop early one day and had dinner with Karen and the kids on the deck. We finished eating early and sent the kids upstairs to do their homework. The air was turning cold and once again it was feeling like autumn. A few of the neighbors had their fireplaces working and the smell of the burning logs made me want to snuggle close to Karen.

"Getting cold, hon?" I said, noticing the tip of her nose turning red. "I'll go upstairs and get you a sweater."

I went up to our bedroom closet and hunted for our matching wool cardigan sweaters. They were never something that we wore together in public. We actually bought them as a joke. When we were dating, we promised ourselves never to dress alike, like some of the older married couples Karen had known. Karen bought them as a Christmas gift, more or less to awaken me to the fact that we were the old married couple we used to make fun of.

I found Karen's neatly folded in her drawer, but I had some problem locating mine. I hadn't worn it for almost a year. Probably because I couldn't find it.

"Chris," I called from the hallway. "Have you seen my brown wool sweater?

"No, Dad," he yelled back.

"Connie, have you seen my sweater?"

"It's in my closet!"

I walked into her room. She was lying on the floor, chewing gum and talking on the phone.

"I thought you were supposed to be doing your homework," I chided her.

"I paid Chris to do it," she answered, smiling up at me.

She was waiting for my reaction, but I was getting too smart for her. I ignored her.

"What is my sweater doing in your closet?" I asked, throwing open the closet door and scanning the crowded cubbyhole. It smelled of old sneakers, cardboard boxes and bubblegum.

"How am I supposed to know? You're the one who put it there," Connie snickered. She bobbed her head and rolled her eyes, as if to let me know I was going senile. "When I first saw it, I thought it was a dead animal."

I retrieved the sweater, which was lying, partially hidden, under a big carton marked "bombs and stuff." I decided to let sleeping artillery lie, but as I left Connie's room, I couldn't resist one more volley: "Get off the phone," I commanded as I cleared the threshold.

She ignored me.

I put my sweater on and slipped my hand into my left pocket to check for old gum wrappers, loose coins and other assorted junk. What I found instead was a treasure. It was Bill's tiny gift for Byron, still wrapped in the comics page. I had forgotten all about it.

I sat at the bottom of the stairs and carefully unwrapped the Sunday funnies from the box. Inside were Bill's dogtags, wrapped in a piece of yellowed writing paper which bore a single, hand-written line: *Mike, wear these until Byron's old enough to wear them. Love, Bill.*

I felt as if I were being strangled. For a moment I couldn't breathe. That was just like Bill, always there when I needed him. I slipped the tags around my neck and let them rest, cold against my collarbone. I realized at that moment, that long after Byron came home to stay, after the Derzack family and Baby Byron faded from the public's eye, there would still be a battle to fight, a war to wage.

I was now officially a soldier. My tour of duty was to be served in areas like Pinegrove Terrace with children like Charles. That was Bill's legacy. Now it was mine.

Postscript

IKE AND KAREN DERZACK will be testifying in front of a state senate hearing on children and youth welfare issues. The Abandoned Baby Act has gained bi-partisan support and is expected to be passed into law. A new act based on Illinois' ACT 1886, which places the best interests of the child over family reunification, has been drafted and will be going before the Pennsylvania Senate. It, too, is expected to pass into law.

Children and Youth Services and especially Jane Worley have come under fire. Shortly after the September hearing, Jane Worley was forced to resign as the director of CYS. She was given two weeks to clear out. There are rumors of an independent audit into CYS's activities.

Shawntee Ford, who was murdered by her father after CYS failed to supply a court-ordered criminal check to the judge, is finally getting attention by the press. They are probing for answers.

Lucy solicited an undercover cop for money in exchange for sexual favors. She was arrested for prostitution.

Judge Lerner still sits on the bench of Family Court. His nights, no doubt, are still restless.